DigitalAssassination

Richard Torrenzano
and Mark Davis

Digital Assassination

PROTECTING YOUR REPUTATION, BRAND, OR BUSINESS AGAINST ONLINE ATTACKS

ST. MARTIN'S PRESS NEW YORK

www.stmartins.com

Library of Congress Cataloging-in-Publication Data

Torrenzano, Richard.
Digital assassination : protecting your reputation, brand, or business against online attacks / Richard Torrenzano, Mark Davis.—1st ed.
p. cm.
Includes bibliographical references and index.
ISBN: 978-1-250-01369-9
1. Public opinion. 2. Reputation. 3. Internet—Security measures.
I. Davis, Mark W. (Mark William), 1955– II. Title.
HM1236.T67 2011
005—dc23 2011025849

First Edition: November 2011

P1

RT: *To my family*

MD: *To Rebecca*

Contents

Acknowledgments

THE AUTHORS EXPRESS sincere thanks to our agent, Leah Spiro of Riverside Creative Management, for her knowledge of the publishing world and her uncanny ability to find the right fit. We consider ourselves very lucky to have started out with the best of all possible agents.

Leah led us to many resources, one of the best is Anne Greenberg, whose sharp editorial eye and deep knowledge of many complex subjects proved critical for us more than once.

We also thank Neil Livingstone, chairman and CEO of Executive Action, LLC, a leading global security expert, for his guidance in helping us navigate through the secretive world of digital attacks. Thanks also go to Adam D'Luzansky for his insights into recent changes in digital technologies.

And we thank our long-suffering colleagues—Clark S. Judge, founder of The White House Writers Group; Edward A. Orgon, president, The Torrenzano Group; and everyone from our firms who were gracious with their help and understanding during our absence while researching and writing this book.

We are also deeply grateful to our editor, St. Martin's Press Editor in Chief George Witte, and especially John Murphy and the entire editorial, marketing, and PR team for their encouragement, support, and guidance.

DigitalAssassination

1://The Digital Mosh Pit

ON JUNE 5, 1968, for reasons known only to himself, Sirhan Sirhan fired a bullet into the head of Robert F. Kennedy at the Ambassador Hotel in Los Angeles, killing him.

In May 2005, a Nashville man, for reasons known only to himself, used Wikipedia to fire a bullet directly into the reputation of John Seigenthaler, former Kennedy aide, civil rights hero, and newspaper publisher, character assassinating him to the core.

The Wikipedia entry reported that Seigenthaler:

> was the assistant to Attorney General Robert Kennedy in the early 1960's. For a brief time, he was thought to have been directly involved in the Kennedy assassinations of both John, and his brother, Bobby. Nothing was ever proven. . . . John Seigenthaler moved to the Soviet Union in 1971, and returned to the United States in 1984.

Was the entry correct? Did it matter?

It did to Seigenthaler. "At age 78," he later wrote in *USA Today,* "I thought I was beyond surprise or hurt at any negative said about me. I was wrong. One sentence in the biography was true. I was Robert Kennedy's administrative assistant in the early 1960s. I also was his pallbearer."[1]

Did the entry really harm Seigenthaler?

At that time, one of the authors was asked to pen an introduction of Seigenthaler for a speaker at a charitable event. Though not fooled by the Wikipedia entry, the writer took pause, consuming valuable time and attention to sort out the story in advance of the event. There is no telling how many others linked to John Seigenthaler were similarly perplexed . . . or actually believed it.

The entry sat on Wikipedia's page for 132 days, and was picked up uncritically by two widely used information automatons, Reference.com and Answers.com.

For those 132 days, Seigenthaler's character was assassinated—not the man himself, but his reputation, his avatar constructed of words spoken and written. When such an assassination happens, however, more than a shadow self is murdered.

Digital assassination can murder opportunity—carefully cultivated brands or businesses, jobs or job offers, celebrity, and personal relationships. Character assassination has led to heartbreak . . . and even death by suicide.

The world witnessed a vivid example of character assassination in the digital arena on September 22, 2010, when Rutgers University freshman Tyler Clementi jumped from the George Washington Bridge into the Hudson River. Two students had used a webcam to secretly stream on the Internet Clementi's sexual encounter with a man.

"There might be some people who can take that type of treatment and deal with it, and there might be others, as this young man obviously was, who was much more greatly affected by it," New Jersey governor Chris Christie observed in the aftermath of the tragedy.[2]

Clementi's digital assassination relied on a media that is instantaneous, vivid, works 24/7, has global reach, an eternal memory, and can organize crowds to attack individuals. But we are wrong if we imagine the character attacks the Internet enables are something entirely new.

More than half a century before, in the McCarthy era, a group of Republican senators went to a Democratic colleague, Lester C. Hunt of Wyoming, and suggested that the arrest of Hunt's son in a homosexual prostitution sting could be kept quiet if Hunt were to announce his retirement from the Senate. Days later, Hunt sneaked a rifle under his coat into his Senate office and blew out his brains.[3]

> The malevolent can assassinate character, brand, reputation, celebrity, business, or life with emotional violence.

FOR DECADES, Steve Jobs was not just the cofounder of Apple. To millions, he *was* Apple, the most successful and visible CEO of our generation.

Years before Jobs took his most recent medical leave of absence in January 2011, equity market short sellers and other financial vultures tried to exploit Apple's stock by spreading rumors about his long struggle against pancreatic cancer, followed by a liver transplant.

Why has Jobs been so important? Apple is a company with a soul, dominating the market by meeting consumer cravings for a fusion of design and functionality—the essence of cool. Jobs and his team certainly know how to excite the 4G spot of millions of technophiles.

"Design," Jobs purportedly said, "is not just what it looks like and feels like. Design is how it works."

The soul of Apple, however, seemed to disappear in the mid-1980s when Steve Jobs was forced to step aside for a soda executive he had recruited. And the soul of Apple, their mojo, reappeared only when Jobs came back.

Will there be an Apple after Jobs? By the second decade of the century, Jobs had been at the helm so long, his DNA so instilled in the corporate culture, the company will almost certainly continue being the Apple we have come to know. For years, however, the best way to damage Apple was to try to digitally assassinate Jobs.

In 2008, a teenager on CNN's iReport, its "citizen journalism page," reported that Steve Jobs had suffered a heart attack. The result? This teenager's digital attack caused one of the world's best-known brands to lose millions of dollars in stock value within minutes. The traffic of rumors was so thick that Jobs publicly accused hedge funds and short sellers of profiting off Internet rumors about his health.[4]

"Millions of people, from hard-core computer geeks to high-finance Wall Street martini drinkers, hang on every word related to Apple," observed Tom Krazit of CNET News. "Sometimes that can have consequences."[5]

Like losing millions of dollars in a single day.

greedy can assassinate your brand, reputation, or stock with lure of pure fiction propelled by the Internet's instant international reach.

WHEN WILLIAM SHAKESPEARE had Julius Caesar opine about the dangers of men with a "lean and hungry look," the Bard could have been describing James Carville, the political operator and organizing genius behind the successful presidential campaign of Bill Clinton. Carville, who fires deadly innuendos with a vulpine smile, is a good man to have in a foxhole—provided it's your foxhole and he's your man.

Needless to say, Carville has made his fair share of enemies in Washington, as has his wife, Mary Matalin, an equally acid-tongued Republican who once worked behind the scenes for both presidents named Bush.

Bipartisan couples are not rare in Washington. But pairing two operatives with so many years of back-alley political skulduggery against each other's bosses is exotic, a spectacle as alluring as if Lucrezia Borgia had matched up with Niccolò Machiavelli. Needless to say, the sparks fly between them—sparks of political anger and underlying attraction that makes for great theater. And so Carville and Matalin have become fixtures on television political talk shows.

One day it seemed as if the tension between them had spun out of control. The circuits of the nation's political gossip networks overloaded when it was reported that James Carville was arrested after firing a gun into a sofa, plunging a knife into a wall, and physically abusing Mary at the couple's Rockville, Maryland, home. The online story, under the byline of Lee Canular of the *Montgomery County Ledger,* was aired on a national radio syndicate and was e-mailed back and forth between every politically connected person in both parties.

A few facts began to surface. The Carvilles lived in Virginia at that time, not in Maryland. There is no *Montgomery County Ledger,* nor is there a reporter named Lee Canular—the last name is the same as the French word for hoax. Carville had not been arrested by the Rockville police or any other police for anything. And there is no reason to ask James Carville when he quit beating his wife.[6]

Unknown people use the Internet for unknown reasons to muddy brands and reputations without fear of a reckoning.

DID YOU KNOW that "Roddy Boyd Sucks It Like He's Paying the Rent"? Or that he left *Fortune* magazine to "slither into his own unique and arrest-warrant-laden world (that's him, just above the child porn guy.)"?[7]

Roddy Boyd is a journalist whose reporting often appears in Time Warner's *Fortune* magazine. The person posting this diatribe is not a forty-year-old man in pajamas living in his mother's basement. The man who wrote this message—and many other entries of similar ilk—is Patrick Byrne, former Marshall Scholar (Cambridge), Stanford PhD in philosophy, and CEO of Overstock.com, the Utah-based online retailer represented by the sexy ads with German actress Sabine Ehrenfeld ("It's all about the O"). Overstock is a major player in Internet retail that competes with eBay and Amazon.com.

The arrest reference is in a blog linked to the police log in what appears to be from a *Greenwich Post* article on January 22, 2009. This item refers to Boyd's arrest over a failure to appear in court after a previous arrest for running a light while under a suspended license and allegedly without auto insurance. The reference to child pornography has nothing to do with Boyd, except that the next case listed in the Connecticut police log concerns a man charged with downloading numerous images of child pornography. This apparently was the worst thing that could be found out about Boyd.

"I am one of only two reporters—the other is my former *Fortune* magazine colleague Bethany McLean—apparently evil enough in his [Byrne's] eyes to warrant a reference to oral sex and ejaculation in his assessment of our ethics and reporting skills," Boyd drolly blogged on a Slate site.[8]

Byrne has called reporters lapdogs and hedge fund quislings. This CEO accused another reporter of being "on the take, and get[ting] paid off somewhere in order to do hatchet-jobs-to-order."[9]

Why is Byrne burning up his keyboard? The CEO seems convinced that he and his company are the victims of character assassination by equity short sellers and hedge funds that encourage the spread of negative media stories about his and other corporations, paving the way for quick and dirty profits. And to back it up, Byrne initially funded DeepCapture.com, though it is not part of Overstock. It purports to reveal, says its mission statement, "that powerful actors have been able to influence or take control of not just the regulators, but also law enforcement, elected officials, national media, and the intellectual establishment."[10]

Who is the assassin here and who is the victim?

Some observers believe Byrne has a point to make against some hedge funds and perhaps some journalists. Overstock did succeed in winning $5 million from one hedge fund, Copper River (formerly Rocker Partners), though the fund characterizes the settlement as a payoff to end years of meritless litigation.[11]

Opinions will differ about the merits of Byrne's underlying arguments. But it is hard to imagine Byrne's board of directors and shareholders of a NASDAQ-traded company are pleased with his aggressive and unorthodox approach to representing Overstock.

> The new social media environment enhances the vulgarization of business culture by airing vituperation among elites.

FINE INDEPENDENT FILMS have been made for less money than some production company's budget for their Oscar campaigns. About $20 million was lavished in 2000 promoting *Gladiator*, which eventually won five Oscars, including one for Best Picture.[12] By 2011, Sony's Oscar campaign for *The Social Network* had invested $55 million in ads and the re-release of the film in 603 theaters.[13]

Much more than vanity is at stake. Win an Oscar for Best Picture, and the global and digital rights to a film are worth many times more than the expense of such a campaign. Not surprisingly, some of the money is spent not just on raising the profile of a film, but promoting and spreading some disqualifying dirty linen—often a spun or distorted fact—about a competitor's film.

Was there ever a surer bet for the Academy Award's Best Picture than Steven Spielberg's 1998 *Saving Private Ryan*? At the time of its summer release by DreamWorks, *Saving Private Ryan* became an instant classic—managing to shock viewers into tears who considered themselves long since jaded by war-movie violence. When Oscar time came, *Ryan*'s only real competition was *Shakespeare in Love*, a romp through an Elizabethan comedy of errors.

Cowritten by playwright Tom Stoppard, produced by brash mogul Harvey Weinstein of Miramax, *Shakespeare* was indeed a good film.

But it was a comedy (no comedy had won Best Picture since *Annie Hall* in 1978), and it was at times more than a little predictable.

"But journalists and critics on both coasts report that they were recipients of negative Miramax spin," Hollywood insider Nikki Finke wrote in *New York* magazine, "including comments from Weinstein himself, who opined to at least one major critic that *Ryan* 'peaks in the first twenty minutes.' "[14]

When *Shakespeare in Love* won Best Picture in 1999, the Hollywood elite grinned at what they saw as a triumph of publicity and politics over art.

By 2002, Oscar-season disparagement had migrated to the Internet when Universal's *A Beautiful Mind* came up against Weinstein and Miramax's *In the Bedroom. A Beautiful Mind* used startling reverses, plot twists, and animation to take us into the schizophrenic mind of John Forbes Nash Jr., a Nobel Prize–winning mathematician who lost—and regained—his grip on sanity. It was a tour de force for actor Russell Crowe, more well known for his physicality on screen and his brawling off screen than for his acting skill. Equipped with nothing more than dowdy clothes and a wax pencil on which to frantically scribble formulas on a bay window overlooking the Princeton University campus, Crowe made us believe that he possessed a vast and luminous intelligence that allowed him to peer deeply into the very fabric of reality. Director Ron Howard convinced us that we could follow Crowe as his character's hold on reality shatters and his mental phantoms slither into the full light of day.

As Oscar night approached, Hollywood was ablaze with ugly gossip from the Drudge Report, not about Russell Crowe or Ron Howard, but about the film's subject—the Nobel Prize winner, John Forbes Nash, who was rumored to have been a raving anti-Semite and a sexual weirdo. Matt Drudge reported that three academy members had changed their votes after learning that Nash was guilty of being a "Jew basher." Nash himself took this charge in stride, noting that when he was ill, he had said and done a great many strange things—he once believed he was the emperor of Antarctica. He allowed that he might very well have made some anti-Semitic utterances.[15]

Questions, fueled by bloggers, kept coming: Why wasn't this in the story? Why did Howard and screenwriter Akiva Goldsman choose to leave out details about Nash's complex sexual life? The answer, of course, is that like all moviemakers, Howard and Goldsman streamlined and skewed history, adapting it to the screen. Somehow, however, a campaign was under way in Hollywood to make this artistic choice seem as if it were some kind of sordid scam, if not an outright cinematic scandal.[16]

In the end, *A Beautiful Mind* was too good to be derailed. It won Best Picture. But Hollywood insiders said that the negative campaign from an interested source did real damage to the film's chances.

"This may not be the worst year in Oscar history, but it's pretty low," Pete Hammond, a film historian and consultant for American Movie Classics, told *The New York Times*. "To accuse the subject of a film of being anti-Semitic when you know that a lot of the people who will be voting on the Oscars are Jewish, well, that's really down and dirty. . . . It's getting nastier. It's like a political campaign now. You get these so-called Oscar consultants who go out there thinking, 'What kind of dirt can we dig up?' "[17]

In 2010, the Academy of Motion Picture Arts and Sciences banned *The Hurt Locker* producer Nicolas Chartier from attending the Oscars for sending out an e-mail disparaging competitor *Avatar,* while Hollywood insiders report that the little digs in Chartier's e-mail were mild compared to some of the sponsored attacks they were seeing every day.

> Powerful competitors knock worthy projects as easily as a race car can tip an opponent into a tailspin.

Something Old, Something New

Digital assassins gone mad with money, sex, power, and envy will use technology to fire a malicious story to weaken, wound, or kill you. But not all attacks are digital assassinations.

Brands, companies, products, and celebrities can be criticized and subjected to the rough-and-tumble of free speech—a truth made apparent when an Amarillo jury in 1998 found Oprah Winfrey not guilty of libeling the Texas beef industry for airing a show on mad cow disease.

Character assassination is certainly not to be confused with bad publicity based on wicked acts, hypocrisy, incompetence, or lack of due diligence. Representative Anthony Weiner of New York, Tiger Woods, former senator and presidential candidate John Edwards, former South Carolina governor Mark Sanford, and former New York governor Eliot Spitzer were not character assassinated. They self-destructed, killing their own reputations.

The same can be said for Toyota in its apparent lack of due diligence in the sudden-acceleration debacle, BP's repeated careless actions leading up to the Gulf oil spill, or the bad odor from the decision by Merrill Lynch CEO John Thain to spend $1,400 on a trash can as part of his million-dollar makeover of his office during the worst recession in seventy years.

These are clear examples of character suicide. So what then is digital character assassination?

Digital assassination begins as a willful act by someone who wishes to do harm through the Internet. It unfolds as a deliberate campaign to spread harmful lies that the assassin has concocted about you or as an attempt to take a fact about you grossly out of context or embellish it, making an ordinary shortcoming seem ghastly. Words are then forged into swords to be thrust into the gut.

Digital assassination is most effective when others—as knowing conspirators or unknowing parrots—are incited by social media to thrust swords of their own. The result is multiple slices and stabs, leaving a permanent, searchable Internet record that continues to harm your brand, fan base, business, or reputation among friends, customers, investors, or other media on a 24/7 basis.

This power of the new digital assassin to destroy is as powerful as YouTube, but as old as civilization. Character assassination was a weapon in the arsenal of the ancients, from palace intrigues against Jewish advisers to the king of Persia, to the philippics employed in the class struggles and civil warfare that consumed Rome in the time of Cicero and Mark Antony.

Character assassination is deeply woven into the fabric of American political life. America's revolutionary leaders, nostalgically remembered as our Founding Fathers, indulged in endless acrimonious backbiting. They used Latin pseudonyms and pamphlets to attack each other. They hired character assassins and subsidized vituperative partisan presses. The next chapter seeks lessons for the digital age from the savage, covert war Thomas Jefferson and Alexander Hamilton waged against each other through various journalistic outlets, flinging taunts that were well-understood references to each other's personal vulnerabilities in an effort to blackmail and dishearten.

This tendency to fling mud and ruin reputations was checked somewhat in the twentieth century by the rise of mainstream media—newspapers, wire services, magazines, radio news, and then television news—that relied on mass subscriptions and advertising to liberate editors and reporters from the tyranny of business and political patrons. The mainstream media had its biases. But it did something no character assassin has ever done. It tried to be fair and often succeeded.

The establishment media at its zenith illuminated all that could be seen. But the sun began to set on such media with the close of the twentieth century.

In this new century, we find ourselves surprisingly close to the nineteenth-century era of barbed commentary, slanted accounts, and subsidized attacks. The migration of these smears from paper pamphlets to screens, however, is about more than the evolution of print into more vivid media.

With the new technology, character assassins have more than a few new platforms from which to attack. Digital technology enables spontaneous groups to emerge instantly, bringing the power of social media to the age-old human tendency to character assassinate.

The Internet empowers a motley collection of anarchists, libertarians, leftists, and hackers known as Anonymous to spontaneously organize hundreds of sites to continue Julian Assange's cyber WikiLeaks campaign against Washington, D.C. Social media lets ordinary people do what tyrants and terrorists could not—make a frontal assault on the U.S. government and win.

Assassins with little effort and little cost can now contact your customers or stakeholders, employees and colleagues, lovers or friends, fans, and even former high school coaches and teachers, to contribute a few keystrokes that can add telling details to form a collective portrait of your monstrosity. Such smears then become a permanent part of your digital reputation—one you can subsume, but not hide from the world.

In the days of the old media, you had obvious ways to counter a bad story. There were ombudsmen, op-eds and letters to the editor, advertising opportunities and plenty of competitors willing to let you tell your side.

Now, when a negative thread appears about you on the Internet, you'll never know for sure who read it, how it was received, or whether a separate targeted campaign was mounted to directly deliver it to your friends, customers, clients, employers, and significant others. Today, in this new media, you may never know how deep the wound is until it manifests itself in the form of murdered opportunity, both personal and financial.

So then, what can be done?

We take an analytical and anecdotal approach to the new phenomenon of digital assassination. This is needed because many books today tend to get lost in technology, as well as its platforms—Twitter, Facebook, Yelp, and the rest—as if the basis of the problem was technology itself.

To be sure, new technology is transformative. And it is overwhelmingly good, improving the way we live, work, shop, educate, and romance. It changes societies with unprecedented transparency.

This technology, however, also has a dark side. We explore how that dark side can threaten your reputation, brand, and business from online attacks.

The first two chapters show how principles of human behavior, not technology, are the driving factors behind this dark side of the Internet. In chapters 3 through 9, we reveal the seven forms of digital attacks, how they can destroy business, career, and life.

In these chapters, we draw on stories from the left, the right, and the center—from ancient times; the American Founding Fathers; our experience working with world leaders, CEOs, and corporate boards; and pulp dramas right out of the tabloids—not to make you feel sorry for the victims, but to create object lessons useful for you.

We will explore what is timeless about the uses of this technology and what is new.

Many victims of digital assassination in these pages might include people whose personalities you find grating or whose politics you find offensive or both.

Never mind.

This is not a political book. It is about understanding the nature of attacks, as a basis to prepare you to act in your defense.

In chapter 11, we arm you with seven strategies, as well as tactics and keystrokes, you need to blunt and reverse attacks. This chapter presents ways to be ready for a surprise onslaught and to monitor your presence in cyberspace, and provides a simple game plan and actions to take when an attack occurs.

Whether you are a corporate executive or manager, doctor, lawyer, accountant, consultant with a large group or singular sensation, shop-keeper or restaurateur, model, designer, celebrity, parent, or grandparent, this book will help you understand the nature of these digital attacks and how to prepare for them and respond.

> No one is bulletproof in the digital world. Take steps to show a digital assassin you are not an easy mark.

2:// America's First Bloggers

> One of our greatest presidents [Thomas Jefferson], our greatest Founding Father, is also the one we've got the goods on in terms of being a jerk.
>
> —**Stephen Colbert**, interview on "Monticello," *American Icons*

MILLIONS OF PEOPLE feel adrift on the Silicon Sea. There are no welcoming shores visible on this horizon, only mysterious kingdoms with fanciful names like Tumblr, Twitter, Digg, Delicious, Foursquare, Second Life.

If you are older, you might sometimes feel like you have been given the exhausting task of exploring these unfamiliar shorelines to classify a whole new zoology, as if it were up to you personally to define the ecological niche each distinctive new service occupies in the world of social media.

In truth, understanding the technology is the easy part. All you have to do is to Google, Bing, or Yahoo! anything you don't understand. Go to that site, and it will show you what it does. If you want to know more, read consumer or media reviews from leading sites like mashable.com, as well as the mainstream press. Clear answers in everyday language are at your fingertips.

If you are younger, you navigate the virtual world with ease. What is harder for all generations to grasp is that behind the technology is greed, malice, desire—the age-old motivations of money, sex, power, and envy.

Many take information from you—where you go, whom you talk to, what you decide to post—and commoditize it, even weaponize it.

So age needs to approach technology with greater skill, while youth needs to approach technology with greater wisdom. For everyone, the most difficult things to anticipate about new technologies are the possible creative uses for them and humans' myriad reasons to use them in spiteful ways.

How do we recognize age-old patterns of attack in the new media? And in which ways can technology endow human malice with awesome new muscle?

Too much of commentary about the misuses of Internet platforms gets lost in the power and breadth of this technology. True, the Internet, no less than the Industrial Revolution, is reshaping every aspect of our life. One in eight couples married in the United States met through social media. Facebook is the world's largest country.[1] User-generated content is forcing business to be responsive to the customer as never before. Adaptive information technology may be our best hope of educating the planet.

Digital technology is an enormous force for good. But the cyberutopians overlook the fact that because digital technology is woven into almost everything we do and think, this technology also has a raging dark side, which includes digital assassination.

Some current books tend to get lost in the modality of expression, as if the basis of the problem was the technological platforms themselves. Rather than get lost in these technologies and platforms, we must first understand the broader strategic patterns from which character attacks surface on digital platforms. This book starts with the insight that the underlying issue is not the proliferation of dangerous technologies, but the amplification of human meanness.

To fully understand how character assassination works in our digital world, we need to look to history. This chapter will examine a conflict from late 1700s America, when newspapers came damp with printer's ink. This struggle reveals seven key ways to destroy a target's character. We will examine each of these seven "swords" to understand how they are amplified by digital speed, magnitude, and the capacity for spontaneous organization.

Blackmail, Slaves, and Sex

Every day, millions of bloggers—some paid, some not; some tired, angry, or blowing off steam—fill the Internet with attacks on brands, products, companies, or individuals. It is all too easy to get hung up on the technology and forget that what we are dealing with are for the most part just words.

The practice of using words to slip a knife into the ribs of a rival is as old as Rome—and as American as Thomas Jefferson and Alexander Hamilton. This chapter takes an in-depth look at a historical struggle that involved power, sex, and skulduggery.*

This story reveals the seven swords of character assassination exposed by a feud between prominent early Americans, those we call America's first bloggers. Jefferson and Hamilton—each embodying an ideological polarity of early America—waged a long subterranean war that began in Washington's cabinet between the secretary of state and the secretary of the treasury. The weapon of choice in their duel was the exposure of each other's sex lives. What transpired in this early period provides a model for understanding the dangerous trends proliferating in our digital age.

Hamilton Sexposed

On a July day in 1791, in Philadelphia, Alexander Hamilton had a lapse in judgment that would become a gift to his enemies. He took a visit from Maria Reynolds, an attractive and vulnerable twenty-three-year-old mother abandoned by her husband James to fend for herself and their daughter. She sought help from the sensitive and sympathetic Hamilton, one of the young nation's most prominent men.

When Hamilton promised to give Maria $30, he made a point of delivering it personally. Maria pointedly invited Hamilton upstairs to her bedroom, where, he later admitted, "it was quickly apparent that other than pecuniary consolation would be accepted." In fact, for almost a year, Hamilton—married to Elizabeth Schuyler, one of the most beautiful and socially connected women in New York State—made regular visits to the young Maria, entering her rooming house through a back door.

Hamilton must have known of Maria's husband. James Reynolds was a hustler who was making a fortune swindling Revolutionary War

* For a detailed but riveting history, see Ron Chernow's *Alexander Hamilton* (New York: Penguin, 2004).

veterans and their widows out of their back pay. Returning to Philadelphia and to his young wife, Reynolds saw the married Hamilton as a new mark. He wrote a letter about "the poor Broken harted woman" that must have shot a bolt of fear through Hamilton's heart: "I would Sacrefise almost my life to make her Happy. but now I am determined to have satisfation."

As it turned out, satisfaction could be had not in the form of a duel, but in the form of a government sinecure. Hamilton refused to install Reynolds in an office, but he did pay $1,000 in blackmail to James Reynolds, about $23,000 in today's money. There would be many more such "contributions."

After a brief attempt at restraint, Hamilton returned to the affections of the young Maria. As he did, more requests for payments came from James Reynolds. In effect, Hamilton was now paying Reynolds as both a blackmailer and a pimp.

In 1792, James Reynolds was arrested for, among other things, an early American version of identity theft, claiming to be the executor of a soldier's estate. From his jail cell, Reynolds got word of the affair to several political detractors of Hamilton, including future president James Monroe.

Hamilton came clean, admitting to the whole squalid arrangement to congressional inquirers. Monroe held on to the copies of the incriminating documents, which eventually found their way to his fellow Jeffersonians, including James Callender, the scurrilous smear artist secretly subsidized by Jefferson. Jefferson himself tried to get the U.S. House of Representatives to censure the Treasury Secretary for mixing up federal accounts, as well as other charges.

Hamilton survived by throwing himself into a prodigious effort to respond to each charge. This lunge for Hamilton's jugular was a mistake, for Thomas Jefferson's private life was at least as vulnerable as Hamilton's. And Hamilton knew just how to strike back at Jefferson.

Jefferson's Secret Desire

After leaving office, Hamilton took up writing under the pen name of Phocion in the *Gazette of the United States* in 1796, ridiculing the southern fear that emancipation would result in miscegenation, when in fact the slavemaster (unmistakably Jefferson) "must have seen all around him sufficient marks" of racial mixing. A few days later, Hamilton referred to "evidences of aristocratic splendor, sensuality, and epicureanism" on the plantation.

Four days later, Jefferson's allies anonymously referred to the Reynolds affair in the Republican *Aurora*. "Would a publication of the circumstances of that transaction redound to the honour or reputation of the parties and why has the subject been so long and carefully smothered up?"

In other words, Hamilton employed a front to tell Jefferson that he knew that the sage of Monticello was using a slave for sex. Jefferson, likely through the pen of an ally, was telling Hamilton, that he'd better shut up about that, or the whole world would know about Maria Reynolds.

For a time, both Jefferson and Hamilton had acceded to the reputational equivalent of mutually assured destruction. Jefferson's Charlottesville neighbors had long gossiped about the widower's closeness to his slave, Sally Hemings, and the resemblance of her children to the master of the house.

And here matters rested until Callender went public with the Reynolds story, using the sex angle to prop up the old charge that Hamilton had been cooking the federal books.

Under attack, Hamilton adopted the same response as he had done before Congress. He published ninety-five pages of personal confession, letters, and affidavits that led the reader through a thorough account of the affair, Hamilton's long slide into the grasping hands of James Reynolds, and documentation absolving him of any betrayal of his public duty.

Did it work? The Jeffersonian press had a field day, raising the question that if Hamilton admitted to being a rake, why should we not believe he was also swindler? Most readers saw something else. They recognized in Hamilton's confession the desire to obtain the respect of his countrymen for his achievements as a statesman at the expense of their opinion of his private behavior. Even then, there were sections of Hamilton's pamphlet that read almost like an eighteenth-century version of the Starr Report. It offered, in modern parlance, too much information.

Jefferson had little time to gloat. In this all-out war of character attack by paid partisans, neither party would escape unscathed. In Jefferson's case, it was not so much the hidden hand of Alexander Hamilton as it was the undependability of his own paid assassin.

The same James T. Callender who prospered on Jefferson's payroll became embittered when jailed under President Adams's Alien and Sedition Acts, and vengeful when Jefferson, now president himself, refused to pay off his potential blackmailer with a government appointment. The president did make a private "charity" payment. Callender was insulted but took the money.

In 1802, Callender accused Jefferson in the Richmond *Recorder* of fathering several of the six children of Sally Hemings. Callender's revelation came at the worst possible time for Jefferson, early in his first term as president.

The Reputational Fallout

Jefferson could have followed Hamilton's strategy of issuing a confession. He could have tried, like Nixon, a "limited hangout." He could have lied like Clinton. Instead, Jefferson maintained a dignified and glacial silence. Fourteen years later, Jefferson explained his approach to the scandal in a letter to a supporter: "I should have fancied myself half guilty had I condescended to put pen to paper in refutation of their falsehoods, or drawn to them respect by any notice from myself."

The scandal in our time, of course, is not that Jefferson likely loved a woman of color, but that he owned her and their children—and continued to own them when he could have given them their freedom. This personal failing throws into stark relief the contradiction of Jefferson, human liberator and slaveholder.

In matters of character, we are sometimes forced to choose between current comfort and damnation for posterity. Hamilton sullied his reputation while safeguarding his place in history. Jefferson protected his presidency at the expense of his reputation for all time.

Now, how is all this relevant today?

The Seven Swords of Digital Assassination

Digital attacks are more about words and strategy than media and technology.

The Internet has power that no other media has ever offered. Power in the form of instantaneity, 24/7 global reach, eternal memory, deep search capability, and instant retrieval. But what was the American Revolution if not a social media movement drummed up by newspapers, pamphlets, and polemical engravings, such as Paul Revere's rendition of the Boston Massacre?

As with the paper world, the digital world has its Facebook prostitutes and digital exposés. But out of the Jefferson–Hamilton stealth reputation war we can identify seven distinct strategies of attack, seven swords of character assassination augmented by the new power of the Internet age.

In the coming chapters, we will examine how each of these seven swords slash and wound in the twenty-first century.

The First Sword of Digital Assassination—New Media Mayhem

From the printing press to the personal digital assistant, new media has been a disruptive force that upends regimes and overturns authority of every kind. This can be seen in the eighteenth century, when mass circulation media in the form of paper pamphlets, magazines, and daily newspapers trafficked in gossip and skewered monarchs and presidents alike. This cacophony of anger helped inspire colonial rebellion in America, social turmoil in England, and bloody revolution in France.

Today, new media organizes leaderless revolutions in Libya, Tunisia, Egypt, and elsewhere, allowing WikiLeaks to set the U.S. government on its heels and bloggers to confront global corporations.

The Second Sword of Digital Assassination—Silent Slashers

Silent Slashers are severe cuts to one's reputation from anonymous attackers. In early America, anonymous pamphlets and leaflets aired personal and political attacks too venomous for attribution, freeing attackers from having to own up to their remarks. Federalist leaflets depicted Jefferson as a swindler, an atheist, and a Jacobin who wanted the streets to run red with revolution. Republican leaflets portrayed John Adams as planning to marry his sons into the British royal family in order to establish monarchies on either side of the Atlantic. Many of these broadsides were from Silent Slashers—anonymous, destructive, and well circulated.

Today Silent Slashers have instantaneous and global reach. They appear, disappear, and reappear with a new angle of attack.

The Third Sword of Digital Assassination—Evil Clones

Impersonators can create an evil caricature of you, an avatar self that revels in its faults. In early America, the Jeffersonians attributed bogus quotes to John Adams to create a false representation of him as a "champion of kings, ranks, and titles," just as Federalists exaggerated Jefferson's Enlightenment views so as to make him seem atheistic and as dangerously radical as Robespierre.

Today digital technology allows anyone to instantaneously spawn an evil clone, a perfectly believable avatar, of anyone else, in online images as well as words.

The Fourth Sword of Digital Assassination—Human Flesh Search Engines

Attackers can crowd-source private information, turning gossip into actionable intelligence, using these unearthed secrets to incite mobs ready to tar, feather, and even lynch. Callender teased out intelligence about Jefferson and, in casual conversation while in jail and, later, with Jefferson's neighbors over fence posts and in taverns. The story had already been put together for him: Crowds can perform investigations better than any individual.

Today digital assassins appeal to global audiences to collect secrets about individuals from old teachers, colleagues, and ex-lovers—and then call on the crowd to launch attacks on that target from every possible angle.

The Fifth Sword of Digital Assassination—Jihad by Proxy

Organizations with noble-sounding names and mission statements can disguise attacks for donors with less than the civic good in mind. Jefferson's campaign against President Adams was organized through Committees of Correspondence, modeled after the effective revolutionary political communications organs of the same name, that produced attacks and spread dirt from organizations that appeared to be citizens acting out of high motives.

Today there is a panoply of front organizations, nourished and funded by special interests, that launch online attacks on environmental, health, and patriotic grounds that are utterly disingenuous.

The Sixth Sword of Digital Assassination—Truth Remix

Ordinary human imperfection can be exaggerated, turning commonplace failings and vices into horrendous crimes. In the eighteenth century, Jefferson tried to transform Hamilton's personal scandal into a financial one, and Hamilton tried to link Jefferson's complicated life to the charge of being a dangerous radical. They reduced shades of gray into deepest black.

Today the traditional media has been replaced by a blogosphere that creates falsities out of truth in order to compete for ratings and clicks.

The Seventh Sword of Digital Assassination—Clandestine Combat

Throughout history, when all else fails, enemies or competitors simply purloin each other's secrets.

This was done to Hamilton by Jeffersonians who leaked the confidential investigation of the Reynolds affair, and by Hamilton who secretly interviewed cabinet officers, getting them to leak stories that portrayed President Adams as unstable and "mad." At the end, water seeks the lowest level. Character assassins are desperate enough to take what they cannot find.

Today, the open architecture of our critical technologies provide hackers unprecedented opportunities for outright stealing.

THESE SEVEN SWORDS are examined in the chapters ahead. We will reveal age-old patterns of attack and emerging new capabilities powered by technology in the digital age.

In *Thirteen Days*, a movie about the Cuban Missile Crisis, the Robert McNamara character looks at a war-room map of the U.S. Navy blockade of Cuba. McNamara tells a top admiral that a naval blockade at the brink of nuclear war is not a blockade. "This is language," he says. "A new vocabulary, the likes of which the world has never seen! This is President Kennedy communicating with Secretary Khrushchev!"[2]

This was eloquent but wrong.

Instead, what was being used was an old vocabulary of power projection that seemed new because it was transmitted instantly and for far higher stakes. What had changed was speed and magnitude. The same is true of digital technology today.

> In a digital world, age needs to approach technology with greater skill. Youth needs to approach technology with greater wisdom.

3:// The First Sword

New Media Mayhem

> Clothes make the man. Naked people have little or no influence on society.
>
> —**Mark Twain**

NEW MEDIA is still evolving in fast-forward, shaped by Darwinian forces that mold increasingly lethal forms of digital assassination. This first sword of digital assassination, new media mayhem—from Gutenberg's printing press to Google's Android—is a disruptive force that roils governments and challenges authority in all its forms.

This new global media environment oddly takes us back to the level of a disgraced inhabitant of a small village of a prior era, condemned for life by gossip. It is impossible to doubt that we live in a global village of character assassination when:

- Fortune 500 companies and individuals alike rely on computer systems wide open to hacking and exploitation.
- Negative images are sticky, eternal, and prone to spread like kudzu in a Google environment.
- Nongovernmental organizations (NGOs) are often in cahoots with secret donors, the media, and ambitious prosecutors to target the successful.
- Media institutions that might have mitigated the damage have been replaced by the clowns and barking seals of a digital circus.
- Companies, brands, products, and people must monitor anything said about them through nights, weekends, and holidays

in order to keep pace with the tech-enabled demons inhabiting the Internet.
- We are surrounded by potential "shame famers" grasping for attention.
- Business competitors are as apt to inspire or spread the defamation about you as they are to rush to your defense.

The Global Bookie and the Hilton Effect

Exquisitely sensitive to customer needs, Google has tried to live up to its unofficial motto, "Don't Be Evil"—winning the applause of human rights activists by standing up to censorship by the People's Republic of China. Google is the first big Western company willing to risk abandoning the world's largest market over an issue of principle.

The problem with Google isn't its business ethics or its heart, but the way its algorithms wind up reinforcing the Internet's dark side. Google doesn't mean to be evil. It means to track billions of click-throughs to see how hot topics, sales, ads, and pricing trends fluctuate—information that is worth billions of dollars to marketers.

Google excels at this because it is a heuristic learner. That is, Google learns by its experience with you. It excels at seeking optimal solutions based on rough approximations of your somewhat inaccurate and sometimes misspelled search terms. As it learns what you like, Google hones in on your preferences to find more of what you like.

"Another light side of informatics is Amazon," says Leo Yakutis, an IT expert who started his career troubleshooting product support for Microsoft and is now a digital hound, a private investigator who detects breeches in corporate firewalls and traces attacks back to their source. "Amazon predicts and recommends things that you want for the future. That's what happens when what is out there about you is used for a productive purpose."[1]

Just as Amazon predicts what kind of book you'll want, and Google can track and remember your searches, so too can search engines follow the tastes of the crowd to rank search results by popularity. These capabilities are truly transformative, shifting the commercial paradigm from mass marketing to social media and putting unprecedented power in the hands of consumers.

But it isn't always the cream that rises to the top. It is the sensational that draws the most viewers and inspires them to link to one another. And negative emotions draw the most links of all. A razor-sharp attack in the Huffington Post or the National Review Online will immediately attract cross-links and chatter from a thousand blogs and Twitter accounts. Negative items that shock the most rise even faster.

In late 2009, people around the world who searched for an image of the First Lady of the United States found among the top results to come up was not one of Mrs. Obama's official and press portraits and candid shots, but a grotesque melding of her face with that of a chimpanzee.

"People gimmick the system to get their stuff up higher and higher," says James Lee, a social media expert and president of The Lee Strategy Group in Los Angeles. "Google keeps trying to improve its searches, but people keep finding ways to skew the system. If you want to intentionally defame someone, it's an easy process."[2]

The process is easy even when defamation may not be intended.

In a landmark case, Barbra Streisand unintentionally demonstrated how the sticky nature of the Internet can spread unwanted information even when no malicious force is at work. The diva was following the rules of old media when she sued to keep an environmental activist and Pictopia.com from posting aerial photos of her beachside mansion. At the time, the photo was sandwiched with more than 12,000 other coastline photographs.

The publicity from Streisand's lawsuit for $50 million in damages had the effect of blowing hard on a dandelion gone to seed—the obscure site soon had more than one million visitors.[3] The picture wafted all across the Internet, like so many dandelion seeds, into too many places to monitor or count. Since then, the tendency of cease-and-desist letters to spread unwanted or damaging information or images has been called the Streisand Effect.

So it is almost impossible for an offended person to compel the total removal of something off the web that has already achieved some notoriety without making it more widespread. Since Google's caching of the web gives it virtual omniscience, the effort at old-fashioned damage control also guarantees that the offending pictures, video, or words never really go away.

Two days after Tyler Clementi committed suicide, Yakutis checked to see how far the actual sex tape had circulated. "It was on over a thousand English-speaking servers," he says. "How are you going to clean that up?"

The media focuses on the catastrophic stories of Internet exposure and suicide like Clementi's. But there are many more young people who will pay a more subtle price. "Digitally defaming a grandma in her seventies is not really that effective if she doesn't use the media," says Yakutis. "But make a charge of assault against a young football player, no matter how little foundation for the charge, it can't go away for him—ever."

Nor does an inflammatory comment a young person makes online. "Young professional athletes have lots of testosterone, lots of ambition, lots of money, and low maturity," Yakutis says. "So say a young football player bad-mouths his coach on Facebook or Twitter. Every tweet from the beginning of Twitter in 2006 is now indexed at the Library of Congress."

"Your indiscretions will be able to be seen by generations and generations of graduate students," Stanford scholar Paul Saffo told *The New York Times*.[4]

And when a posting does start to fade, archival retrieval services like the Wayback Machine act as digital time capsules to make sure that everything that once was on the Internet can remain on the Internet. "You touch the Internet and it never forgets," says Bill Livingstone, a former high-level political operative turned security expert. "Your criminal record can be wiped clean in seven years, but not if you can still find it on the Internet."[5]

This Streisand Effect is what happens when you fail to understand how Google operates.

The Hilton Effect is what happens when you fail to understand who is in control of the pattern of attacks and counterattacks. Consider how Google's rating by popularity acts as fuel for salacious Internet destinations like that of Perez Hilton's Hollywood gossip site. This shock blogger until recently had a habit of drawing penises over the faces of celebrities he doesn't like. He also inserts snarky captions. One Hollywood celebrity, a picture posted of her looking out the window from the driver's seat of her car, has Hilton's added caption "Crack Is Wack," thus implying that she is a crack addict.[6]

The opening salvo of an attack on such a site may be highly clicked. If the public gets engaged in the story, the counter to the attack is thus also assured of high ratings, boosted by links and algorithms to a few keywords, which sets up even higher ratings for the next attack.

More dirt means more eyeballs, which means greater ad revenue.

The Hilton Effect was on full display in 2009, when a Miss USA judge, none other than Perez Hilton himself, asked California beauty contestant Carrie Prejean where she stood on gay marriage. No matter how you feel about gay marriage, the digital subtext of this media drama is perhaps the greater story, one that reveals new media as a force greater than any debate it amplifies.

Prejean replied with an answer that she later characterized as "biblically correct" rather than politically correct. Within minutes, the beauty queen's no to gay marriage became a top feature on Internet searches and YouTube clicks, propelled by both angry people passionately in favor of gay marriage and people who greatly opposed to same-sex unions.

Perez Hilton, the self-styled queen of all media, quickly responded with a video flaming Prejean as a "dumb bitch" who had made the biggest PR mistake in pageant history. Thus Hilton's attack became a top Internet search term; his vitriolic interpretation was laid on top of her answer, creating a negative context for it.

When Prejean appeared on NBC's *Today* show two days after the pageant, she shot back that she was being victimized for giving an honest answer that was close to those given by then presidential candidates Obama and Hillary Clinton. Prejean's response overlaid Hilton's comments, putting her back on top on YouTube.

Hilton and his allies subsequently revealed Prejean's old modeling pictures, which they argued were salacious (part of a nipple was showing), and exposed the evangelical Christian Prejean to the charge of being a hypocrite. Then Prejean responded with a detailed explanation of how the pictures came to be and added another counter about how she had been mistreated.

And so on, the Hilton Effect game continued, each hand grabbing a higher part of a seemingly endless stick. Whether they knew it or not, Prejean and Hilton were in business together, his gay, blue-state yin countering her straight, red-state yang, and vice versa, for months on end.

Who won?

Google won. The corporate giant serves as the smart bookie who wins both sides of every bet, selling ads all along the way.

> **Global Bookie and the Hilton Effect:** For people, brands, or companies attacked on the Internet, Google's algorithms assure that every defense will hype every attack—and every counterresponse—for as long as the sheer ugliness of a fight is interesting to onlookers.

A Pirate's Dream

Ever wonder how vulnerable you are to digital pirates?

By now, everyone has read about Russian gangs and brigades of sophisticated hackers organized by the People's Liberation Army of China. But do these sophisticated hackers really target individuals, brands, or businesses? Do I really have to be worried about the computers in my offices, in my home, as well as my accounts with companies I do business with?

The average American is exposed to about 34 gigabytes of data and information each day. The average American youth, eight to eighteen years, devotes 7 hours and 38 minutes a day to entertainment media (10 hours and 45 minutes, if you include multitasking).[7] As that data flows into your devices, data about you is constantly flowing out—and not always to benign sources.

Reported privacy breaches occur all the time on a monumental scale. In 2010, Facebook, MySpace, and other sites were discovered to be releasing vast amounts of personal information about millions of users through apps and advertisers.

Then there is the more sinister work of "black hat" hackers. A Data Breach Investigations Report issued in 2009 by Verizon's RISK team could account for 90 data breaches compromising 285 million records in 2008.[8] Reported breaches have occurred with T-Mobile, American Express, PepsiCo, and Merrill Lynch.[9]

Bank of America in 2011 found itself in the crosshairs of unwanted attention from WikiLeaks. Even video games are subject to mass exposure of personal information. In May 2011, Sony acknowledged that digital pirates waged a highly sophisticated attack that potentially compromised more than 100 million online-gaming accounts, including its popular PlayStation Gaming Network. Industry insiders concede there have been innumerable other breaches—likely tens of millions of them—that companies do not want to report or even acknowledge internally.

Some basic truth about your computer emerged when a major IT company told the authors it decided to investigate just how seriously cyberattacks had penetrated the average computer—*your* computer. The company's engineers purchased a garden-variety PC from a chain retailer. They installed in it the best off-the-shelf antivirus, anti-spyware protection, and firewall software packages available. Then they connected this PC to the Internet. They did not use it for anything. They just tracked the flow of code into and out of the machine.

Within four hours the engineers detected the first ping by a potential hacker. In two weeks more sophisticated software from a computer in Canada slowly embedded itself in the PC and started running its own software. The Canadian computer soon set up links between the enslaved zombie PC and a computer in Singapore, which used the PC to attack a network in Poland.

This wide-open nature of any computer attached to the Internet, whether wired or wireless, is something that many executives understand intellectually but do not incorporate into their actions. Witness John Deutch, a polymath who earned a PhD in chemistry at MIT and served as President Bill Clinton's director of the CIA. This supremely intelligent man—at a conference one of the authors saw him taking notes in the form of a string of calculus variables—apparently did not know or accept how a computer worked. He took a CIA computer home with him, one laden with classified files containing—judging from the government's subsequent reaction—some of America's most closely held sources and methods. Deutch became the subject of an intense investigation after a routine audit of his computers by the CIA showed that he had connected it to the Internet, and on occasion someone with access to his computer used it to visit pornography websites.[10] Deutch might as well have left a briefcase full of secrets in Tiananmen Square or on the front doorstep of the FSB in Moscow.

Bill Clinton pardoned Deutch on his last day in office.

Before WikiLeaks revealed the extent of the government's vulnerability to pirates from within, attacks from China accessed sensitive data in four computers used by a staffer to U.S. Representative Frank Wolf specializing in foreign policy and human rights, likely compromising the identity of human rights sources in China.[11] Long before Google objected to China's infiltration of its Gmail accounts and corporate information, an attack linked to the People's Liberation Army forced the Pentagon to shut down part of a computer system serving the office of Defense Secretary Robert Gates.[12]

While black hats can't match the prowess of foreign governments in accessing federal computers, they have more than enough skill to get into any digital device you own. So if you are wondering if your computer or laptop is compromised in some way, you can stop worrying.

It is.

The ease with which digital assassins and potential blackmailers can access your machines for damaging information to use against you is limited only to the extent that there is nothing in any message you have ever sent, any website you have ever visited, or any secret—including financial details, account numbers and PIN numbers—that you would not want anyone to know about, in any of your computers.

> **A Pirate's Dream:** You are not somewhat exposed. The open nature of computing allows our systems to be easily boarded by digital assassins.

Corporate Warfare

Corporate executives once adhered to a code similar to that of white-shoe law firms. They would refrain from running down one another's products, brands, ethics, or character in ads or anywhere else. The peace between corporate giants of postwar America mirrored the uneasy Cold War peace. The damage such conflict would create was seen as an unthinkable risk, the corporate version of mutually assured destruction.

In the twenty-first century, however, this code seems as outdated as the top hats presidents once wore to their inaugurals. We are now in the age of combative advertising that began with the cola wars of the 1980s. Some negative ads are good natured and jocular in tone. In a set of 2009 commercials, after a Verizon ad lampooned AT&T's coverage, AT&T responded with a lawsuit, then a humorous response with actor Luke Wilson slowly downloading himself with Verizon.[13]

Others are meant to draw blood. Jenny Craig made a little dig at its principal diet-industry competitor, Weight Watchers, on its website and in a 2010 TV ad in the critical post-holiday season in which actress Valerie Bertinelli donned a lab coat to claim that a major clinical trial showed that "Jenny Craig clients lost, on average, over twice as much weight as those on the largest weight-loss program!"[14]

This was a direct attack on the credibility of Weight Watchers spokeswoman Jenny McCarthy, who was boasting she had lost 75 pounds on the Weight Watchers program. Weight Watchers sued, claiming that Jenny Craig was lying. There had been, Weight Watchers claimed, no such "major clinical trial." The case was soon settled with Jenny Craig being forced to drop the ad.[15] These two corporations came off looking like two Roller Derby queens—Valerie and Jenny—throwing elbows and body slams.

Then there is Burt's Bees, the homespun maker of "Earth-friendly" personal care products. When Burt's Bees attacked its competitors, it did so not by attacking their brand, but by arousing fear about competitors' ingredients. One Burt's Bees Internet ad states that the lip balm from leading competitors (such as ChapStick) contains petroleum, which the ad helpfully adds is "a nonrenewable hydrocarbon made from crude oil . . . sometimes used to stop corrosion on car batteries."[16] Few customers realize that this eco-friendly brand with a logo that looks like it came straight from the *Farmers' Almanac* is in fact now a division of Clorox—a sign that even top Fortune 500 companies are willing to punch low and hard.[17]

In May 2011, Facebook was deeply embarrassed when it was caught using global PR firm Burson-Marsteller to pitch negative stories meant to put Google in hot water with the federal trade commission.[18]

Indeed, low-grade corporate warfare is constantly being waged between technology giants through patent trolls, insider blogs, and corporate talking points that company lobbyists thrust in front of senior congressional staffers and regulators. Time and again, it seems that technology companies that are against regulation as a matter of principle are more than willing to see harsh regulations imposed on their competitors.

What has changed is not just the willingness of companies to attack each other's products, but to launch real attacks on the lives of each other's brands or businesses.

Corporate Warfare: When a brand, product, executive, or company are digitally assassinated, shots may very well have been fired by a peer competitor.

The Iron Rectangle

Political scientists have long written of an Iron Triangle between congressional committees, the bureaucracy, and special interests. The American political scene today is more of an Iron Rectangle made up of new players. Money and politics shape and define the digital conversation.

It works like this: Trial lawyers, many of them überrich, troll for deep-pocket corporate victims to attack with class-action lawsuits. These trial lawyers funnel large sums (often laundered through foundations) into the second corner of the rectangle, activist nongovernmental organizations (NGOs).

The activist "scholars" of these NGOs are then inspired to act as opposition researchers to level a debatable but explosive charge, whether environmental (killing rivers!), health (cancer clusters!), or other hot-button claim (sweatshop!), against the target company, brand, or executive. The NGO spreads around the dirt in slickly produced reports and video clips, often with a voice-over by a naive Hollywood celebrity. All this publicity stimulates the third corner of the rectangle—the media—to ring like a chuckwagon dinner bell.

NGOs such as the National Resources Defense Council or the Center for Science in the Public Interest are powerful and well funded. They have institutional agendas no less ambitious than those of Exxon or Citigroup. Yet many journalists and bloggers uncritically accept any claims these NGOs put before them as if these came from pure and objective sources.

The media, whether old mainstream or new online, are more than willing to trumpet these stories as scandals and raise the heat to create a basis for public action. This in turn engages the fourth and final corner of the rectangle, politicians—federal and state regulators, members of Congress angling for a TV or video bite, and especially state attorney generals, who (close to the trial bar, usually his or her biggest contributor and future employer) often hire on behalf of the state—surprise!—members of the trial bar who initiated the whole controversy.

Eliot Spitzer, long before his own disgrace and resignation as New

York governor in a sex scandal—a man many on Wall Street dubbed the worst character assassin of the last decade—perfected this game of state attorney general as avenging angel. The power behind this Iron Rectangle, however, begins and ends with the trial bar, which has revenues that far exceed those of Intel, Microsoft, or Coca-Cola.[19]

The tobacco settlements and successful asbestos class-action verdicts have left trial lawyers with billions of dollars more to invest in pioneering new charges with a coterie of bespoke scientists, oily PR firms, and pliable NGOs, thus pushing claims against new deep-pocket victims through corporate character assassination.

The Iron Rectangle: Ready-made character assassination machines driven by powerful and moneyed interests.

The Rise of the "Digital Estate" and Gossip Girls

Big media is often accused of being liberal, biased, and urbane. But if ABC, CBS, NBC, or CNN made an assertion, it was in the open. You knew who was reporting the allegation, even if they did quote unnamed sources. There was also a predictable cycle to the news in the last century that worked, in most instances, to ferret out the truth.

Wire services, radio network news, and newspapers gave more thoughtful analysis and local TV sent out reporters to validate information. In the end, major networks, *The New York Times,* and *The Washington Post* defined what was newsworthy.

It was a creaky and flawed system based on fallible, biased human beings. But it (mostly) worked.

Today the old networks continue to cover news largely as they always have, but with a rapidly shrinking audience. Fox News covers the news differently, with a conservative bias, but also with enough credibility to grow market share exponentially. In a sign of Fox's growing media dominance, in 2010 and May 2011, Bill O'Reilly went mano a mano with one of the great wits of the left, Jon Stewart of *The Daily Show.* It is impossible to imagine such ideological diversity, not to mention unrestrained debate, in the days of Dan Rather and John Chancellor.

While declining ad revenues have forced newspapers and TV stations to pull their last remaining news bureaus from state capitals and make deep cuts in their news staff, a new animal—online "sponsored news"—has begun to occupy this empty space. This is not the Fourth Estate we have long known. This is a new Digital Estate.

On the left, sponsored news is typified by the Huffington Post Investigative Fund, a group of online journalists sponsored by the left-wing Tides Center, the 501(c)3 with connections to the scandal-ridden ACORN.[20] On the right, sponsored news is supported by the Franklin Center for Government and Public Integrity, a 501(c)3 that supports investigative journalist watchdogs who reveal profligacy and conflicts of interest in state capitals.[21]

In both cases, these organizations are not required by law to reveal the identities of their ultimate donors—and they do not.

Journalists in both camps do profess adherence to the code of ethics of the Society of Professional Journalists. Both sides undoubtedly strive to report the truth as they see it. Franklin Center journalists broke the story that the Obama administration was bragging about saving or creating jobs with stimulus dollars in congressional districts that don't exist. The HuffPo investigative journalists broke the story that the payday lending industry spent record sums on lobbyists to try to stay out of Washington's various proposals for financial reform.

So both report with a given slant to expose a set of targets to satisfy the worldviews of their sponsors and readerships. The HuffPo Investigative Fund is not likely to go after a scandal in the Obama administration, and journalists supported by the Franklin Center are not likely to fact-check Sarah Palin.

As mainstream media retreats, there are fewer and fewer journalists who would be willing to go after sacred cows on either side of the ideological divide.

Meanwhile, on national TV, the signature news of today comes not from a magisterial network anchor, whether Fox, NBC, or the gray lady of *The New York Times,* but from biased stories from Gossip Girls like Extra, ET, and TMZ who serve every prurient taste ("who's gay and who's not," "fat celebrities on the beach!"). This is what is taking over the golden slot, the dinner hour that was once the province of Walter Cronkite and Peter Jennings.

People who once scoured the society pages of *The New York Times* turn to anonymous reviewers like Socialite Rank, with comment boards that offered unsourced descriptions of cocaine use and lurid sex.

The old major networks are often forced, sometimes with mock reluctance, to report gossip as news. So if TMZ or Perez Hilton drives a story far enough on the Internet, old media is forced to cover it with the fig leaf that the very spread of the gossip itself forces them to treat it as news.

Rising over the exotic creatures of this vast and ever-changing new media ocean is the sun, which is of course Google.

Gossip Girls: Victims of character assassination should expect little fairness and no ombudsmen from this new Digital Estate.

Damage at Light-Speed

"Everywhere you go, everyone has a camera," says comedian Robin Williams. "It's not Big Brother anymore, it's Little Snitch."[22] The Internet is the new camera of the twenty-first century. It is always on.

Little Snitch hides in video cameras, cell phone cameras, and tiny pinhole cameras disguised in pens or on lapels or in reading or sunglasses. It can arrive in your office in the hands of Michael Moore, or it can already be in your office. James O'Keefe, half of the "pimp and prostitute" hoax that brought down ACORN, pled guilty for masquerading as a telephone technician to get into the telephone exchange of Senator Mary Landrieu, Democrat of Louisiana.[23]

It is not enough to watch what you say. You have to be careful what you read. Representative John Conyers, a Democrat from Illinois, chairman of the House Judiciary Committee in 2010, was riding on an airplane when he was caught by another passenger's camera phone ogling photo spreads in an adult magazine.[24]

A device that weighs next to nothing can have the instant, broad, and permanent impact of a thousand-pound bomb. Remember the explosive impact online photos of prisoner abuse at Abu Ghraib had on Donald Rumsfeld and the Pentagon? Or the crushing impact on actor Alec Baldwin when his telephone tirade against his daughter went viral? Or the coup de grâce to Mel Gibson's reputation when his girlfriend leaked his rants to Radar Online? All it takes is a few sound bites or devastating images to fashion a "TubeBomb" on YouTube, a visual IED to take out you, your brand, your product, or your company.

Restaurants, who rely on the trust of easily turned-off customers, are particularly vulnerable to TubeBomb attacks. A KFC in California and a Burger King in Ohio were the first fast-food chains to be Tube-Bombed by employees taping themselves performing disgusting pranks (in these cases, workers filmed themselves soaking in restaurant kitchen sinks).[25]

Then in 2009 came the mother of all pranks, when two young Domino's Pizza employees in rural North Carolina filmed themselves sneezing and blowing their noses on Domino's food and other grotesque behavior. By the time 750,000 people had viewed the video, Domino's was reeling and struggling to get out the word that the two now-fired employees had not actually served the disgusting pizza to customers.

About forty-eight hours later, Domino's president Patrick Doyle posted a sincere YouTube response in which he thanked the online community for allowing him to take immediate action—issuing felony arrest warrants for the employees and sanitizing the store. He ended his two-minute apology with an impassioned talk about the damage to Domino's local, independent owners and the company's 125,000 employees.[26]

This was a bold move, a light-speed reaction according to the standards of classic media relations. In this new global, digital world, however, the authors advise clients to view eight hours as one digital day. By this standard, Doyle was late by five digital days. "The lag in response time left the online conversation to grow and fester, and the story continued to proliferate throughout social media channels," wrote Patrick Vogt in *Forbes* magazine.[27]

A truly effective response would have been mounted *within hours.*

Sales still sagged. Within months, Domino's unveiled a new humility campaign, launching a total repositioning of its product.

Damage at Light-Speed: Renders digital assassination a form of asymmetrical warfare with the attacker always having the ultimate advantage—surprise.

Shame Famers

Most people become celebrities because, like Tiger Woods or John Edwards, they do one thing exceptionally well. The fact that this preceding statement may have prompted you to giggle illustrates the extent to which scandal can utterly overshadow achievement.

The sexual predations of wayward people is matched by the publicity predators they seem to attract, for whom scandal is their only claim to fame. This was not true of the infamous women of history, from Cleopatra to Catherine the Great, who were resourceful queens who manipulated empires and commanded armies. Their sexual predations only inflamed their existing reputations. But in today's digital world Paris Hilton was what?—an "heiress"—when her sex video went viral and made her a household name.

That kind of viral shame fame would have been impossible without the Internet. For this new kind of celebrity, scandal is the only reason for fame—with big potential to inflict collateral damage on everyone they know. Few people who are publicly embarrassed like Paris Hilton actually find their shame to be a golden road to riches. But that doesn't keep thousands from trying.

Witness Duke University 2010 graduate Karen Owen, who created a multimedia "Fuck List" PowerPoint thesis of the men she had slept with, rating their attributes complete with a professional-looking case-study approach, including bar charts. The fact that she may have foolishly believed it would be shared with just a few friends did not stop it becoming a global sensation—with a flood of queries from agents, publishers, and movie producers.[28]

Or consider the women in the Tiger Woods scandal. There was a time not so long ago when being publicly identified as an adulteress was a badge of shame and would have had severe consequences for one's career or marriage prospects. At the very least, most women would have been mortified to have their parents, family, boss, and friends know that they engaged in this behavior.

Not Jaimee Grubbs, the cocktail waitress who sold her story to *US Weekly* and told it to VH1's *Tool Academy*, or any number of other women who came out of the woodwork of various golf clubs and bars to tell their Tiger tales. The willingness, even eagerness, to blithely disclose sordid details to millions of strangers is a new kind of exhibitionism that is a prime enabler of character assassination.

A record of sorts was set in this arena when YaVaughnie Wilkins, the former mistress of Charles Phillips, president of Oracle, made her announcement to the world. After Phillips broke off their relationship, Wilkins became famous—infamous being hard to achieve these days—by spending a fortune to post photos of her snuggling with the married Phillips on gigantic billboards in New York City, Atlanta, and San Francisco.

In years gone by, wives were most likely to go public to embarrass a wayward husband. Now it is the other woman.

Another source of shame fame comes from young men who lack any memory of the chivalric code that males were once taught by their fathers. Levi Johnston is a prime example of the new age of shame fame.

Soon after his wedding plans with Bristol Palin were scrapped, Johnston trashed his onetime fiancée and her family on the usual round of celebrity talk shows. He revealed a number of personal family secrets, posed nude for *Playgirl,* and shopped a book and a movie deal. It doesn't matter where you come down on the political spectrum or what you think of the Palins. Johnston has taken boorishness to a new level.

The likelihood is that most of these Shame Famers will live to regret their roll in the mud. Ten years from now when the easy money has long since run out, they will bitterly regret having defined themselves for life.

Or maybe not. For many people, having once been on national television and in the pages of *People* magazine is the definition of success, regardless of the reason. This exhibitionistic drive is more than a danger for the wayward. It is a positive danger for organizations, good and bad actors alike, that can be reduced to shambles by a character assassin posing as a whistle-blower.

It is not a far step from a Shame Famer to Mark E. Whitacre (memorably played by Matt Damon in Steven Soderbergh's *The Informant*), who alerted the FBI to price-fixing at Archer Daniels Midland and served as their undercover agent, while simultaneously defrauding the company of $9 million. Later, when Whitacre was stripped of his legal immunity as a whistle-blower, *New York Times* reporter Kurt Eichenwald reported in his masterful chronicle, on which the movie was based, Whitacre tried to implicate the FBI by falsely accusing agents of destroying tapes.

Shame Famers: Suicide bombers who have nothing to protect can take out victims by the busload.

Blood and Sand in the New Digital Arena

Many people are somewhat knowledgeable about social media. Some are adept at using it for product publicity and promotion. But most still do not have solid plans and strategies to counter digital attacks.

The Internet is now a central feature of risk management for brands, products, or reputation. Yet most corporations have yet to become as sensitive to what is said about them online as many restaurants, doctors, and local businesses are to their reviews on Yelp. In the face of a digital onslaught, the prevailing instinct is still to circle the wagons . . . or Toyotas or BP tankers or Goldman Sachs trading desks.

In short, businesses or individuals, celebrities or nonprofits choose to stroll unprotected through this new war zone. Many sense but don't truly understand how the law treats digital media differently from offline media. Many still do not know that Section 230 of the Communications Decency Act of 1996 distinguishes between an interactive computer service provider—who is held harmless from liability—and an information content provider, who can be sued.

Take the case of a post on an AOL bulletin board that attached the phone number of an innocent man to cruel, sick humor about the bombing of the Alfred P. Murrah Federal Building (advertising T-shirts with the slogans, among others, "Visit Oklahoma City . . . It's a BLAST!!!" and "Putting the Kids to Bed . . . Oklahoma 1995").[29] The Fourth Circuit Court of Appeals upheld a lower court decision in favor of AOL.

One federal judge explained the logic behind this seemingly unfair law:

> Interactive computer services have millions of users. . . . The amount of information communicated via interactive computer services is therefore staggering. The specter of tort liability in an area of such prolific speech would have an obvious chilling effect. It would be impossible for service providers to screen each of

> their millions of postings for possible problems. Faced with potential liability for each message republished by their services, interactive computer service providers might choose to severely restrict the number and type of messages posted.[30]

In other words, if interactive computer service providers—not just AOL, but Google, Bing, Wikipedia, eHarmony, Facebook, and countless others—as defined by the Section 230 of the Communications Decency Act, were held responsible for anything and everything posted, the Internet as we know it and everything that depends on it would shut down.

That is why you may be able to sue *The New York Times* for running a letter to the editor that defames you, but you cannot successfully sue nytimes.com for a slur someone posts on the comments section of an article. In the digital world, only the content provider—the person who posted the malicious comment—can be held responsible.

The rub is that this person in many cases can be almost impossible to identify. While Section 230 keeps defamation suits from shutting down the Internet, it also encourages many websites to take a lackadaisical attitude toward defamation, forcing victims to spend a lot of time, anguish, and money to get their attention.

Most who are attacked on the Internet do not understand that assassins are playing under different rules from those in the offline world. Victims do not comprehend the fight they face to protect their company, brand, reputation, careers, marriages, and livelihoods because, being decent people themselves, they don't appreciate the many reasons attackers attack.

Why do people digitally assassinate?

The facile answer is because they can.

And they can because new technology platforms today allow a vengeful individual to have an impact as never before. The same power of social media that enabled Barack Obama to raise $650 million in small donations to run for the presidency also enables the nastier side of democracy. Social media can awaken citizen power. But it can also create a digital lynch mob.

The old motivations of money, sex, power, and envy are at play.

Take the money motivation. This can include powerful interests looking for profit: trial lawyers looking for a payout, ambitious politicians looking for trial lawyer contributions, unions looking for raises, TMZ and other Gossip Girls looking for higher Google or TV ratings, or corporate competitors looking to clear space for themselves on shelves in their marketplace.

The attacker might also be looking for blackmail. At the high end are racial and environmental organizations that certify corporations for their good behavior, in effect indemnifying them from class-action lawsuits. Fail to pay and the certification may give way to one character attack after another, followed by class-action lawsuits from associated trial lawyers.

At the low end are defamation poachers, bloggers who complain knowing that a complaint to a responsive, customer-oriented company can often result in a free pass, voucher, or a new replacement item.

Others are out to shove you to the political left or right. They believe if they apply enough pressure, they can use your reputation or that of your company or brand to advance their political goals.

And then are old lovers, disgruntled or former employees, and irrationally incensed customers who want to deface your storefront and reputation. They want to flame you and the Internet provides an anonymous way to do it.

These attackers just want to create agita, Italian slang (from *acidus*), a term doctors now use for severe acid indigestion. Others seek to commit a little vandalism—perhaps to sever Tiger Woods from his sponsors; to humiliate, superimposing penises or wisecracks about crack cocaine on celebrity images; or to attack a man's heart, such as linking John Seigenthaler, friend of the Kennedys, to the Kennedy assassinations.

And some just want to kill. If digital assassination results in ruin or death, all the better.

In the movie *The Dark Knight,* Batman (Bruce Wayne) has trouble deciphering the motives of his nemesis, the Joker. Michael Caine's character, the butler Alfred Pennyworth, speaks of his past experience tracking a bandit.

> Alfred Pennyworth: A long time ago, I was in Burma, my friends and I were working for the local government. They were trying to buy the loyalty of tribal leaders by bribing them with precious stones. But their caravans were being raided in a

forest north of Rangoon by a bandit. So we went looking for the stones. But in six months, we never met anyone who traded with him. One day I saw a child playing with a ruby the size of a tangerine. The bandit had been throwing them away.

Bruce Wayne: So why steal them?

Alfred Pennyworth: Because he thought it was good sport. Because some men aren't looking for anything logical, like money. They can't be bought, bullied, reasoned, or negotiated with. Some men just want to watch the world burn.[31]

4 // The Second Sword

Silent Slashers

> If you know the enemy and know yourself, you need not fear the result of a hundred battles. If you know yourself but not the enemy, for every victory gained you will also suffer a defeat. If you know neither the enemy nor yourself, you will succumb in every battle.
>
> —**Sun Tzu,** *The Art of War*

SILENT SLASHER ATTACKS are wounds that go unnoticed until you've walked ten paces past your attacker only to feel something warm and sticky soaking your shirt. Silent Slashers enjoy this advantage of wounding targets anonymously without exposing themselves to scrutiny.

Today the Internet empowers digital assassins, allowing undocumented charges and concocted images to ping around the globe at light-speed. But we make a mistake if we suppose that this represents something new in human nature.

Writings on the Wall

In HBO's acclaimed series *Rome,* Julius Caesar and his wife are being carried on litters by slaves when they encounter a wall crammed with offensive graffiti referring to Caesar's relationship with his mistress, Servilia. Several include messages that have ready cognates in English, "Caesar Servilia Futatrix," and "Servilia Caesaris fellator." Each of the graffiti, commissioned by an enemy, is underscored by an appropriately graphic line drawing. Caesar turns stiff and red-faced as onlookers glare at him and his wife while they are forced to pass beneath the offending messages.[1]

The scene, though fictional, is inspired. How many modern politicians have had to endure similar embarrassment in real time, not from graffiti on a wall but from a glowing screen?

Graffiti in particular can be seen as the ancient world's Silent Slasher equivalent of today's Internet message boards. Graffiti allowed anonymous artists to post digs at the rich and famous with impunity, spurned lovers to attack their rivals, the humblest to humble the powerful by scrawling on their walls or defacing their family's expensive mausoleum.

Just as the leaderless revolutions of Twitter today can rock regimes from Tunis to Tehran, so too did graffiti help undermine the Emperor Nero, especially after the great fire that swept Rome on July 18 in AD 64. As the Roman historian Suetonius records, disrespectful graffiti about the matricidal emperor began to appear on the walls of Rome.

Count the numerical values
Of the letters in Nero's name,
And in "murdered his own mother":
You will find their sum is the same.[2]

The legend that Nero sang of the sack of Troy while the city burned to the ground gained widespread circulation in graffiti that depicted him chanting "to the lyre with heavenly fire."

Resentment grew over the Golden Palace Nero was building in the cleared-out city.

The Palace is spreading and swallowing Rome!
Let us all flee to Veii and make it our home.
Yet the Palace is growing so damnably fast
That it threats to gobble up Veii at last.[3]

A portrait of the young emperor on one of his grand estates makes him a ridiculous figure, with a scruffy beard and fish eyes.[4] Though Nero tried to divert attention by scapegoating the Christians, it wasn't long before the relentless verbal attacks from the walls of Rome presaged a revolt across the empire that forced Nero to commit suicide much as Twitter and Facebook comments helped generate the political whirlwind sweeping the Muslim world today.

One of the richest sources on daily life, commerce, and politics in the ancient Roman world is from the walls of the excavated city of Pompeii. "I am amazed that you haven't fallen down, O wall / Loaded as you are with all this scrawl," scribbled one artist.[5] Some Pompeian graffiti read as if they were plucked from a modern-day chat room:

> If you bugger the fire, you burn your prick.

The Latin word for fire in this sentence, scholar Mary Beard tells us, can also mean the title of a minor municipal official.[6]

Some of the graffiti work like ancient world blog comments. One young man, Severus, wrote of a rival for the love of Iris:

> Successus, a weaver, loves the innkeeper's slave girl named Iris. She, however, does not love him. Still, he begs her to have pity on him. His rival wrote this. Goodbye.

Successus answered in terse, Instant Messaging style:

> Envious one, why do you get in the way? Submit to a handsomer man and one who is being treated very wrongly . . .

Severus gets the last word:

> I have spoken. I have written all there is to say. You love Iris, but she does not love you.[7]

It is a pity that Iris the slave girl herself never added her feelings to the wall. Imagine reading one graffito after another, as a fast-walking Pompeian might as she moved quickly through the side streets and byways of Pompeii, and the experience seems like reading a message board.

Read in sequence, they have the same bathroom-wall vulgarity and random flashes of wit as any chat room. Consider:

> Restitutus says: "Restituta, take off your tunic, please, and show us your hairy privates."

> Lovers are like bees in that they live a honeyed life.

> Antiochus hung out here with his girlfriend Cithera.

Theophilus, don't perform oral sex on girls against the city wall like a dog.

Blondie has taught me to hate dark-haired girls.

Whoever loves, let him flourish. Let him perish who knows not love. Let him perish twice over whoever forbids love.

I don't want to sell my husband, not for all the gold in the world.[8]

Many offered Yelp-like reviews on the outside walls of taverns on the quality of their food, wine, or service. Some of the messages are the same commonplace reportings that make up so many contemporary Facebook postings, such as the Pompeian who felt the need to declare, "On April 19th, I made bread."[9]

What comes through the ages to us is the same burning desire by spurned lovers, disappointed customers, and various favor seekers to find expression in venomous words, just as Internet users do today on a billion screens. Of course our human eye instantly perceives graffiti as the product of one individual hand. This is harder to remember in the twenty-first century, when any online post can have the same visual authority as *The New York Times.* Now, with the creation of tools like Google's Sidewiki—which allows visitors to scrawl comments across a sidebar on any website—graffiti is a fully digital phenomenon.

In graffiti through the ages, words are weapons, anonymity is always available, and candor can be a vice.

Disfiguring Faces and Reputations

Liskula Cohen, a tall, blond New York City model, was enjoying drinks with friends one winter evening at the Ultra nightclub on January 14, 2007, when a friend of a twenty-five-year-old off-duty doorman, Samir Dervisevic, lifted a vodka bottle from her table and served himself. Cohen objected. Dervisevic threw a drink in her face. Then he called Cohen the c-word.

Cohen did what most women would—she tossed her drink in his

face. Dervisevic smashed the vodka bottle and ground it in her cheek, drenching her white Ralph Lauren minidress in blood. Cohen needed forty-six stitches to repair the quarter-size hole in her face. Dervisevic pleaded guilty. The lithe Canadian-born model was still stunningly photogenic, but in the world of flawless fashion photography, her bookings fell off.[10]

Cohen was attacked again a year later, only this time defaced by a Silent Slasher attack that also had the potential to affect her fashion-career prospects. This slash, however, came when she achieved unwanted notoriety in a blog that—evidently unconcerned with its truth or falsity—awarded Cohen the title "Skankiest in NYC."[11]

> How old is this skank? 40 something? She's a psychotic, lying, whoring, still going to clubs at her age, skank.
>
> Yeah she may have been hot 10 years ago, but is it really attractive to watch this old hag straddle dudes in a nightclub or lounge? Desperation seeps from her soul, if she even has one.[12]

In the second assault, Cohen (who was actually in her thirties) was the victim of a Silent Slasher.[13] Until the advent of the telephone, voice mail, and then the Internet, graffiti could be read by only a few.

> New technology platforms provide graffiti artists with anonymity and global reach, while wikis give them a crowd to hide in.

Borat at Yale

One frequent source of Silent Slasher attackers is the message board of AutoAdmit, an online discussion forum for law school students founded by a young insurance broker in Allentown, Pennsylvania.[14] Amid the questions about appropriate shoes for a big law firm (which link to an image of a classic black shoe from a men's store) are observations, speculations, and verbal ejaculations about the sex lives of women attending some of the nation's most prestigious law schools.

One woman, an anonymous poster claimed, is a herpes-infected slut who got into Yale Law School through bribery and lesbian sex with an admissions officer. Another has gonorrhea, yet another post alleged, and won a passing grade in a class by performing oral sex on a dean. She also "deserves to be raped." An African American law student at Vanderbilt Law was said to have, of course, been "gangbanged" by four Cincinnati Bengals. All of these posts were fictional attacks.

Follow the threads, with their hundreds of "cunts," "fags," and "bitches," and you will quickly make out the jocular, frat-house gutter talk of young men. Something else is at work. Frequent racist rants against "niggers" and "rat-faced Jews" have the air of parody, as if the real joke is on anyone square enough to seriously imagine that these attacks represent real opinions.

Journalist David Margolick, in a sharply written 2009 profile piece in Portfolio.com, interviewed an academic who nailed the vicarious pleasures of AutoAdmit, which gives "its patrons a peculiar, vicarious kick: It allowed people who were straitlaced and risk-averse enough to want to be lawyers in the first place to become briefly, crazily irresponsible. They could spout outrageous lies, or, in the manner of Sacha Baron Cohen, invent entirely new personalities for themselves, invariably as homophobes, racists, or misogynists."[15]

So what's the big deal?

Google.

AutoAdmit's trolls posted their comments about the targeted women with enough frequency to put their rants at the very top of any search about them. Indeed, these postings seemed to have been deliberately designed to shove aside good material about the women and make sure that prominent keywords would make ugly falsehoods would be the first thing any prospective employer would see at the top of a search engine results page (SERP).

So what appears as offensive but juvenile tripe on AutoAdmit becomes deadly serious defamation when algorithms enable horrific sexual imagery to dominate background checks. It is for this reason, a later lawsuit alleged, that one of the Yale Law women, who had published in top legal journals and interned at prestigious law firms, interviewed with sixteen law firms for summer jobs but received no offers.[16] The African American law student who was supposedly "gangbanged" felt so intimidated that she changed law schools.[17]

> Harm comes in many ways. Most people don't see racist slurs in the light of post-racial irony.

Lighting Up Targets

Silent Slashers also can put individuals and whole countries in the crosshairs of geopolitics. One recent senior U.S. official, deeply involved in the war on terror, was surprised to find that his Wikipedia biography had an unusual level of detail on his family members, listing the full names of his adult children and where they lived. It was of official concern that they were included in his Wikipedia page by political detractors in order to enhance the likelihood that his family members could be targeted by Al Qaeda.

Silent Slashers have an abundance of old techniques to draw from the predigital world.

The late Vasili Mitrokhin, the former chief archivist for the foreign intelligence arm of the KGB, revealed in a book that he wrote with Cambridge historian Christopher Andrew that one of the most successful disinformation campaigns ever mounted by the KGB was the planting of the story that the United States had bioengineered HIV/AIDS, which the CIA subsequently spread throughout Africa. The Soviet Union may be long gone, but to this day many educated Africans believe that HIV was born at the U.S. Army Medical Research Institute of Infectious Diseases at Fort Detrick, Maryland.[18]

Or consider the case of "Hitler's Pope." Over the last thirty years, a rising chorus of scholars and journalists have contributed to a portrait of Eugenio Pacelli, Pope Pius XII, as having at best mounted a timid response to Nazi persecution of Europe's Jews. Some go further, believing Pacelli had a thinly veiled sympathy with the Third Reich's anti-Semitism and tacitly approved of Hitler's goals.

Now a growing body of counterscholarship is beginning to suggest that not only is this portrait off the mark, but that Pacelli himself was such an ardent defender of Jews and consistent opponent of Hitler that he deserves recognition by Israel as a non-Jew who took great risks to oppose the Nazi regime and save large numbers of Jews. The weight of the existing evidence is sufficient to convince Martin Gilbert, the Oxford-educated historian, official biographer of Winston Churchill and preeminent scholar of World War II and the Holocaust, to say: "I think the time has certainly come, in the light of what we now know, for the pope to be put forward for nomination at Yad Vashem in the Department of the Righteous."[19] (The complete Martin Gilbert interview can be seen at http://www.barhama.com/PAVETHEWAY/gilbert.html.)

The argument will not be settled until all the relevant documents in the Vatican archives are released and fully assessed. But if the mainstream understanding of Pope Pius XII for forty-eight years has been a monstrous and unjust inversion of the truth, how could so many get it so wrong? Intellectual opinion first began to turn against Pius XII with the enthusiastic international reception of a play, *The Deputy,* by a German writer, Rolf Hochhuth, that portrays Pius XII as so obsessed with protecting church property that he agreed to look the other way as Hitler completed the Holocaust—a play Martin Gilbert says he didn't find "historical in any way."[20]

It has been alleged that *The Deputy* was part of a deliberate disinformation campaign. According to Ion Mihai Pacepa, a high-ranking Romanian intelligence agent who defected during the Cold War, the image of Pius XII as a coldhearted Nazi sympathizer was deliberately disseminated in the West as part of a decades-long character assassination by the KGB, including its secret conception and production of *The Deputy.* The apparent purpose of this assassination campaion was to drive a wedge between two religions prominent in the West, and destroy the reputation of the Vatican worldwide.[21]

> Whether or not this in fact occurred in *The Deputy,* the dark arts of disinformation on the Internet have the potential to insinuate any falsehood, provided it is lurid enough.

User Name Cowardice

The anonymity afforded by server farms and domain proxies allow Silent Slashers to go about their business. For more casual attacks on a business, the pseudonymity of review sites can be enough.

When writer Andrew Ferguson went looking for information on hotels, he wrote in *Forbes Life,* "I learned that the local Hilton was a terrific bargain with pleasant service and an excellent central-city location, and that I would be charmed by the little sequined unicorns laid by the maids on the pillows every night. It was also, I learned, scrolling down, a hellhole manned by human ferrets, with overflowing toilets and mephitic smells that had tragically ruined the honeymoon of vox12populi and I wantmyrum, who were now exacting revenge by describing their nightmarish experience on every message board they could find . . . How seriously am I supposed to take the views of a person who identifies himself as 'boogerman'?"[22]

The nature of largely anonymous reviews can also be hell for the people on the other side of the check-in desk. When the business partner of one Detroit restaurateur entertained the client of a record label at the hotel bar, a guest mistook the musician for a prostitute. The guest posted an anonymous review describing the misunderstood scene on TripAdvisor. The restaurateur says reviews can sometimes be "a cesspool of negativity."[23]

> The worst aspect of Silent Slashers' negative comments is that they are read by Google's spiders, automated web crawlers that scuttle across websites to index pages for searches—boosting slander rankings.

Hackers' Paradise

With as little as a $100 digital video camera and a $400 laptop computer, Silent Slashers can post words, images, and video through such sites with little fear of being traced. Any small-time operator can set up a website and enjoy administration rights to control the site with complete anonymity. All it takes is a prepaid credit or debit card, which can then be used to purchase a website from a privacy service such as Domains by Proxy, affiliated with the domain registrar Go Daddy, which assures private registrants that "your identity is nobody's business but ours."

There are, to be fair, a number of legitimate reasons why someone might put up a website anonymously, including a desire to avoid domain-related spam, to hide from stalkers, and to enjoy more privacy. If you're trying to identify a Silent Slasher, however, consulting the public Whois directory of domain owners will often show only domainsbyproxy.com (or the relevant domain service) as the owner. In the United States, if a legal action is pending, a court can force a hosting company to reveal who is behind a given site. In Great Britain, where libel laws are strict, it is easier to use the law to identify someone hosted in that country. But it takes legal expenses to obtain discovery.

Sophisticated investigators with resources to burn can still locate website owners, even if they are not listed in WHOIS. "If you want to put up a website without fingerprints, there are so many pieces you have to be aware of to be anonymous, or else it won't work," says Bill Livingstone, the sought-after American security expert who works out of Europe. But hiring an investigator is also an expense.

Even then, Internet service providers under court order or digital investigators may still not be able to track the offender. In lax jurisdictions such as Australia, Iceland, and the Netherlands, authorities protect virtual identities from exposure or prosecution for anything short of child porn or snuff films. The international rise of server farms in these countries—where server capacity is clustered—makes it difficult to trace anonymous Internet attacks. "The Australians value freedom of speech above any other country," says Leo Yakutis, the digital hound. "Australia has truly anonymous servers. You can set something up, and it can't be taken down. You can try to block it or DoS [denial of service attack] it. But you can't take it down." The Netherlands is another country that attracts server farms criminal hackers use for phishing and other crimes.

Iceland is yet another hackers' paradise, where some prominent lawmakers are openly sympathetic to WikiLeaks. Walk along Reykjavik's urban waterfront, and you will encounter a fisherman's row, picturesque old wooden clapboard buildings with freshly painted trim and brass fixtures near wharves where most of the boats are pleasure craft. The fishing fleets may be gone, but that doesn't mean there isn't any fishing going on. "If you made a thermal image of these buildings, you would see that they are very hot, with big coolers," Yakutis says.

In California, such hot spots with high electrical use and coolers would indicate that someone is growing indoor marijuana. In Reykjavik, it means server farms. "Because Iceland has two Internet backbones going through it, it has become a haven for some very weird stuff," Yakutis says. Of course, a lot of the work being done on the servers at fisherman's row is legitimate. Some of it is gray, or at the edge of legality. Some of it is black.

Some of these international hosts, whose landing pages promise not to bow to lawyers or law enforcement, have information on servers from twelve different places around the world. Just determining the jurisdiction of a site by country can be impossible. And in the relevant place, the law may simply not exist. "A third of the world has a lot of laws, a third of the world has some laws, and a third of the world has no laws," Livingstone says. "Depending on where you are oriented, you can do a lot of things and not break the law. You have a lot more rope."

> There is no lack of remote caves in which Silent Slashers can hide, plan, and launch attacks.

Rumors and Google Bombs

On the Internet, even Netflix can be turned into a weapon. One jilted boyfriend, looking to get even with his ex-girlfriend, posted a screen shot from her Netflix account. Under the caption "My girlfriend cheated on me, so I rated movies in her Netflix account until I reached the desired result," he recommended the poster icons for movies he thought she would appreciate: *The Scarlet Letter, Unfaithful, Indecent Proposal, Whore,* and *Slutty Summer.*[24]

This technique of conflating names is a low-tech version of the practice of Google bombing, which manipulates search results so that a search for one person or thing leads the searcher to something satirical or defamatory.

Google bombs began as the manipulation of search engine algorithms as ridiculous broadsides. The classic Google bomb in 1999 yielded the top result "Microsoft" for the search "more evil than Satan himself."[25] Since 2003, the top result for the search "French military victories" leads you to a phony Google results page that asks, "Did you mean French military *defeats*?"

A humor magazine Google-bombed a site that sold merchandise for George W. Bush fans; in 2003 it was linked to the text "dumb motherfucker." This may be funny to Bush critics, but it wasn't a bit funny to the merchants who were trying to capitalize on that president's popularity in Red State America.[26]

French president Nicolas Sarkozy's Facebook page regularly comes up from a search for *trou de cou de Web* ("asshole of the Internet"). Other world leaders and political parties, from countries as disparate as the Philippines and Estonia, are hit with similar links. In 2007, humorist Stephen Colbert enlisted his audience to create enough links so that his website would rank number one in the search for "big brass balls," though he settled for "greatest living American."[27]

A similar technique, keyword stuffing, surrounds a victim's appearance on search engine result pages with defamatory URL names and troublesome descriptions. The nomenclature gets a bit fuzzy here—some also call this technique Google bombing—although the search company, for obvious reasons, doesn't like having its name linked to a shady practice.

Just before the 2010 midterm elections, Chris Bowers of the Daily Kos and Neil Stevens of RedState got into a heated exchange over the propriety of using tactics that Bowers calls "Grassroots SEO" and Stevens calls a "pagerank scam."[28]

The issue, once again, is Google bombing, which Bowers frankly admits he advocates, using the same anchor text to link many blogs and many websites together to make "the most damaging news article" about a Republican congressional candidate one of the first things on a potential voter's SERP.[29]

RedState's Stevens indignantly demanded that Google impose its digital "death penalty" on the Daily Kos for this behavior; although frankly, campaign operatives in both parties will tell you they would be committing political malpractice if they failed to use search techniques against their opponents.[30] Nor can Stevens expect much help from Google, though its spokesmen say the company does not condone Google bombing.

"If you look up Google's policies, Google bombing is legal," Leo Yakutis says. "There is no law against it. There is no Google policy against it."

What is against Google policy is to proliferate meaningless, repetitive anchor text and link it to artificially drive up the ranking of a given search term. "The Google search engine is a mathematical formula," Yakutis says. "In the same way that you hear about an Ivy League team that went to break Vegas, so too can you break Google because it is an index, very mathematical."

In these cases, Google does enact the "death penalty" on those who use link farms or other automated means to generate links, or who excessively link reciprocally or to sites with no real information just to artificially drive search results. But Google has no ability and really no desire to stop Silent Slashers from making organic links that reflect their interests. If that interest happens to be your defamation, then so be it.

Google bombing can surround your name, brand, business, or product on search results with sheer ugliness.

Same Tricks, Different Day

Saul Alinsky, the left-wing Chicago organizer who godfathered Hillary Clinton's entry into politics and who is often cited by Barack Obama for having inspired him to get into politics, wrote a handbook, *Rules for Radicals*. Though himself an anticommunist, he had a distinctly Leninist zest for psychological warfare and the employment of the threat of defamation to wrest power from enemies.

Alinsky's rules would later be picked up and perfected for the other side by Republican operatives, from Lee Atwater to Karl Rove.

"Pick the target," Alinsky wrote, "freeze it, personalize it, and polarize it."[31] Alinsky's methods are ideal for the Internet age, where Silent Slasher campaigns inspire a thousand cuts by creating a self-replicating rumor. Rumors flourish best when the subject is important to the targeted "rumor public"—a subset of people who have reason to care about your reputation, brand, product, or company, but must contend with ambiguous information.

A famous 1947 study by psychologists Gordon Allport and Joseph Postman reduced the power of a rumor to this equation:

$$R \sim i \times a$$

This equation holds that the circulation of a rumor (*R*) will increase with the importance (*i*) of the rumor's subject to the listener *times* the ambiguity (*a*) in reliable information about the subject. It is multiplicative because if either of the two variables—*i* or *a*—reaches zero, the rumor zeroes out and stops.[32] To take a trivial example, if Lindsay Lohan is important to you and she disappears for a spell behind the walls of a county correctional facility, the ambiguity—indeed, the invisibility—of her situation will make you more susceptible to outlandish rumors about what happens to her behind bars.

Whole countries can be plunged into a stew of rumor. One of the authors was a student in Greece during the 1974 revolution and that country's limited war with Turkey over Cyprus. The bar of his hotel was abuzz with "news"—that the deposed king of Greece had marshaled an army in Yugoslavia and was marching through mountain passes south to take Athens. Another rumor held that the Turks had resigned from NATO and joined forces with the Soviet Union to mount an amphibious attack on Greece.

Each rumor had the ring of truth because in the absence of legitimate news under Greece's ruling junta, each was equally probable. "Rumor will race," Allport and Postman wrote, "when individuals distrust the news that reaches them."[33] When there is a vacuum of information, people will fill that vacuum with speculation, which can be taken as fact—a classic PR nightmare.

We are affected by rumors we know likely are not true, especially where food is concerned. In the late seventies, the McDonald's and Wendy's hamburger chains were reeling from stories that they used ground worms as additives in their hamburger patties. "Just the thought in the back of one's mind of worms in hamburgers was enough to steer one to a pizza parlor," sociologist Fredrick Koenig observed in the 1985 classic, *Rumor in the Marketplace.*[34]

With the spread of information technology, the ability of Silent Slashers to deliberately perpetuate rumors increased. Church newsletters spread the story that one CEO or another had confessed a corporate allegiance to Satan on national TV. The first recorded incidence of such a rumor being spread by computer occurred in 1982 when someone in Kansas with access to the computer system of the Union Pacific Railroad used it to send the message "Satan is afoot."[35]

In the Internet age, shadow groups harm people and companies by putting up unattributed sites that collate any defamatory thing said about a company on Twitter feeds and other sites.

≣ Digital assassins distribute rumors with unprecedented precision.

Trajectory of a Rumor

Who uses these tactics? In the 1980s, sociologist Koenig discounted the probability that business competitors are behind the generation of rumors. When the New York Stock Exchange had a larger, much more active trading floor, an observer standing in the press gallery could observe a rumor pass from one side of the room to other, rolling through the trading floor like a wave. As it did, the facial expressions of humor, sadness, or excitement passed along with the wave. "It is more difficult to 'start' a rumor by composing it and planting it somewhere than most people realize," Koenig wrote, adding that "it is more realistic to think of rumors as emerging and evolving than as being 'started.' "

Besides, he wrote, any business competitor that did engage in this behavior might victimize itself, for rumors "once they get started, they have a life of their own . . . The risk is much like that in using poison gas in warfare: The wind may force change and blow all the gas back over the initiating forces."[36] There is a tendency of similar businesses to get hit by the same rumor, as Wendy's and McDonald's both were by the ground-worm rumor.

Two caveats need to be added here. First, a sophisticated and deliberate smear campaign, backed by doctored documents or documents taken out of context, like the *dezinformatsia* efforts of the KGB, can start rumors. Two, Koenig's astute observation in the commercial world may no longer hold up in an age of information technology.

Consider the legendary case of Procter & Gamble and charges of satanism, which began as a Silent Slasher starting a rumor among churches. The rumor died out, only to be resurrected through technology by a competitor. How this case evolved over time shows how technology is changing our understanding of how rumors propagate.

In 1980, *The Washington Post* reported a rumor about P&G that "the crescent moon-faced logo with a cluster of stars is a symbol of witchcraft, Satan or both." The *Minneapolis Tribune* traced one of the sources of the occult rumor to a high school club division of the Youth for Christ. By 1982, church newsletters made much of the curls in the Man-in-the-Moon's beard, which were said to be a mirror image of 666, the number of the beast, while the thirteen stars evoked a passage from Revelations.[37]

P&G managed to stamp out the rumor with statements from the Reverend Billy Graham and other evangelical leaders in mass mailings to churches and with media campaigns.[38] It also threatened to sue. The last tactic, Koenig writes, was particularly important in calling "public attention to the company's strong legal stand against the rumor, not necessarily to obtain legal redress." The campaign and the P&G strategy succeeded—an analog strategy perfect for an analog world.

But in the mid-nineties, the rumor, stoked by technology, returned with a vengeance. Why? A federal jury in 2007 awarded P&G a $19.25

million judgment against distributors from its competitor Amway (though Amway itself was dismissed from the lawsuit). The cause of action was related to a series of messages distributed through a voice mail network reaching salesmen in many states.[39] The rumor should have been dead, but it was resurrected because of technology.

Of course social media can quickly correct bad information. Bloggers finding fault with a national news story caused Dan Rather to prematurely lose his anchor's seat. But social media can also perpetuate rumors—from Area 51 tales to Barack Obama's supposed lack of American citizenship.

> Competitors use technology to stoke rumors and spread them to the four winds.

"Positive Slander" and Google Bowling

An early twentieth-century psychologist noted that rumors are often spread by the "grandiose," those with "the desire to figure as a person of distinction, to occupy the center of the stage, to have the eyes and ears of the neighbors directed admiringly toward us."[40] When a Silent Slasher leaks sensitive political or corporate information, it is often to buy some measure of goodwill and admiration at the employer's expense.

When one of the authors served on the White House staff, more than once he read in the news the exact opposite of what had actually happened in the West Wing. Such malicious leaks are the currency of the White House. Often leakers can be identified by the way in which the reporter will put the leaker at the periphery of a bad event. Prolific leakers can sometimes be identified by profile puff pieces written about them by White House beat reporters. So every White House chief of staff is always on the lookout for descriptions of a staffer as strangely heroic.

This awareness makes another Silent Slasher technique even harder to spot—the malicious leaking of praise. Here's how this works in the White House: Imagine you are a high level staffer. After a meeting in the Oval Office, the president has initially bought into an ill-considered proposal. So you politely but firmly intervene, pointing out the flaws in the proposal to the president. The president listens to you, reverses course, and nixes the proposal. This happens every day in the fevered improvisational atmosphere of the White House.

A classic Silent Slasher technique, then, is to leak the story of the good staffer going to the mat to protect a dim-witted president from harming himself. For these purposes, it is okay if the story makes the Silent Slasher himself look like one of the dopes. In fact that is optimal—it insulates him from suspicion.

As for the Silent Slasher's victim, his mother may want to clip out the story and place it in the family album. But the poor chump will have been made to look to the president like a vainglorious bastard who is willing to sell out his chief executive in order to get a one-day bump in the press.

A digital analogue of this technique, called Google bowling, can knock down competitors like bowling pins. Google bowling harms brands and businesses by using technology to puff them up. Most businesses engage in search engine optimization (SEO), a technique to raise the rankings of one's own website. Google bowling works just the opposite way. When Google determines that a business or brand has been using automated spam to artificially raise its profile, it will ruthlessly kick its website down in the rankings, often with no appeal and little explanation.

One prominent website for black hat hackers makes a sales pitch:

> Google bowling is a tactic to consider only after you have exhausted all on site SEO.
>
> It will probably take more than a few infractions to affect a site[']s rankings. We don't recommend even trying to Google bowl a competitor with less than $2500 worth of search engine spam.
>
> It may take tens of thousands of dollars of **Google bowling** to affect all the sites that rank above you for a keyword phrase—with no guarantee of success. Some sites cannot be effectively Google bowled at all.
>
> But if you make a significant amount of money per sales, why not give it a try?[41]

A Silent Slasher can then procure a black hat to mount an obvious, automated Google bomb on behalf of a competitor. For a short time, the competitor will be deluded into thinking that his firm has bottled lightning as it zooms to the top of the rankings. Then the Silent Slasher can laugh into his sleeve when Google kicks that competitor down the rankings and punishes the website.

> . . . if your competitors [*sic*] starts using tactics like poorly cloaked doorway pages and buying site wide links, they may get **penalized, sandboxed or even banned.**
>
> So, why not take the initiative and buy this search engine spam for your competition??[42]

Character assassins have long known that good news can be deadly.

Wicked Wiki World

In Hawaiian, wiki means quick. A technologist in the mid-1990s saw the word on the Wiki-Wiki bus shuttle at Honolulu International Airport and applied it to a website that allowed for rapid open content creation and editing by a crowd. So a wiki today is any website that allows for open creation and editing.

The ability of strangers to spontaneously cooperate and create new software or content is a startling new power of social media, with consequences examined in chapter 6. Wikipedia—which self-assembles like Hoyle's proverbial tornado that sweeps through a junkyard to create a 747—is the one wiki that, after Google and Facebook, defines the digital domain.

John Seigenthaler's ordeal, which opens the first chapter, is worth examining in some detail, for it shows how easily Silent Slashers can hide among the palm trees in the wiki forest. A former editor of Nashville's daily the *Tennessean*, John Seigenthaler Sr. performed heroic work for Attorney General Robert F. Kennedy during the era of civil rights and the Freedom Rides. Seigenthaler had close calls, including one instance in which he was knocked unconscious with a lead pipe after being overrun by a mob of white supremacists. He later served as publisher of the *Tennessean* and founding editorial director of *USA Today* before founding the Freedom Forum's First Amendment Center at Vanderbilt University in Nashville.

Now in his eighties, still going to the office, John Seigenthaler plays the role of éminence grise with disarming humor. One September day in 2005, a leading Nashville businessman and longtime friend called Seigenthaler to ask if he had seen his Wikipedia post.

"No," Seigenthaler replied.

"Google yourself to the Wikipedia link and sue the bastards," the friend said with a laugh.

So Seigenthaler did.

The piece had been posted since late May. After he took in the sentences that linked him to the murders of John and Robert Kennedy, his initial reaction was to snort in disbelief. It wasn't until several days later that Seigenthaler got a demonstration in the reach and harm such a comment can do when he received a phone call from a young woman who had interned at the First Amendment Center and was now studying at the University of Hawaii.

She had told international students about her great experience with the First Amendment Center and John Seigenthaler. Naturally, the first thing the students did was to look up Seigenthaler's Wikipedia page. They were perplexed. The former intern was in tears. "You have to do something to get that down because these people believe it," she told him over the phone.

Another call from his son, also John Seigenthaler, the former weekend anchor for NBC News, forced him to take a harder look at the impact of the posting. "Look, Dad, you're not the only John Seigenthaler around, so don't take this lightly," he said. "Your son is John Seigenthaler and your grandson Jack is John Seigenthaler."

Reflecting on that conversation, John Seigenthaler acknowledges that his son understood the full reach of Wikipedia in a way he did not. The younger Seigenthaler told his father that there were twenty-four mirror sites that had picked up Wikipedia. "At that point, I got a little pissed off," Seigenthaler said.

A couple of weeks went by as the elder Seigenthaler struggled over what to do. He looked up an archive interview between Jimmy Wales, the cofounder of Wikipedia, with Brian Lamb at C-SPAN, "an old, close friend." In the interview, Wales had asserted that Wikipedia's thousands of volunteer editors correct mistakes within minutes.

Seigenthaler called Brian Lamb, who gave him Wales's telephone number in St. Petersburg, Florida. After listening to Seigenthaler's complaint,

Wales replied that he didn't happen to know of Seigenthaler, but was certain the entry was too outlandish to be true. He promised to retire the comment to Wikipedia's archives.

"Do you . . . have any way to know who wrote that?" Seigenthaler asked.

"No, we don't," Wales said, though he stressed that he wanted to. The comment came from an anonymous contributor, Wales said, although he could trace the contributor's Internet Protocol address, the online equivalent of a home address. Seigenthaler had already turned to a young, tech-savvy employee at the First Amendment Center who had traced the IP address to Bell South, but no further.

Seigenthaler told Wales he was not comfortable with having the Kennedy assassination smear even in Wikipedia's archives, given that thousands of Wikipedia administrators and editors could still see it. "We ended that conversation without much satisfaction on my part," Seigenthaler says. His lawyer, after talking with Bell South, came back with the news that Seigenthaler would have to file a "John Doe/Jane Doe" lawsuit, committing him to prosecuting the claim in order to get the identity of this "biographer."

"You know, if you are the founder of the First Amendment Center at Vanderbilt, you shouldn't be thinking of suing anybody for saying bad things about you," Seigenthaler said. "So it never really did cross my mind."

In investigating the posting, Seigenthaler learned a particularly galling fact. The biography had been posted on May 26. Soon after, an eagle-eyed editor saw that the first entry of the defamatory portion of his biography had spelled the word "early," as "e-a-l-r-y," and corrected it. "So Jimmy's administrator caught it the same day, corrected the misspelling, and left me a suspected assassin who had defected to the Soviet Union for thirteen years," Seigenthaler said.

Stymied, Seigenthaler decided to make his case on the more familiar turf of mainstream journalism. Six months after the post, Seigenthaler wrote a very personal piece in *USA Today* detailing his ordeal. "And so we live in a universe of new media with phenomenal opportunities for worldwide communications and research—but populated by volunteer vandals with poison-pen intellects," Seigenthaler concluded. "Congress has enabled them and protected them."[43]

After the editorial ran, "I was flooded immediately with e-mails and phone calls from people who had suffered, not always from Wikipedia, but suffered similar distress" from digital attacks. The editorial made Seigenthaler a Silent Slasher piñata. As for Wikipedia, Seigenthaler's friend the late writer David Halberstam said, "it's like somebody lifted the lid on a running sewer." One attacker wrote that Seigenthaler had raped Jacqueline Kennedy.

As Seigenthaler's article got media attention, *The New York Times* business editor Larry Ingrassia, known for incisive reporting, sent a memo to reporters reminding them not to rely on Wikipedia. In this midst of this ordeal, Seigenthaler soon heard from Daniel Brandt, the San Antonio editor of wikipediawatch.com, a site that documents Wikipedia's mistakes, shortcomings, and—in Brandt's eyes—its essentially flawed nature. Brandt is so tenacious that he finally wore down Wikipedia, forcing them to delete his own biography altogether.

Brandt went to work and called about two weeks later to say that he had found a "reverse page" on the Internet that revealed that the IP number also served a small delivery company. "I had never heard of [it]," Seigenthaler said. "I did what any run-down, aging investigative reporter would do, I ran to the city directory and there it was."

Word was passed to reporters, who flooded the little firm with a dozen or more calls from journalists. Soon after, a man walked into the First Amendment Center with a signed letter of apology.

Following Digital Bread Crumbs

Not everyone has a Daniel Brandt in their corner. Did Seigenthaler have any other options? Essentially one: Follow the advice of Seigenthaler's friend and "sue the bastards."

Of course, Section 230 would have prevented Seigenthaler from winning a lawsuit against Bell South and Wikipedia. Nothing, apart from Seigenthaler's conscience and sensibilities would have kept him from suing to get to the information content provider—the man who wrote the slur—and winning. Of course a sophisticated Silent Slasher who used anonymous web hosting paid for with a debit card or a public IP address with a cheap, toss-away computer would be beyond the realm of a subpoena.

"Many people have said that when they do it to enough members of Congress, that we'll get regulation," Seigenthaler said. "I go the other way on that. I deplore what is happening, but Jimmy [Wales] could have solved this a long time ago if he really wanted to be an editor. He calls it an 'intellectual democracy.' It's a libertarian approach. The last thing I would want to do is urge repeal of Section 230, although I will admit that after forty years as a journalist, the threat of a libel suit—it can sharpen the mind."

Golfer Frank Urban "Fuzzy" Zoeller Jr., former Masters and U.S. Open winner, was ready to sue after he was defamed by a malicious, untrue Silent Slasher Wikipedia entry describing him as an alcoholic who beats his wife and children after polishing off a fifth of Jack Daniel's chased with Vicodin. He traced the attack back to the IP address of a law firm in Miami. But the identity of the actual writer could not be found. It might have been someone who was visiting the office. Or, as in many of these cases, it could have been someone in close proximity to a company's wireless hot spot.[44]

As we will see in more detail in later chapters, attackers can always use proxy servers in wireless hot spots to hide their ID.

≣ You cannot sue those who you cannot find.

Wikipedia's Dirty Underwear

John Seigenthaler is far from being the most high-profile victim of Wikipedia. That particular honor would have to go to Jimmy Wales himself. One day in 2008, Rachel Marsden, a Canadian editorial writer and former Fox News commentator, whose tart prose in favor of conservative viewpoints often prompts reporters to dub her the "Ann Coulter of Canada," posed on eBay modeling a medium black T-shirt that she had put up for sale, along with another article of clothing. In the image, Marsden is looking straight into the camera, eyes fierce and set, a slight smile.

"Both of these items have been washed, twice, with Tide extra-strength liquid detergent," Marsden posted. "Otherwise, they would not be in salable condition. I took them out of GitMo style isolation from a plastic bag in my closet (where they were placed to prevent the ongoing terrorism of my olfactory senses) and washed them out for the purposes of this auction."[45]

Marsden said that Jimmy Wales, the cofounder of Wikipedia, had left the clothes in her New York City apartment, before he broke up with her "via announcement on Wikipedia." It was "such a classy move that I was inspired to do something equally classy myself"—sell Wales's undergarments on eBay.[46] She also posted this March 2008 response to Wales:

> I only have one thing to say to you: You are the sleazebag I always suspected you were, and should have listened more carefully to my gut instincts—and to my friends. No, in fact, you are much, much worse than I ever expected. You are an absolute creep, and it was a colossal mistake on my part to have gotten involved with you.[47]

The Marsden–Wales saga, a sensational story of a high-profile breakup in full view of a global audience (including the release by Marsden of steamy sexual Instant Messaging conversations), is as important to policy as it is to prurience. It raises significant questions about wikis and their policies.

Marsden, like Seigenthaler, had contacted Wales about her Wikipedia biography. Her biography as of 2011 still encapsulated a sexual harassment charge she leveled against a university swimming coach, which he countered by saying she stalked him. It also details Marsden's stormy relationships with men that ended in blizzards of accusations and legal complaints.

Whatever the truth (or lack of truth) of any of this, Marsden had contacted Wales—at that time separated from his wife—seeking what she insisted were necessary corrections to her biography. Her account and the IMs she released depict a more responsive reaction to Marsden than Seigenthaler ever received.

The IMs portray Wales as working with Marsden point by point in the disputed material with a chronological dissection of the charges. In messages released to the Gawker media blog, Valleywag, Wales was portrayed as responding.

> jimbo.wales: but the correct timeline is
> (1) wrote about him on the blog
>
> me [Marsden]: hahhahaha

jimbo.wales: (2) he files harassment charges
(3) you post email messages to show how his harassment charges are bullshit

me: you're a sh*tdisturber. :)
right

I only posted the emails after he went public trtying [*sic*] to create trouble
NOT before that.

jimbo.wales: nod
so we can get that sorted
and then this makes the story clearer

me: that's good of you to do. really.

jimbo.wales: ok so then the other thing is . . .
in my email I said, here are some thoughts about this, things that need fixing
and i may follow up if there are clarifications from her
but then I said I am recusing myself from it other than that
i explained that we became friends in IM and that I offered to give advice about your website and that we would be meeting about that

me: ahhhh so you qualified it, and left it "up to them". :)

jimbo.wales: and therefore not appropriate for me to directly edit the article with a conflict of interest

me: which usually, actually, works better than the alternative

jimbo.wales: the truth is of course a much worse conflict of interest than that :) but that will do

me: aaaaaaaaahahaha. lol

jimbo.wales: well this is an internal mailing list of people who specialize in fixing this kind of stuff, so you are in good hands

me: awwww thank you.
how many people are on the list?

jimbo.wales: oh, huh
I have no idea.

me: hahaha so you told them the half-truth. :p

jimbo.wales: depends on what the meaning of "is" is

me: ahahahahahha[48]

Wales acknowledged that he had a relationship with Marsden. He posted that he had worked on her biography before they had met because he "found it not to be up to our standards. My involvement in cases like this is completely routine, and I am proud of it." He also states that after planning to meet Marsden, he disclosed his plans to the Wikipedia team that handles complaints and addresses concerns relating to the Biographies of Living Persons (BLPs). Then he posts he "recused myself from any further official action with respect to her biography."[49]

While the story resides in he-said/she-said land, the fact remains that some biographical entries of living persons will always cry out for correction—such as Seigenthaler's—while others will simply cry out—such as Marsden's. As for Wikipedia, it might take only one credible documentation of favoritism to step out of the role of host and into the role of content creator, and therefore into potential liability.

In the aftermath of the Seigenthaler and other debacles, Wikipedia in April 2009 set out a tighter standard for editors for BLPs that make it harder for Silent Slashers to weaponize them. "Wikipedia is an encyclopedia, not a tabloid," Wikipedia declares in its BLP guidelines. "[It] is not Wikipedia's job to be sensationalist, or to be the primary vehicle for the spread of titillating claims about people's lives, and the possibility of harm to living subjects must always be considered when exercising editorial judgment."[50]

An entry must therefore have a neutral point of view, be verifiable, and contain no original research. Facts must be anchored to publicly accepted sources of information. Contentious material about a living person that is unsourced or poorly sourced should be removed without waiting for discussion. Wikipedia's BLP standard also forbids "feedback loops" in which a contributor quotes his own material.

Wikipedia must still rely on the integrity and competence of armies of faceless volunteer administrators, editors, and contributors. Those who feel stymied in their efforts to add, correct, or defame still often resort to sock puppetry, the use of separate digital identities to reinforce an edit, as well as meat puppetry, the recruiting of proxies to do the same.

> Wikipedia remains only as good, or as bad, as the crowd that edits it.

Takeaway—Fighting Silent Slasher Attacks

In Roman times, one simply repainted the walls. Today it can cost thousands of dollars to hire a specialist to perform digital forensics, the kind of service that Daniel Brandt performed free for John Seigenthaler. Even when the identity of the attacker is obvious, one can easily spend $5,000, $25,000, or more to have such a company verify the identity of a posted statement and provide a technician to testify in court.

Of course not everyone is as reluctant as Seigenthaler to call in a lawyer. For most people, a lawsuit remains the easiest way to track down a Silent Slasher. This is the path chosen by the two Yale Law women who were subjected to AutoAdmit's campaign of abuse. With the help of Reputation Defender, they filed claims against almost thirty pseudonymous attackers. The use of a beauty contest photo of one of the women allowed the lawsuit to allege copyright infringement, which elevated the case to the tougher standards of federal court.[51]

Not all, but some of the men who made the postings were outed (the scofflaws were smart enough to make their IP addresses untraceable). Some of the men settled. One was eaten up with contrition. ("I said something really stupid on the fucking Internet, I typed for literally, like, 12 seconds, and it devastated my life," he told journalist David Margolick.)[52]

Perhaps most important, legal action forced AutoAdmit to clean out the threads, reducing most of the trash to distant search results. If you search these women's names now, most of the material at the top of the search highlights their ordeal and their response to it. Their names cleared, one woman headed to a top law firm in New York, the other to work for the International Criminal Court in the Hague.[53]

A legal but stealthy method to ferret out the identities of people who might be stalking or snooping around you is to set up a conspicuous website and use tracking software to capture the IP addresses of all visitors. "One of the advantages of having a website up is to see who's looking at you," Livingstone says. This works unless the visitor takes pains to hide his digital fingerprints.

More must be done than just combat Silent Slashers. One must counter the rumors they create. Remember the Allport and Postman rumor equation: If either the importance of a rumor or its ambiguity can be reduced to zero, the rumor itself evaporates. As P&G did by contacting churches, one must locate and address what Allport and Postman refer to as susceptible populations, or "rumor publics."

The opposite is true. You don't want to pack the rumor equation with even more weight. Dismissing the rumor without giving it new life and fresh color is harder than it seems. The exact wording of a response, then, is of maximum importance.

An extreme example of this was the task McDonald's faced in killing the rumor about ground-up worms being added to its patties. It wisely elected not to use the word "worm," but to deny rumors about "protein additives" and then launch a slick ad campaign about McDonald's "100% U.S. Government-inspected beef."[54] McDonald's approach succeeded brilliantly in reducing the rumor to zero.

A similarly nuanced approach is needed in confronting rumors today.

Tough response strategies that worked brilliantly in the offline world would evoke the Streisand Effect in a nanosecond today. When the Stroh Brewery Company came under fire for allegedly slipping cash under the table to bankroll the presidential run of the Reverend Jesse Jackson in 1984, Stroh's ran a newspaper ad offering $25,000 to the first person to identify who started the rumor, and left the number of a Chicago detective agency to call with any information or evidence. It is hard to imagine an Internet equivalent today without tremendous blowback.[55]

The AutoAdmit case reveals a superior strategy, that of public shaming and counter social media efforts. The power of AutoAdmit, after all, rested on a perverse incentive. Even those who were offended by it felt they had to read it to see what might be posted about them. This drove traffic, giving the defamations greater reach. Elena Kagan, Harvard Law's dean before President Obama appointed her to the U.S. Supreme Court, helped break this vicious cycle by asking her students in an e-mail to boycott this "new and highly efficient mechanism for malicious gossip."[56] It seems to have worked. Unique visitors to AutoAdmit are a fraction of what they were.

Whatever the response—a lawsuit against AutoAdmit or Amway distributors, a traditional media campaign against Wikipedia, or a counter social media campaign—victims must understand the potential lethality of a Silent Slasher attack.

In many attacks, attackers leave behind some kind of signature. Sometimes it is intentional, a fragment of themselves they place as a boast or a joke. Certainly the code writer of the Stuxnet virus, which caused the centrifuges in the Iranian nuclear program to go haywire, had a sense of humor, as well as a sense of history.

In 2010, discovered buried deep in the code of Stuxnet was an ancient word, "Myrtus."[57] Some scholars believe this is an allusion to the Hebrew name for the Biblical Esther. If the word was a deliberate clue or taunt, it was an appropriate one. Esther, the covertly Jewish queen to the Persian king Ahasuerus, had saved her people. She had detected and stopped court politicians who were generating a Silent Slasher attack, an anti-Semitic rumor campaign that had caused the king to assent to a pogrom.

Who did this? Israel's cyberwar Unit 8200? Another power seeking to point the finger at Israel?

> Whoever the code writers, they are people who appreciate the deadly, silent power of a rumor.

5://The Third Sword:

Evil Clones

You are who Google says you are.

—**Anna Vander Broek**, "Managing Your Online Identity"[1]

IDENTITY THEFT IS AS OLD AS the story of Jacob and Esau, when one brother used a bit of goatskin to fool his blind father into giving him his shaggy twin's inheritance.

By now every consumer knows that Evil Twins flourish on the Internet in the form of phishing scams, those phony but official-looking websites that come complete with a company logo over photos of smiling employees. Many people are just becoming aware of Evil Twin wireless networks, rogue Wi-Fi base stations that jam legitimate wireless providers to con you into providing your confidential information. Some are still taken by surprise by a related tactic, Evil Clones, which can slam your brand, business, or personal reputation by stealing your identity to make it appear as if you have done something stupid, wrong, terrible.

Christianne Carafano, a voluptuous actress noted for appearances on *General Hospital* and *Star Trek: Deep Space Nine,*[2] was a victim of Evil Clones. For a beautiful woman, she had an unusually desperate profile on the dating site, Matchmaker.com.

The site's format involves sixty-two questions, for which the profiled person provides self-descriptive answers. Carafano's were unusually blunt and to the point.

"Main source of current events?"

Playboy, Playgirl, read Carafano's profile.

"Why did you call?"

Looking for a one-night stand.

In addition to alluring pictures of Carafano, the profile stated that she was looking for a "hard and dominant" man with a "strong sexual appetite," and that she "liked sort of being controlled by a man, in and out of bed."[3]

The worst aspect of Carafano's profile? It provided her home address (a violation of the site's policies) and a Yahoo! e-mail address with an autoresponder that, when contacted, replied, "You think you are the right one? Proof [sic] it!!" The e-mail provided her telephone number as well as her address again.[4]

For days, as sexually suggestive messages began to fill her voice mail, Carafano was unaware that this profile had been posted by someone using a computer in Berlin on Matchmaker's Los Angeles site. When she returned home from a trip, Carafano found a sexually explicit fax that threatened her and her son. Phone calls, voice mail messages, letters, and e-mail from anxious men began to flood into her house.

When she learned of the source of all this unwanted attention, Carafano had her assistant contact Matchmaker on a Saturday to demand the profile be taken down. The customer service representative initially said that only the person who posted the profile could do that. By Monday morning, presumably when higher management got involved, the profile was blocked and soon deleted. Feeling unsafe, Carafano and her son stayed locally in hotels and sometimes away from Los Angeles.

Carafano filed suit against Matchmaker for invasion of privacy, defamation, and other torts. An appellate judge found her to be the victim of "a cruel and sadistic identity theft"—but nothing more. The case, after a few twists and turns, was resolved before the U.S. Ninth Circuit Court of Appeals. In order for Matchmaker to be held liable under Section 230, the court held in *Carafano v. Metrosplash,* the company would have to have been considered an information content provider. Simply providing a template, even sixty-two detailed questions, the court found, was not enough to make Matchmaker a liable content creator.

When all was said and done, only the information content provider, the unidentified person in Berlin, was at fault.[5]

Evil Clones attract hordes of attackers like ants on honey.

Fouling the Nest

The authors uncovered a struggle between a young man and a young woman, the scions of rich and powerful families, who dated while they worked for rival financial services firms in a major North American city. They were not, however, typical MBAs in love.[6] They were citizens of the People's Republic of China, highly educated, perfectly fluent in English. Each of their families had set them up at top American corporations to get experience for their future careers back in China.

The couple worked hard, played hard, and stayed close . . . until the boyfriend started showing signs of being too possessive.

After a period of tension, the young woman broke off their relationship. Rather than get drunk or write a hate letter, this ex-boyfriend, being a creature of his times, resorted to a twenty-first-century form of retaliation. He opened his laptop and set out to do a number on her. He invaded her office e-mail account to send catty comments about the personal foibles, physical appearance, and hygiene of her superiors at the firm to other workers, all under her name and IP address.

Fortunately for this young lady, she had a wealthy father in China with the resources to hire the best digital hounds to find out what had happened. At first glance, the e-mails appeared perfectly legitimate, coming straight from her office e-mail. After a little digging, however, the hounds discovered that the jilted boyfriend had made one critical mistake. Some of the e-mails went out from the young woman's IP in the United States address while she was visiting her parents in China.

Investigators were eventually able to track the e-mail back to the boyfriend. He had used one of the most common means to crack her e-mail. While they were still dating, the boyfriend had installed a simple key logger, software that recorded her every stroke.

Once exposed, the ex-boyfriend lawyered up. At first the young man's lawyer offered only counterthreats and indignation. When all the evidence was aired, a settlement was reached.

In this case, the young woman's father could afford to write a check for $50,000 to start the process of forensic investigation, an amount few could easily afford. But in truth, the stain of such an incident never truly rubs off a young person's career. "You have to ask what effect did this incident have on her?" says one person close to this case. "Even if everyone understood, it was not a positive event for her career. Everyone is going to remember she is the one who had the crazy boyfriend." At the very least, she exhibited poor judgment. And every superior who was targeted in the e-mails—likely from some real gossip the young woman once shared with her ex-boyfriend—will remain insulted.

Even the exonerated pay a reputational price.

Candidate Clones

A recent victim of Evil Cloning is S. R. Sidarth, who between his junior and senior years at the University of Virginia followed the senatorial reelection campaign of George Allen with a video camera on behalf of Allen's opponent. Allen, the front-runner who at the time was also considered a leading Republican candidate for the presidency, famously referred to the American-born son of immigrants from India as a "macaca." This odd racial slur derailed Allen's political career and elected Sidarth's candidate, James Webb, to the Senate.

Two weeks later, a conservative blogger assailed Sidarth for his AutoAdmit postings in which the young man confessed to having sex with a transvestite while high on methamphetamines. Sidarth, of course, had posted no such thing. Someone had created an Evil Clone of Sidarth to digitally assassinate him.[7]

Similar Evil Cloning tactics have been used at one of the world's best universities. In 2010, as two young men ran against each other to head the Harvard Republican Club, an e-mail from McKinsey & Company arrived in the in-boxes of at least several Harvard undergraduates and members of the Republican club. This e-mail included an invitation to sign up for "one of 25 exclusive fast-track interview slots, available only to those who attend our event."[8]

For business-oriented undergraduates, as Gawker put it in its usual crass (but accurate) terms, "waving a McKinsey gig in front of Harvard College Republicans is like waving a crack salad with crack dressing in front of a crackhead."[9] Unfortunately the private gig, an exclusive recruiting event at MIT, happened to fall at the very same time as the Harvard Republican Club was to hold its election. A second, more important problem was that McKinsey had not sent the e-mail.

After one of the candidates accused the other of forging the e-mail, the accused dropped out of the race (while proclaiming his innocence). What is the truth? As in many of these kinds of investigations, the digital breadcrumbs thin out and disappear. As a board member of the Harvard Computing Society informed the *Harvard Crimson,* "messages sent from the Gmail web client usually show the IP address of the website's servers rather than the unique IP address of the sender."[10]

Evil Cloning also hit the 2008 presidential elections with the emergence of phony domains—RudyGiulianiForum.com, MittRomney forum.com, and the online Fred Thompson Forum. "Most posts adopt the persona of a supporter of the candidate, while offering views that amount to over-the-top parodies of genuine boosters," wrote Sarah Lai Stirland, a Wired News reporter, who determined that these phony forums used the same software, the same hosting company, and a common IP address. After Stirland exposed deceptive spam promoting Ron Paul's candidacy for president, it was her turn to be the victim. Someone made an Evil Clone of Stirland's digital identity confess that her story was a fraud paid for by Giuliani supporters. The impersonation of Stirland and her confession was believable enough to inspire a YouTube attack on *Wired* as a paid attack dog for Rudy Giuliani.[11]

Another new permutation of the Evil Clone is the concern troll. Here's how it works: A concerned Democrat under the user name IndieNH posted pieces in 2006 on liberal blogs in New Hampshire giving tepid support to Democrat Paul Hodes, set to oppose U.S. Representative Charlie Bass, a Republican, while expressing the concern that Hodes could not win. "I am going to look at the competitive race list to figure out where to send another donation and maybe help out in other ways," IndieNH posted. "Maybe CT or NY for me—they are at least close by."

When site managers traced the IP address, they found that the messages came from official computers inside the U.S. House of Representatives. After an investigation, Representative Bass, the Republican, fired a top aide for posting the phony Democratic blog entries.[12]

Evil Clones can also take more vivid form. Doctored Internet images of actor Jake Gyllenhaal show the actor stretching in a beefcake pose in white briefs. Legal action by Gyllenhaal, however, seems to be evoking the Streisand Effect. "We're keeping the photo up, since it hasn't been proven fake and because their letter bumped it from 'funny and cute' to 'actually newsworthy,'" Queerty.com told the press.[13] It is easy to do this to anyone's image with Photoshop, though close inspection reveals that the head in the picture is not quite matched to the body. With the exponential increase in the power of cheap digital imaging, within a few years these kinds of smears will become fully pornographic, incorporating realistic, full-motion video.

Given the ease with which Evil Clones can be created, they now spill into all areas of modern life, from Harvard Yard to the boxing ring.

High Society Hit Parade

"Next time you think about skipping that certain gala, wearing that unknown designer, dating some weird band member, beware. We're watching. And your ranking is on the line!" So warned Socialite Rank, a website that the *New York Post* called "the hilariously bitchy anonymous cabal!"

A profile piece by Isaiah Wilner in *New York* magazine reported that the now-defunct site Socialite Rank not only elevated "unknown women to unlikely prominence" but also included comment boards "with catty and frequently venomous remarks," including allegations of cocaine abuse. "And what made it more eerie—like the voice of a Bitch God bellowing from the heavens—was that no one knew who was speaking," Wilner observed. "The Rankers hid behind their anonymity, as did the commenters who wrote in with their own harsh judgments."

One target of the site was Olivia Palermo. In 2007, Socialite Rank alleged that she had e-mailed a long list of people prominent on the New York social scene to beg "for acceptance, privacy, and forgiveness" for being such a desperate, raving sycophant. Socialite Rank gave Olivia its "final verdict," booting her from the website and its rankings. That Palermo herself quickly denied that she had sent the message was of far less interest.[14]

Evil Clones often take the guise of penitents who want to publicly confess.

Evil Clone Stock Scams

On a spring day in 2007, Engadget, the slick and highly respected consumer electronics weblog, received a startling e-mail from a trusted source within Apple. The company was issuing a bad-news release. Apple announced a delay in the delivery of the new version of its Mac OS X operating system, Leopard. Worse, Apple announced it was being forced to delay the production of its iconic iPhone. "This one doesn't bode well for Mac fans and the iPhone-hopeful," Engadget opined. Leopard had already been delayed, so news of another delay sounded credible. Apple's stock dived 2.2 percent.[15]

In truth, the product delay was as real as Steve Jobs's later "heart attack" in 2008. Someone had used Apple's internal e-mail system to spoof Engadget into producing a legitimate-sounding story that had rocked the investment world.

The flaw in these kind of bear attacks, or short-and-distort securities fraud, is that the trail often leads back to the perpetrator. The fraudster has the problem of explaining to the SEC the remarkable coincidence of his shorting stocks before the phony announcement. The classic case in the Internet age was a bear attack on Emulex, which caused the California IT equipment maker in 2000 to lose $2.5 billion in value. Investigators quickly located the twenty-three-year-old intern for a wire news service working out of a community college who had made $250,000 from short-selling Emulex shares—and secured a guilty plea and a multi-year prison sentence.[16]

A likelier scam is the pump and dump, which involves putting out good news on a company, often an announcement that the company has developed a breakthrough product ("promising cure for a wide variety of cancers!") or news that it is being acquired at a high stock price ("Warren Buffett invests millions!"). Small science-based companies whose stock prices can be volatile are the most frequent pump-and-dump victims. In such a scheme, the perpetrator, already holding shares for some period and clever enough not to be linked to his phony news, simply dumps his shares the instant the phony news bump ups share value. The perpetrator can be harder for the SEC to find since pump-and-dumpers can be lost amid the hordes of other people cashing out at the word of unexpected good fortune.

Years ago, such scams were perpetrated through faxes and snail mail.

The news was not instant because of the nature of those communications. These schemes then worked as well for short sellers as for pump and dumps. While technology has made pump and dump the better play, the motive—greed—is exactly the same as it was in the days when traders gathered under Wall Street's buttonwood tree in 1792.

In 1987, Gordon Gecko in the first *Wall Street* movie said, "Greed is good."

It was not then. It is not today.

While new services are wising up, performing journalistic due diligence when presented with a market-moving news releases, some fraudsters are still managing to stay ahead of the curve. In June 2010, PR Newswire and Business Wire, two of the most prominent distributors of business news releases, fell prey to spoof releases. One phony release put up on PR Newswire read: "Obama Orders Full Investigation of General Mills Supply Chain Following Food Recalls"; it indicated that the administration was preparing a massive investigation and regulatory assault on General Mills.[17]

When a reporter from the Minneapolis–St. Paul *Star Tribune* was approached by the writer of the phony news release, the man said that his motive for the hoax was not financial but political. "It's not to manipulate stock prices, but to serve to discredit Obama," the "media contact" said.[18]

Another phony release—this one fallen for by Business Wire—seemed to support a pump-and-dump scheme, announcing that in a 5–4 decision, the U.S. Supreme Court had ruled in favor of Javelin Pharmaceuticals in a product liability suit. Adding a little novelistic detail, the phony release had Javelin thanking Justice Clarence Thomas, who "was particularly influential in swaying the vote our way."[19]

In both the General Mills and the Javelin attacks, the perpetrators posted almost at midnight.[20] Both General Mills and Javelin were quick to spot the releases and seek retractions. In the case of General Mills, however, human action could not beat the automated news links, with headlines and stories appearing on Dow Jones Newswire, WSJ.com, and Fox Business News.[21]

> The greedy manipulate financial markets with old ploys wrapped in new technology, making good news bad news, and bad news even worse news.

Fatal Masquerade

The Lancet medical journal reported that an eighteen-year-old Italian man was depressed over a breakup, a heartache that deepened when his ex-girlfriend "friended" many new young men while "unfriending" him. *The Lancet* found it interesting that when the young man connived to get back on her Facebook page, the sight of her photos exacerbated his asthma, causing him to experience a frightening shortness of breath. Perhaps the ex-girlfriend would have suffered shortness of breath if she had been aware that her ex was on her site masquerading under a new nickname.[22] Indeed, another young man might have sought a friend request from his ex-girlfriend using the photo of, say, an attractive girl plucked off the Internet, with an interesting profile that made imaginary connections to her school and work, all under a new name.

The creation of Evil Clone identities out of whole cloth has been the central feature in a number of high-profile cyberbullying cases, some ending in death.

The iconic cyberbullying case of Megan Meier is worth revisiting. A thirteen-year-old girl in Dardenne Prairie, Missouri, Megan was thrilled to make a new friend on her MySpace page, a sixteen-year-old boy named Josh Evans, in September 2006. Megan thought Josh, who had a pet snake and looked handsome in his posted photo, was cool. Josh thought Megan was "sexi." Megan responded: "aww sexi josh ur so sweet if u moved back u could see me up close and personal lol."[23]

Megan, who struggled with self-esteem issues and was on antidepressants, was elated to know that there was a boy sensitive enough to see her true worth. The relationship, however, remained online. Josh had moved and did not yet have phone service. Over time, however, Josh turned on Megan. His communications became more critical, more undermining. On October 5 he posted, "I don't like the way you treat your friends, and I don't know if I want to be friends with you." The fracas attracted other teens, who hurled obscene insults at Megan.

On October 16, 2006, Josh finally suggested that "the world would be a better place without you."[24] Megan went to her room, sobbing. Twenty minutes later, her parents found that the teen had hanged herself in a wardrobe closet. She died the next day in a hospital.

The ugly potential of Evil Cloning caught the attention of the American public when it came to light that Josh did not exist. He was a digital creation that prosecutors would later attribute to Lori Drew, then forty-seven, a neighbor of the Meiers. Drew's daughter and Megan had once been best friends, even vacationing with the Drews, before becoming estranged. Concerned that Megan was spreading rumors about her daughter, Lori Drew allegedly conspired with a teenage employee of her home-based business, Ashley Grills, to create the digital persona of Josh, in order to spoof Megan into revealing what she was saying about Drew's daughter.[25]

According to Ashley Grills, Lori Drew, her daughter, and Grills took turns concocting the messages from "Josh." Drew, through her attorney, denies that she created the Josh Evans MySpace account or directed anyone to do so, though "she was aware of it."[26] Drew says the project belonged to Ashley Grills, a defense that a repentant Grills denied on *Good Morning America*.

Under a grant of immunity, the teen co-conspirator, Ashley Grills, later testified that it was she who had sent the fatal cruel message. She sent the message, she later said, to make Megan so angry that she would quit communicating with Josh, allowing Ashley to close the book on the digital setup.[27] Soon after, Grills said Drew ordered her to shut down the account and to say nothing more about it. Lori Drew attended Megan's funeral and said not a word to her parents about what had happened. Had it not been for the contrition of Ashley Grills, who revealed the plot six weeks later, Megan's parents might never have known who prompted their daughter to commit suicide.

Lori Drew was prosecuted in a federal court in Los Angeles (where MySpace servers are located), only to be found guilty of a misdemeanor violation, which the judge later set aside. The prosecution had based its case on the Computer Fraud and Abuse Act aimed at hard-core hackings. The contention was that by violating MySpace's terms of service forbidding fake identities and harassment, Lori Drew had become in effect a hacker.[28]

What happened next shows how much leeway the law gives those who create Evil Clones. Ashley Grills testified that like almost everyone else, the little cabal that created "Josh" had not read MySpace's terms-of-service page before clicking the "I Agree" button.[29] U.S. District Judge George Wu dismissed the charges, noting that if Lori Drew could be convicted of being a hacker, the precedent "basically leaves it up to a website owner to determine what is a crime," criminalizing a mere breach of contract.[30] Internet free speech proponents breathed a sigh of relief. The State of Missouri passed a law that took a more modest stance, adding the Internet to written and telephone communications as the means of transmitting illegal harassment.[31]

And Lori Drew? It was her turn to be the victim of anonymous Internet attacks. A digital mob assembled Lori Drew's personal information, including her e-mail address and a satellite image of her house. Someone hurled a brick through her kitchen window.[32]

An Evil Clone can be a wholly imaginary person and yet draw you to ruin.

Did I Write That?

Liberia is a country recovering its tranquility and reputation after being torn apart by rampaging armies of child soldiers. Since its founding by former American slaves, Liberia has often been in the grip of self-serving elites known to divert national wealth into private bank accounts.

The latest cycle of violence wound down slowly in the face of a broad-based reform movement led by courageous women, both Christian and Muslim. A fair election was held, one that brought Harvard-educated Ellen Johnson Sirleaf to the presidency. During her tenure, Sirleaf negotiated major reductions in Liberia's debt, began a national healing process with a Truth and Reconciliation Commission patterned after that of South Africa, and began to restore Liberia's reputation as a reliable business partner.

Liberia's flag itself is in a sense its major export. Liberian-flagged vessels encompass more than a tenth of the world's commercial fleets. Liberia gave a contract to the Virginia-based Liberian International Ship and Corporate Registry (LISCR) to manage the activities of 3,500 Liberian-flagged vessels that carry more than 112 million gross tons and bring more than one-third of the oil imported to the United States.

That contract for the Liberian Registry comes up for renewal every ten years. Run on the U.S. side by businessman Yoram Cohen in Northern Virginia, the contract has been estimated by outside experts to be worth $10 million to the foreign partner; for Liberia, it represents a very large percentage of its national revenue. When the contract was last up for renewal, the ship company and the Liberian government were attacked in a way that left both sides dumbstruck.

A raft of e-mails between Cohen and one of his aides to Willis Knuckles, a minister in Sirleaf's government, appeared in FrontPage Africa, a muckraking online journal dedicated to uncovering corruption in Africa. The e-mails were unambiguous in their meaning. So was their origin. They had come from the company's computers in Vienna, Virginia, to the computer in Knuckles's office in Monrovia.

On August 15, 2008, the press reported this e-mail was sent from a Cohen aide to Knuckles:

> You are the man! What would we do with out our PR man. It is only prove to me again that the issue of the pr men is extremely essential. Anyways please inform Madame President that her concerns will be addressed. Yoram told me that he has already informed you that the first payment of US$1 million will be made after our contract is signed.[33]

This revelation put Cohen at immediate risk of investigation and prosecution under the U.S. Foreign Corrupt Practices Act. Knuckles—whose pleas of innocence were not helped by the fact that by this time he had already been forced to resign from the cabinet after a pants-down photo of him having sex with two women went viral—faced prosecution under Liberia's Penal Code.

As FrontPage Africa reported this story, even President Sirleaf herself might have been in jeopardy. Africans seized on a message reported on the Internet in which Knuckles was reported to have written to Cohen and his aide:

> I have been assured by the President that the process will not be opened to bid. I was also told by her at the symposium some harsh words might be used at LISCR. But keep in mind, that in order for her to look transparent she has to be on the offensive don't take it personal its just for show.[34]

The story was picked up by the international press.

There is certainly no lack of muck for muckrakers to rake in Liberia. The editor of FrontPage Africa would spend a few days in Liberia's most notorious and dangerous prison in 2011 for contempt of court after publishing a letter questioning the ethics of a Liberian Supreme Court justice, before being released by the government.[35]

The IP addresses for the e-mails were legitimate. The messages had been sent from the respective computers of the holders of these accounts. But they were false. As reported in the media, Cohen called in investigators, who discovered a sophisticated act of industrial espionage, which they believe came from a jealous competitor corporation. "Somebody wanted a piece of that contract," a digital forensic investigator opined. "Somebody wanted to cut Yoram out. So they hacked his e-mail server, took e-mails from Willis Knuckles, took e-mails from Yoram, altered them, resent them, making them look like they were doing bribes and other things against U.S. laws in an attempt to defame them, so the Liberian government would not renew the contract."

Every e-mail has a mathematical value associated with it called a checksum, which serves as a kind of digital fingerprint. The press later reported that the James Mintz Group, an investigative firm contracted by the Liberian government to determine the veracity of the e-mails, confirmed that the e-mails had been altered. "But proving what's been altered and explaining that in a way that anyone would believe was a very difficult process," one digital hound observes of the publicized reports of this story. "Someone took a legitimate e-mail, added sentences and subtracted sentences to change both what it was stating and the tone in which it was stated. On the other hand, this is not a new approach . . . Forgery is a five-thousand-year-old pastime."

Although no one knows for sure, the forger who crafted the Evil Clone e-mails may have been acting for a corporate interest jealous of LISCR's contract. After the investigation cleared LISCR, the Liberian government renewed its ten-year contract with the American firm.

In the Liberian ship case, the American company recovered its business, but it was still—eighteen months after the cyberattack—working at a breakneck pace to safeguard its computer operations. The Liberian government had to spend $350,000 to conduct an independent investigation that included the Mintz Group to confirm what LISCR already knew—that the e-mails were fraudulent. With IT help, lawyers and detectives, it is likely that LISCR's cost also ranged in the hundreds of thousands of dollars.

The cost to the attacker? Not counting the hacker's time, close to zero.

Criminal Matryoshka Dolls

Some impersonators have the same criminal intent that forgers always have had. Just as every consumer is by now aware of phishing sites, so too are retailers worried about brandjackers who might use automated programs to search for a lapse in the renewal of their brand's website—with the intent of snatching up their brand equity to sell cheaper, knock-off merchandise.

Toward the end of the last decade, many top brands were facing up to 10,000 attempts at brandjacking a week.[36] Other programs catch those who misspell URLs. "A lot of that real negative stuff is coming out not just on the consumer side," social media expert James Lee says. "It is also coming out in the nonprofit world."[37]

Even a tragedy can be brandjacked. In the aftermath of the 2010 Haiti earthquake and the 2011 Japan earthquake and tsunami, sites appeared like mushrooms after a spring rain to lure the compassionate into donating to a phishing site. Crimes like these pay because cybercriminals are not bound by the physical location of their hardware.

"If you access a server from any place, it can leave a trace telling where you probably are," Bill Livingstone says of tactics used by those seeking to operate websites with anonymity. "But you can cloud the trail by going to Internet cafés, using secondhand computers when accessing the server where the website is hosting. And if you go to a Starbucks Wi-Fi in Vienna one day, London the next, you can be very hard, if not impossible, to accurately trace."[38]

For consultants who wish to wage opposition-issue campaigns for businesses without fingerprints or legal liability, there are more sophisticated methods to throw digital hounds off the scent. They might use mind tricks, such as Americans employing British spelling. Some use untraceable services that automatically switch servers around the planet, from Latin America to Europe to Asia.

Many campaigns are sponsored by shell companies. "You can also create companies in some parts of the world and you have no idea who they really are," Livingstone says. "In Russia and the more lawless countries that came out of the Soviet Union, they like to use cutouts, dozens of companies that own companies that own companies. Russians, for example, might use a local law firm, under client privilege, to set up a company in New Jersey."[39]

> Tracking an IP address can become an endless series of digital matryoshka dolls.

YouSuck.com

Cybersquatters register a corporate or trademark domain name in bad faith, snapping up a site so they can sell it to the owner at an inflated price. Name-jackers will go after a prominent professional, a lawyer, or a doctor, buying up adjacent permutations of his name—and again, make it available for a steep price.

The law mandates a dispute resolution process, which works well for brands and trademarks, but not so well for individuals. Actor Kevin Spacey had to go through extensive legal maneuvers to shut down a namesake domain, which linked to a commercial celebrity fan site.[40]

A related phenomenon is the use of "sucks" or "sux" after the name of a company or person, which represents legitimate criticism or the character assassination of a brand, depending on your point of view. This all started when William Porta flew Alitalia to India for a wedding, only to have Alitalia lose his luggage. Porta had to attend the wedding—as the best man—in ill-fitting, inappropriate local clothes instead of formal wear. When Porta was further angered by Alitalia's reneging on one promise after another for assistance, then compensation, in 2000 he founded the website www.alitaliasucks.com. This site has but one purpose, to tell you the many reasons the content provider believes that Italy's signature airline generates massive suction.

Alitalia sued. In a filing in Porta's defense, Public Citizen noted that "nobody looks for a company by going to 'www.companynamesucks.com' . . . Any consumer finding Porta's website in a search engine's list of relevant sites would see a description sufficient to inform them that his was a critical site, and not one sponsored by Alitalia."[41]

The courts had previously held that the First Amendment protects consumers who use trademark names to make critical comments. As a result, Alitalia's suit failed. More than ten years later, Alitialiasucks.com still comes up on the first search page for the airline.

Similar tactics can be used against an individual, without the obviously satirical "sucks." During his tenure as CEO of United Airlines, Glenn Tilton probably had little love for glenntilton.com, a site maintained by United airline pilots. It was a rich and multilayered site with bars that would lead you to what it termed Tilton's operational failures, his alleged customer service screwups, and the Air Line Pilots Association's call for Tilton to resign.[42] In fact it would have been better for Tilton if the site had had the word "sucks" in it. As offensive as that would be for him, at least visitors would not mistake it for Tilton's home page.

Also on the first page of glenntilton.com was a result that led you to Untied.com, which reproduces the look and feel of a United page. It tells you that "Unless you enjoy being eaten alive by bedbugs, you might have second thoughts about 'flying the friendly skies' with UAL." The site, which has been up since the late-1990s, collects customer complaints and tracks lawsuits against the airline.[43]

> Corporations today have to offer customer service as never before because individuals today have the power to punish as never before.

Social Media Satire Attacks

As with Google bombs, brandjacking easily lends itself to satire. In the aftermath of the Deepwater Horizon disaster that spurted millions of gallons of oil into the Gulf of Mexico, British Petroleum began issuing comments even stranger than then-CEO Tony Hayward's self-pitying comments such as "What the hell did we do to deserve this?" and "I'd like my life back."[44] Or the comments of BP Chairman Carl-Henric Svanberg, who doubled down on BP's image problems with a comment that characterized Gulf Coast residents as "small people" (despite an otherwise well-prepared statement for Svanberg's White House appearance).[45]

As America's outrage grew over the continuing coverage of the torrents of oil chugging up from the bottom of the ocean, a @BPGlobalPR Twitter feed began to pollute BP's reputation with quips so bad, they sounded as if they could have actually come from BP.

> We regretfully admit that something has happened off the Gulf Coast. More to come.

> Are people mad at us for drilling in the ocean? Maybe God shouldn't have put oil out there in the first place.
>
> Here's the thing: we made $45 million A DAY in profits in 2009. This really isn't a big deal.
>
> Catastrophe is a strong word, let's all agree to call it a whoopsie daisy.
>
> And this:
>
> At night the gulf doesn't really look that bad.[46]

BP was also hit with viral video skits purporting to be from the company that showed hapless BP employees stunned into inactivity by a spill of coffee across a desk. These skits about BP's response, which open with a shot of a BP building and its logo, was the handiwork of the Upright Citizens Brigade, an improvisational sketch comedy group. In another piece, a faux spokesman in front of a BP logo apologized for that "oil in the Gulf business."[47]

Facebook cofounder Mark Zuckerberg has also been a target of the Upright Citizens Brigade, which had his Evil Clone issue a snarky apology. "It must have come as a shock to realize," says a Zuckerbergish-looking actor, "that when you handed over that personal information to us, we then had that personal information. I am sorry that I took the personal and private data that you typed into your computers and sent to my company and showed it to other people, even when you told me to forget everything that you told me."[48]

Under American law, the obvious satiric nature of Upright Citizens Brigade's videos protect the use of trademarks as a form of critical speech. While the Twitter feeds of @BPGlobalPR can be mistaken for the real deal, it takes only a few seconds to realize that these pieces are comparable to *Saturday Night Live*'s skits depicting screaming people inside a runaway Toyota Prius.

Some of these takeoffs can be pointed, ending with a vicious crunch instead of a laugh. One viral video appeared to be a Kit Kat commercial in which an office worker in a soulless office takes a break by unwrapping the candy bar and taking a bite. Instead of a satisfying moment and the popular company jingle, however, blood starts to squirt from the man's mouth. He doesn't see that he has in fact bitten into the dismembered finger of an orangutan. The point of the video post, produced by Greenpeace, was to protest Nestlé's use of palm oil in Indonesia, which leads to the deforestation of the orangutan's native habitat.

Nestlé, which had already committed to shifting to environmentally certified palm oil, asked YouTube to remove the video. This of course activated the Streisand Effect to ensure it would go viral.[49]

> Countering Evil Clones that have migrated to Twitter and YouTube must be part of any basic crisis plan.

Spokesmen Trolls

Jude Finisterra, spokesman for Dow Chemical, appeared on BBC World TV from Paris, the Eiffel Tower behind him. The anchor was primed to question the spokesman about the thousands of deaths and injuries in the aftermath of the 1984 disaster at the Bhopal chemical plant owned by Dow's Union Carbide subsidiary. "Do you now accept responsibility for what happened?" the anchor asked in the interview that took place twenty years after the Bhopal tragedy.

"Today, I am very, very happy to announce that for the first time Dow is accepting full responsibility for the Bhopal catastrophe," said Finisterra, a trim man with short black hair in a dark suit, white shirt, and dark tie. "We have a $12 billion plan to finally at long last fully compensate the victims, including the 120,000 who may need medical care for their entire lives." Finisterra promised a swift and complete environmental remediation of the site. He then spoke of children who still play in playgrounds and drink water at sites drenched in tons of toxic waste. "It's a mess." The money would come, Finisterra said, from the liquidation of Union Carbide.[50]

By this point, one might think that the BBC would be wondering why a Fortune 100 executive was going to such great lengths to sound like a class-action attorney indicting his own company. He referred to Union Carbide as "this nightmare for the world and this headache for Dow," and offered for Dow to "take full responsibility," a term no general counsel of any corporation in the world would permit a spokesman to offer for a subsidiary's more-than-twenty-year-old actions.

Perhaps the producers at BBC might have connected a little grade-school Latin to the man's name: *finis,* meaning the end, and *terra,* the earth.

Mr. End of the Earth was, of course, a prankster. He was one of the Yes Men engaged in a practice the group calls "identity correction," "culture jamming," "subvertising"—and the rest of us would call a hoax.[51] In the case of the Dow Chemical hoax, the company lost $2 billion in market value before the story was discredited.[52] Journalists reported that the phony story had left residents of Bhopal in tears.

The Yes Men have engaged in brandjacking with dowethics.com, in which it offers a mission statement: "As a publicly owned corporation, Dow is unable, due to share-price concerns, to accept any responsibility for the Bhopal catastrophe caused by our fully owned subsidiary, Union Carbide."[53] The Yes Men also have a News Center with headlines such as "Chemicals are not only for external uses." They offer a devilishly ingenious "Acceptable Risk Calculator," as well as a PR prop, Gilda the golden skeleton.[54]

Sometimes they hit a droll approach that perfectly parodies the bland, button-down style of corporate communications. One Yes Men website, www.gatt.org, parodies the World Trade Organization with zany headlines, such as a phony Wharton Business School announcement of the creation of a new, much improved form of slavery for Africa.[55]

When the Yes Men step out of character, however, they come across as thin-skinned, distinctly unfunny ideologues who see all private enterprise as inherently corrupt. You can see this in their slickly produced knockoff of an Apple website that advertises the new iPhone 4CF, the C standing for "conflict-free" minerals, instead of what it describes as Apple's current sourcing from the violent extraction industry of the Democratic Republic of Congo.[56] When Apple responded with indignation over the Evil Clone, the Yes Men responded, "Apple's heavy-handed and humorless reaction just shows where their big mechanical (and conflict-mineral-rich) corporate heart is at."[57]

But the signature statements of the Yes Men are often made in character as Evil Clones in the flesh. Posing as spokesmen for the U.S. Chamber of Commerce in late 2009, the Yes Men announced the chamber had dropped its opposition to cap-and-trade climate change legislation and called for a carbon tax. The websites of *The New York Times* and *The Washington Post* picked up the phony story. This "news" also became the subject of a breathless Fox Business Network segment until the anchor, Brian Sullivan, was handed a piece of paper and, after an embarrassed silence, announced it was a hoax.[58]

In April 2011, the Yes Men put out a phony press release announcing that GE would "repay" a nonexistent $3.2 billion "refund" to the U.S. Treasury.[59]

In 2009, Yes Men volunteers handed out 100,000 phony copies of Rupert Murdoch's *New York Post,* reversing that publication's traditional skeptical approach to human-caused global warming to announce, "We're Screwed." The rest of the publication included thirty-two pages on climate change, complete with phony Page Six gossip that managed to pull in a green theme.[60] They have also impersonated *The New York Times* and its website.

In a seemingly innocuous keynote luncheon address before an audience in the petroleum industry in Calgary, a Yes Man appeared as spokesman for the National Petroleum Council. Amid the clatter of silverware and hum of an industry crowd, this Yes Man launched into what sounded at first like a boilerplate special. On occasion, heads would jerk back as the Yes Man's remarks became increasingly bizarre. We need "something as useful as whales, but infinitely more abundant," the supposed representative from the National Petroleum Council said. "Why wait millions of years," he asked, to make oil, when you can turn the billions of people who will be killed by climate change into oil? He then unveiled Vivoleum, a petroleum product made of rendered human flesh.[61]

The Yes Men's droll, understated manner for making offensive statements ("starvation is the new black") neatly skewers the corporate style. As with the antics of Sacha Baron Cohen and his Brüno character, the lack of dissent from the audience to the hoaxsters' heartless statements is depicted by the Yes Men as tacit agreement by the corporate community to moral depravity. The reality appears somewhat more benign. After a few dropped jaws, people in the corporate audience obviously clue in. They listen politely because they know that they are watching some kind of circus act. Such overly polite acquiescence helps the Yes Men put audience members in a bad light. It makes a wreck of corporate PR campaigns and press conferences.

When Chevron invested in a "We Agree" ad campaign, the Yes

Men teamed up with two environmental organizations to send e-mails resembling official Chevron corporate messages, directing media to chevron-weagree.com, that included phony news releases with headers like "Radical Chevron Ad Campaign Highlights Industry Problems." The phony site offered PDF files to download consisting of satirical street posters.[62] The Yes Men went on to promote "billboard alteration kits."[63]

As a result, Chevron's multimillion-dollar ad campaign was marred as the stream of approved and satirical information bled together in the reporting.

> Evil Clones, often flesh-and-blood avatars with agendas, use comedy to wreak havoc on brands and companies.

Anatomy of an Online Breakup

The saga of the digital breakup of a middle-aged professional couple shows how maneuvers on the Internet can escalate a domestic quarrel to the edge of violence and personal ruin. This complicated breakup shows how online impersonation techniques can create an Evil Clone to land someone behind bars.[64]

Let's call the couple "Steve" and "Linda." They are middle-aged, each divorced, attractive players on the lookout for something better. Linda works at an upscale specialty business. Steve heads his own small firm. He is burly, sardonic, frank, and profane. She is good looking and irreverent. The attraction was immediate. Their multiyear relationship was physical and fun.

Before they were done, Steve and Linda would both put each other in jail. Their story, told by documents and surprising candor from Steve's perspective, also shows how technology can make breaking up hard to do in a 24/7 Internet age that provides people with little cooling-off time.

One recent summer, Linda went on a business trip overseas. While she was gone, Steve corresponded with "Vicky," a woman he had met on a dating site. He sent her an e-mail and they agreed to meet for a drink. As soon as she returned to the United States, Linda called, "and she's absolutely livid," Steve says. "She wants to know who Vicky is. And throughout the discussion, it is obvious that she not only has access to my e-mails but has copies of spreadsheets, documents, and photographs that are all on my hard drive."

Steve has imported old data into one computer after another for several decades, each time adding fresh layers to the digital archaeology of his life. Buried deep in Steve's personal computer, which he also uses for business, is a folder that contains nude photos of old girlfriends and copies of old love letters. That folder also contains a "list as best as I can remember of women that I've slept with, not for bed-notching purposes, but in today's world for health reasons," Steve says. "Linda has this list. She has all these pictures. She's quoting me verbatim from letters I had sent long ago."

More alarming than the exposure of his private life was *how* Linda got into Steve's computer. Linda had once confided in Steve that a former lover was involved in shady international business deals. After they broke up her ex worried that Linda might report her suspicions about some of his business deals to the authorities. Later, Linda found out, a friend of her ex, a prolific black hat named "Harold," started hacking into her computer to see if there was anything his friend needed to worry about. This is how Harold discovered that Steve was the new man in Linda's life. So for good measure, he also started examining Steve's computer as well.

According to Linda, Harold was the one who alerted her to Steve's flirting. Harold confessed that he had been monitoring Linda's communications, all for the single purpose of keeping her ex at ease. Harold felt comfortable telling Linda this: His friend had already moved to another part of the world and had shifted all his accounts to offshore banks far from any likely investigator. So Harold told Linda that Steve's behavior was so treacherous that he felt an obligation to warn her about him.

Worried, Steve called in a local computer geek company, a consultancy that found that someone had imported a keystroke logger to follow Steve's every computer touch. The geeks encrypted Steve's networks, installed new firewalls, updated his passwords. Still, Steve says more than three years later, "it's in the back of my mind that somebody's always watching."

After weeks of estrangement, Steve and Linda started seeing each other again. Once they were back together, Steve says, Linda "did seem to have unerring knowledge if some woman had written me on some online site." Every time it happened, Steve wondered if he was still being hacked or if Linda had simply gone through the search history on Steve's computer.

One spring night, the couple started sniping at each other at a dinner party. The argument escalated when they returned to Steve's house; early the next morning Linda announced that she wanted out. "You want to go, fine!" Steve shouted at her. He flung the door open and threw her bags out the front door. Linda called 911 and told the police that she had not been physically assaulted but that she feared for her safety.

"The next thing that I know, there are two cop cars at my house," Steve says. "And the cops are asking what's going on, and I'm telling them, hey, we're breaking up, she wants to go, I want her the fuck out of here. I didn't lay a hand on her, I tossed her stuff out. There it is, right there."

The police gave Linda a Breathalyzer test that revealed she was legally intoxicated. They told Steve that if he wanted her off his property, they would have had to tow her car and drive her to a hotel. "At first I'm like, 'What the fuck do I care, get her the hell out of here,'" he says. "Then I come to arguably the stupidest decision I've ever made in my life, which is—I don't need to be *that* much of an asshole. I can just make up the guest room for her. She can just sleep it off and then leave in the morning."

Most people would say, however, that it was the next thing that Steve did on the Internet that might have been the stupidest decision he'd ever made in his life. Linda had confided personal secrets to him. They were secrets no more. "Linda goes to sleep," Steve says. "So I get on Facebook and I'm writing her best friend, Trudy, who didn't know that Linda had been banging someone very close to her while he was engaged to some other woman. I e-mailed some other friend of hers who she worked with, saying, 'Hey, you know, I'm out of the picture, feel free to nail her to your heart's content.' There was on old friend of hers who was panting after her, despite being married and having kids. I sent him the same sort of nasty e-mail. Nothing illegal. I wasn't hacking into her account. Just Facebook being what it is, if somebody is a friend of somebody else, for the most part you can contact them."

In this digital age, however, many people are on social media when they should be sleeping. One of them was Linda. "About three o'clock in the morning she comes flying out of the guest room," Steve says. "She's getting either messages or notification of the messages on her BlackBerry and she knows what I've done. She's just rip-snorting mad, which was, you know, anticipated. I just didn't expect her to find out about it right then and there. But I wanted her [to find the messages] the next day when she got home [and] to be as pissed off at me as possible, so this would be the final nail in the coffin."

After an altercation, Linda could not find her car keys and accused Steve of hiding them. As Steve would later tell the police, Linda flew into a rage and snapped a windshield wiper from his car, smashed a bottle of wine and scattered the glass all over a table, then pushed the table over and broke it, knocked over a dresser drawer, and emptied filthy trash into his printer/fax. She flipped a coffee table, smashed CDs, and broke an inherited keepsake. She stomped on a computer mouse and splashed red wine on the wall.

Photographs submitted to the police do indeed appear to show this destruction. What no one could photograph, however, was Linda's feeling that Steve's e-mails and betrayal of confidence had also ransacked, broken, and smashed her personal life. "When she was out looking for her keys again, I closed the door and locked it behind her," Steve says. This time it was his turn to call 911 to get the police to take her out of his house.

The next morning, Steve decided to file charges for destruction of property. "My interest is not seeing her get arrested," he says. "It was consequences and seeing that I was compensated." That evening Steve speaks by phone with the officer in charge of the case. He doesn't relent, though Steve seeks an assurance that Linda wouldn't be embarrassed by being arrested at work like "a common criminal." It probably didn't seem that way to Linda, who after she surrendered herself was arrested, patted down, fingerprinted, and given a mug shot.

About one week later, the police officer asks Steve to come down to the station to discuss the case. "At this point," Steve says, "I have collected all of my estimates and such, and I've got them along with a list of all the line items, and I'm assuming that is what he wants to talk to me about."

Steve arrives at the station in early evening. To his surprise, the officer "starts giving me a hard time," disputing the extent of the damage. "Have you communicated with her?" the officer asks.

"We exchanged a few e-mails, and there was texting that went on back and forth," Steve replied.

"Well, what about these e-mails?"

The officer shows Steve two of three e-mails that had been sent from his account to hers. One read:

> I'm assuming by now you've had your tour of the County Detention Center and have concluded tat [*sic*] I was indeed successful in convincing them that you did all the damage. Might want to stop underestimating me. You do so at your peril.
>
> This all could have been avoided if you had just responded to me last week. No need to be so rude. What gives you the right to think you can ignore me like that? Or were you simply so consumed with whomever the newest interest might be. Like I said, my money is on "Hank." So sad really. Now you've brought all these problems on yourself.
>
> —S

In this one brief communication, Steve seemed to be congratulating himself for committing the crime of framing Linda with the damage to his house, as well as coercing her for not "responding" to him. In another, he seemed to threaten blackmail:

> Don't forget about all those pictures I have of you in various creative outfits, positions, etc. Wouldn't want them to end up in the wrong hangs [*sic*], now would you? Don't push me. It will not be pretty.
>
> Cheers!—S

A third e-mail from Steve to Linda notes that she blocked his ability to access her Facebook, LinkedIn, and MySpace profiles. Steve said that he had no intention of sending more messages "unless you fuck with me in some very severe and unexpected" way.

Steve stared at the e-mails and wondered if it was possible that he had gotten so angry he'd written these and forgotten that he had. He had definitely written the third message. But Steve's recollection was that he had not sent it, but had wisely (for once) held it in the "drafts" folder of his e-mail. Had he not been under so much pressure from the policeman, he would have remembered that he had accidentally left his laptop with the TSA at an airport security gate. He didn't. Perhaps remembering his Facebook tantrum, Steve instead allowed for the possibility that he had sent the e-mails in anger and suppressed the memory.

"It sounds like me, but I have no recollection of having sent these, and I am not senile," Steve says. "I'll get back to you, and I'll let you know what I find out. Are we done here?"

The policeman says that they are done, "except for one thing."

"What?' "

"Stand up and put your arms behind your back."

The policeman, swayed by the new e-mail evidence, is accepting Linda's insistence that Steve had in fact physically assaulted her the night of the breakup. Now it is Steve's turn before the magistrate. The policeman surprises him by testifying that Linda, on the night they had broken up and both called 911, had "scratches that appeared to be fresh."

When Steve is released, he calls in the computer geeks. In Steve's send box are the threatening e-mails sent to Linda from his account that he now fully realized he had never seen before, along with the angry e-mail he had written, but kept in the drafts folder. That e-mail too had been sent.

The computer consultant scrolled to the bottom of one suspicious message and clicked on "complete header." This revealed the IP address the message originated from, as well as the IP address it was delivered to.

The threatening e-mails Linda had presented to the police had the same origination IP address on it. Hers.

The messages were an Evil Clone tactic that had gotten Steve arrested. Steve believes that at this point Harold was not involved.

"I hadn't given Linda the password to my account, but in arguments over the dating sites, I had given her the password to the dating sites," he says. "In a naive sort of way, all my passwords were amalgams of my children's names plus their birthdays. So all she had to do was guess, and she quickly came up with the right one."

Steve changed his passwords again, this time to a more robust form Linda could not guess. He commissioned a digital forensic report from the computer consultant and had a subpoena sent to his Internet service provider asking for all the times and IP addresses of anyone who had accessed his account over a six-week period.

In the days to come, Linda had another digital ploy. She slapped a protective order against Steve. He was to have no communication by phone, by e-mail, or in person with Linda. Then she claimed he had IM-ed her and had him arrested again—twice.

"Now I am scared shitless," Steve says. "I am on a first-name basis with everyone in the magistrate's office. And I can't get anything done because I am looking out my window every six seconds expecting to see police cars there. She has offered no proof of this whatsoever, and all she has to do is pick up the phone and say, 'He sent me a text message or an IM,' and they're going to come and arrest me again."

Finally Steve got the result of the subpoena, which showed that Linda had remotely accessed Steve's e-mail account. A further subpoena showed that the vile e-mails were sent while Steve's laptop was still in the hands of the TSA. He presented his evidence to the authorities.

The cases against Steve and Linda were mutually dismissed, Steve being told he was no longer at risk of being arrested for violating the restraining order. During his legal preparations, Steve noticed that Linda has signed a statement under penalty of perjury that she had minimal assets in order to get a court-appointed attorney.

"I had been her ad hoc financial adviser for two years," Steve says. "I know this woman is sitting on six figures in savings."

Steve presents his evidence about Linda's true financial condition and her court-appointed attorney to a detective. The gambit works. Linda is arrested again.

Some time later, in the middle of the night, Steve receives one call after another from Linda. After the seventeenth call or so, at 4:00 A.M., Steve picks up the phone.

"She's calling mostly to remind me what an asshole I am," he says. "But she's also throwing in my face things about my personal life that I can't begin to imagine how she knows. She knows I'm seeing a new woman, she knows that my kids are not at home." Linda had gotten back in Steve's system.

The next morning, Steve found five e-mails from his phone company telling him that his PIN number, password, and secret question to his account have been changed. He also discovers a new e-mail address has been added to notifications tied to an old e-mail account. When he checks, the phone company tells him that the account was accessed from Linda's IP address.

"Now I know how she knows about all this stuff," Steve says. "She has deleted my 150 messages, most of which I am saving because there was business information in there that I needed." Steve took his case to the detective who was handling Linda's perjury case. The detective sent an e-mail, "Linda, this is a week before your trial. How is this going to help you? Do I need to add new charges here?"

The detective subpoenaed a number of Steve's digital accounts and all of them registered positive hits. After a plea agreement Linda was sentenced to time in jail—most but not all of it suspended—followed by probation. She could have spent more time in jail had she been prosecuted for malicious prosecution, defamation, and computer trespass.

What were Steve and Linda left with?

Largely due to an escalating feud enabled by technology, each of them had been arrested. Although only Linda ultimately served jail time, it is likely that the forged e-mails represented for her a kind of rough justice approximating Steve's flaming of her reputation before her Facebook friends. Steve could have replaced the damaged goods in his house many times over with what he spent on forensic digital studies, the testimony of digital investigators, lawyers, and other court costs. Worst of all, he had suffered days of mental torment because he had been framed by a digital clone.

> In a bitter all-out flame war between ex-lovers determined to create Evil Clones, there are no winners.

Takeaway—Counters to Evil Clone Attacks

If someone is impersonating you, follow the example of General Mills and Javelin Pharmaceutical by immediately countering the deception. E-mail all your friends, contacts, and business acquaintances. Put up a notice on Facebook. Post a news release.

Don't let it sit for a moment.

As we have seen, some people—when confronted with e-mails they did not send—are at first not certain that they did not in fact send them. Keeping good records and asking a digital hound to compare the checksums of messages are not enough. If you are presented with a nasty e-mail bearing your name, you should be certain that it is not yours because you never send a nasty e-mail or one that is damaging in substance. While your e-mails may contain proprietary and personal information, there should be nothing so essentially wrong about them that you would be in danger of losing your job or getting in legal trouble to see them quoted on the Drudge Report.

If someone impersonates your company in person, follow the example of the U.S. Chamber of Commerce, which sent a spokesman to walk into the Yes Men's phony press conference, interrupt it, and set the record straight.

If someone impersonates you or presents himself as you or your company's spokesmen, you should file a civil suit and explore criminal charges. In January 2011, California enacted a new criminal law against someone who "knowingly and without consent credibly impersonates another actual person through or on an Internet Web site or by other electronic means with the intent to harm, intimidate, threaten or defraud."[65] Like so much else from California, this law is apt to be enacted in many other states, perhaps even on a federal level.

On the other hand, if you or your company is hit with an online satire, many things you could do in response will only make it worse. The courts give wide latitude where humor is used to make a point. There are, however, many fine distinctions to discuss with a lawyer where copyright violations and misuse of trademarks are concerned.

You might use the Digital Millennium Copyright Act to force the Internet service provider to take down the site—if it truly misuses your copyrighted material. Don't use the DMCA, however, if critics are merely using your trademark to criticize or satirize your company. And do not use the DMCA to take down material just because it is offensive to you. Such an Internet takedown order will be obeyed almost immediately. But if your opponent can prove that there was no copyright violation and that you invoked the DMCA without justification, you can be held liable—and the penalties can be severe.[66]

One key to protecting your reputation is to have the best and most up-to-date firewalls and software to protect confidential, personal, or corporate information. You have to be aware of whom you allow to use your computer. And don't provide passcode information to anyone but your spouse. Make those passcodes robust and change them periodically, particularly after any incident.

> Evil Clones can cause trouble with a mate, an employer, and the law. Safeguarding your technology is the best way to safeguard your identity. Quick response is the best way to unmask an Evil Clone.

6:// The Fourth Sword

Human Flesh Search Engines

The mob is the mother of tyrants.

—Diogenes

IN THE 2007 WESTERN *3:10 to Yuma,* Ben Wade, a character played by Russell Crowe, is being held in a hotel in the town of Contention by marshals waiting for a train to take Wade to trial. One of Wade's confederates surveys the seedy frontier town and realizes that it is populated by useful lowlifes. So he promises $200 to every man who kills a marshal. The offer instantly transforms the men of Contention from a crowd of ambling, shiftless drunks into an army out to liberate Ben Wade.

The difference between this scene and today's Internet is that one need not offer $200, just the chance to anonymously harm someone. The Human Flesh Search Engine, a Chinese netizen term that originated on an Internet bulletin board, began by singling out antisocial acts on social media, using crowd-sourcing to locate perpetrators and national shaming to punish them.

> The Human Flesh Search Engine draws on the power of social media, activating digital mobs to launch an attack on a target from multiple directions.

Social Media Gang Bang

The iconic example of the Human Flesh Search Engine occurred when Zhu Guang Bing, a Chinese netizen, in 2003 used crowd-sourcing to track a woman who posted a "crush" video of her spearing the head of a live kitten with her stiletto heel. Zhu and a horde of other outraged netizens tracked the website to a thirty-seven-year-old nurse, in part by connecting the handle of the person who had uploaded the video to the recent purchase of a pair of high-heeled shoes from an online auction site. Once exposed to a relentless barrage of Internet criticism, the woman lost her job and was forced to make a national apology.[1]

In 2005, a South Korean with a camera phone captured a young woman who refused to clean up after her dog. Her outrageous indifference to the complaints of others made the segment a viral video hit. It wasn't long before the Human Flesh Search Engine tracked down the woman, who became known from one end of the country to the other as "dog-shit girl." The human flesh attack went into overdrive, seeking as much personal and damaging information about the young woman as it could dig up, reportedly forcing her to withdraw in shame from her university studies.[2]

One doesn't have to be a scofflaw to become a victim of this fourth sword of the new media. On the comment board of Socialite Rank, Olivia Palermo's protestations that she was the victim of Internet impersonation only made her anonymous accusers circle into a full-fledged human flesh attack. "She's turning into the Anna Nicole Smith of the benefit circle," one vicious commenter posted. "A tawdry, trashy, white-trash circus freak." One of the self-described masterminds of the site told journalist Isaiah Wilner that Socialite Rank worked to reveal real secrets as well. "Once the girls got the fame, their friends revealed their dark demons, their secrets—drug use, sexual pasts."[3]

The Human Flesh Search Engine can easily turn on its creators. In the aftermath of the 2008 Sichuan earthquake, Zhu, the pioneer who had turned the human flesh attack against the kitten killer, learned that his Frankenstein's monster could turn on anyone, making summary judgments without the support of facts or any right of appeal. When Zhu tried to auction off websites for charitable relief, he was accused by social media vigilantes of cashing in on the tragedy. The result was a devastating bombardment. "They said I was going to try and keep the money myself and that I just wanted to get famous," Zhu told the media. "Because I posted my phone number, they hounded me day and night, dozens of calls at home and the office. I couldn't do my work, so I lost my job all because I was trying to do a good thing."[4]

A similar sense of outrage prompted the Human Flesh Search Engine to go after Megan Meier's tormentor, Lori Drew, enabling someone to locate her house and hurl a brick through her kitchen window (see chapter 5).[5]

This is all in keeping with the writings of Gustave Le Bon, a nineteenth-century social psychologist who drew many examples from France's tumultuous post-Bastille history of how crowds can be swept up into violence by their self-reinforcing sense of justice.

> Human Flesh Search Engine vigilantes feed off the irony of "live by the sword, die by the sword."

SHAC Attack

One summer evening Brian Cass, the fifty-three-year-old managing director of Huntingdon Life Sciences (HLS) in Cambridgeshire, England, drove home from work in the dark, and when exiting his car saw three people with pickaxe handles raised above their heads. The rain of blows that followed on his head, back, and forearm left Cass with a three-inch-long head wound. The police considered Cass, who was rescued by his partner and a neighbor, lucky to have survived the attack. A British court later convicted a thirty-four-year-old man, revved up by a human flesh engine attack, of leading the assault.[6]

The attack on Cass was just one episode in a war on HLS, the science-based company that performs animal testing. It shows how Internet incitement and virtual organization can promote violence, even terrorism, against an organization, its people, and anyone affiliated with it. HLS is a research organization that conducts scientific animal tests on medicines, as well as on agricultural and industrial chemicals, to ensure that they meet the United Kingdom's stringent safety standards. British law is among the strictest in the world on how animals may be tested, outlawing the testing of cosmetics, tobacco, and weapons on animals, as well as forbidding experiments on chimpanzees and other great apes.[7]

Although scientists are currently experimenting with replacing animal testing with human tissue cultures, animal testing remains essential to scientific and medical progress. Animal testing, for example, has led to the development of a brain pacemaker that can ease the symptoms of Parkinson's disease.[8]

By the turn of the century, HLS had found substitutes that allowed it to replace half of its tests with nonanimal methods. Even then, the BBC reported, its experiments consumed 75,000 animals a year, including 750 dogs and 190 primates for tests. All the animals used were eventually killed.[9]

This migration toward nonanimal testing couldn't come too soon after a 1997 documentary on Britain's Channel 4, *It's a Dog's Life,* taken by an undercover whistle-blower with a hidden camera. The exposé outraged the British public with scenes of laboratory technicians abusing an uncooperative beagle, punching it to get it to submit to a test, shaking it to force the animal to accept an injection. The televised report also showed that the chemicals being injected were incompetently measured, rendering the experiment valueless and making the dog's suffering without any moral purpose.[10]

In the ensuing firestorm of public outrage, HLS fired the three technicians. Two of them were arrested at their homes for animal cruelty.[11] HLS apologized, portrayed the beagle incident as an anomaly, and tightened up its management and training. It wasn't enough to satisfy the radical animal rights activists of Stop Huntingdon Animal Cruelty (SHAC), whose leaders turned to social media to activate a human flesh attack on HLS. The animal rights group published shareholders' names on the Internet, calling on supporters to "adopt a director" for harassment and intimidation. The attacks soon expanded to include hundreds of employees and executives at client organizations that contracted for the testing, especially those who worked in pharmaceutical companies.

Institutions that financially supported HLS were also listed, including the Bank of New York and the Bank of Scotland Branch Nominees, Ltd.[12] So many suppliers of HLS were scared off that the company had to build its own laundry, cleaning service, and cafeteria.[13]

Simply listing people for "adoption" was enough to make them targets of terror. The campaign of intimidation included late-night phone calls, hate mail, and the delivery of unwanted sex toys. The cars of affiliate executives were bombed with Molotov cocktails. Neighbors of the victims received letters that included a photo of a mutilated monkey (which had nothing to do with HLS), urging neighbors to "let them know what you think about animal cruelty."[14]

One pension fund manager, frightened by bomb threats, sold its 10 percent holdings in HLS.[15] SHAC bragged that its tactics forced Merrill Lynch, Charles Schwab, and Deloitte Touche to withdraw from doing any business with HLS.[16] The campaign of terror extended to the United States, where HLS had a lab in New Jersey.

The Internet was central to organizing human flesh attacks on HLS and its affiliates and vendors, allowing SHAC leaders to keep their hands as clean as possible by simply listing targets on a website. Describing the activists as cunning, a spokesman for Cambridgeshire police said, "These people often go right to the edge of what is legal, which can make it difficult for us to bring a charge."[17] Being on SHAC's Internet adoption list had real-world consequences, as Brian Cass found out.

The campaign of violence also extended to the home of a Japanese executive living in England who worked for a pharmaceutical client of HLS. Four hooded men smashed the windows of his home and tried to smash down his front door. They fled before the police could arrive. The executive and his family were terrorized, "shaken, drained, and utterly bewildered."[18]

While physical attacks tended to turn executives into sympathetic victims, smear campaigns turned out to be a much more effective way of attacking clients. Executives' wives and mothers had their phone numbers listed in swingers' magazines, advertising their services as prostitutes. In at least fifteen cases, letters were delivered to hundreds of neighbors of executives warning them that they were living next to convicted pedophiles.[19]

By 2007, with police now on full alert, the SHACtivists increasingly turned to encrypted e-mail, sharing the names and addresses of targeted HLS suppliers on a "backbite" website.[20] The Internet proved to be the best way to securely incite, organize, and take credit for acts of violence. "Your life is in danger whenever you go to your car after working in the torture chamber," one SHACtivist wrote in mass e-mails to HLS employees. In another e-mail, she added: "Don't even think that your children are safe, if you have any. It doesn't take us long to find out where they go to school and where they live."

After the woman was found responsible for these threats, she was sentenced to five months in prison and later claimed that she was just a "harmless animal lover." Soon activists were posting the "Internet death lists" of executives worthy of execution.[21]

Activists continue to Google bomb the company, surrounding the HLS website with sites offering heart-rending videos of animal cruelty.

Google bombs were especially effective in the United States in driving investment away from HLS. Another bonus: SHAC found that many of those drawn to the cause of animal rights in North America also happen to have computer skills on tap.

"So any company that got tied to Huntingdon, all of a sudden they touched the third rail and the extremists started to come after them," says a security expert who worked the case. "They wanted to make anything around Huntingdon radioactive." [22] As they did, the Internet became the safe place to post demands and take anonymous credit for acts of terror and vandalism.

In this mode, activists splashed red paint on the Manhasset Bay Yacht Club on Long Island, New York, and the Animal Liberation Front proclaimed on an Internet board: "Let this be a message to any other company who chooses to court HLS . . . If you trade in LSR [Life Science Research, parent company of HLS] shares, make a market, process orders, or purchase shares you can expect far worse treatment. The message is simple, don't touch HLS!" Carr Securities, which had been prepared to guide HLS in listing on the New York Stock Exchange, got the message. It put out a statement of capitulation.[23]

Eventually, though, the rule of law prevailed. If the British are well-known animal lovers, they are also tenacious upholders of the rule of law. The more the campaign escalated, the more HLS employees saw themselves as standing for something important. Most stayed on the job. "There is something of the Dunkirk spirit," an HLS spokesman told the press. "We are not going to let these bastards get us down."[24]

The full resources of Scotland Yard and the FBI were employed, and the trail of violence was traced back in 2008 to SHAC leaders, who were tried, convicted, and faced long jail sentences.[25]

Is the SHAC/HLS war a harbinger of digital wars to come, with the anonymity of the Internet facilitating terror? "If you have other options to invest your money, do you need the hassle of threats to your families?" one of the investigators asks. "Do you need to have security assessments to your house, having to monitor all of your facilities, dealing with stink bombs and protests?"[26]

Such experiences have become so commonplace that elaborate security is needed to protect management and the public posture of the company subjected to such tactics. One of the authors experienced this when he held two different senior corporate positions in the United States and

Europe in which he had to provide security to employees from activist terrorists. Employees were protected from attacks on the street and in their homes; the undercarriages of their cars were checked for bombs. In one case, he had to launch a worldwide recall of a popular drink, which an activist group had proudly claimed it had tampered with. This wasn't an idle threat. A number of bottles had in fact been laced with poison.

The power of such campaigns to terrorize are amplified by the reach and anonymity of the Internet, which allows terrorists to name victims, covertly coordinate actions without having to expose cells to discovery, and take credit for acts of mayhem.

> Human flesh engine attacks unleash terror simply by identifying targets on a comment board or website.

Clowns to the Left of Me . . .

In the fall of 2010, Christine O'Donnell's campaign to represent Delaware in the U.S. Senate was on the ropes. With the endorsement of Rush Limbaugh and Sarah Palin, O'Donnell had edged out a political giant, congressman and former governor Mike Castle, to win the GOP nomination.

From that point on, everything went wrong. A twelve-year-old clip of O'Donnell telling Bill Maher on *Politically Incorrect* that she had once dabbled in witchcraft solidified the notion that she was flighty and without substance. Her attempt at damage control—the infamous "I'm not a witch" ad—made her unelectable. That should have been enough to do her in. But somebody felt the need to pour the whole bucket of water on her.

An anonymous man, known only to be in his twenties and living in Philadelphia, posted a "I Had a One-Night Stand with Christine O'Donnell" piece. Gawker.com carried his claim that three years earlier an obviously tipsy O'Donnell lured the young man and his roommates to join her and a friend to go to a local bar on Halloween night. O'Donnell wore a ladybug costume—a claim backed by several digital photos of an apparently lit O'Donnell mugging around in just such a silly costume.[27]

If that had been all there was to the man's story, it would have been the kind of eleventh-hour embarrassment that every campaign faces. The piece did not stop there. Although there is no way to verify its credibility, it turned out nasty. "It really didn't take very long for Christine to make her move," the blogger wrote. "She'd grabbed my hand on the way from the apartment to South Street, so I can't say I was totally surprised when she leaned in to kiss me soon after we arrived at the bar." He noted that he was later surprised to learn that she was fourteen years older than him.

"I don't think I'd heard the word 'cougar' yet at that point, but that's probably what I'd call her," he wrote. "Things got physical on the couch pretty quickly. It wasn't long before we'd moved from the living room to my bed." He promised not to get into the "nitty-gritty details of what happened between the sheets that evening," then divulged that "it wasn't half as exciting as I'd been hoping it would be."

O'Donnell was "a decent kisser," but "as soon as her clothes came off and she was naked in my bed, Christine informed me that she was a virgin." He later came to understand that she was a "born-again virgin." He added the salacious centerpiece of the story, a commonplace anatomical observation that he used to heap ridicule on O'Donnell. Then the man rolled over and went to sleep without having sex with her.

The next morning, the blogger said, he had trouble getting her to leave his apartment before he went off to work. He ended the post by noting that O'Donnell later dated his roommate and likely did not have sex with him either.

Andrew Sullivan, the Oxford-educated, iconoclastic super-blogger now with the Daily Beast and no admirer of O'Donnell, called the post a "cowardly, brutal and misogynist invasion of privacy." Gawker, which had paid for the story in the low four figures, defended itself by saying that O'Donnell's championship of chastity and marriage made her a hypocrite, and therefore fair game.[28]

What were the underlying facts? O'Donnell wasn't married. And if the post is true, she did not have sex. Gawker's defense for such creepily caddish humiliation of a woman is that she, as a self-declared Christian, has on occasion been a hypocrite.

This Internet attack forces us to ask if the age of total transparency makes it possible for any living, breathing human being to champion a given moral standard. Most would agree that a fire-and-brimstone preacher who denounces adultery and homosexuality every Sunday from the pulpit while exploiting young men in his congregation is a hypocrite worth exposing. John Edwards, whose central campaign appeal to female voters was making displays of his unctuous infatuation with his wife while fathering a child with another woman, is clearly a hypocrite. Former Nevada Republican senator John Ensign, who called on President Clinton to resign and spoke of the sanctity of marriage as his reason for a measure barring same-sex marriage while carrying on an affair with the wife of a family friend and top aide, is certainly a hypocrite.

Christine O'Donnell is just an unmarried lady who got silly on one Halloween night, had too much good cheer, and may have let a man see her naked.

> Once a woman becomes a target, the Human Flesh Search Engine can crowd-source her entire private life—anyone who has ever known her—and strip her naked in the public square.

Jokers to the Right . . .

Reverend Carol Howard Merritt is a minister at the Western Presbyterian Church, a short walk from the Watergate building along the banks of the Potomac. A progressive who brings a liberal perspective to theology, Merritt is a voracious blogger, podcaster, and editorial contributor to the Huffington Post, with a significant following on Facebook and Twitter.

When Merritt started writing regularly in 2007, she says she was surprised "how quickly things spread. At first it was very positive, exciting, and interesting how, as a budding writer, I was being read."[29] As her pieces appeared on the Huffington Post, "pretty soon, I began to get nasty e-mails, comments which I tend to ignore."

Before long, Merritt was under attack by a group of people she did not know existed—atheist fundamentalists. Like many intellectual Christians, she had long cultivated many friends who are atheists, finding the give-and-take of ideas with other thinkers bracing. To her surprise, however, a fair number of atheists respond to digital debate with personal attacks.

"Often there is this sense of real woundedness that you can read in their comments," she says. "It's almost like they're oozing with pain from religion really hurting them in some ways."

The worst human flesh attacks, however, came from her fellow Christians, especially a group that has come to be called "heresy hunters." One evangelical preacher goes beyond criticism of Merritt's liberal theology to demonize her as a "pastrix"—a conflation of "pastor" and the sexually charged term "dominatrix."

"For a while he was reading every single thing on the Web I wrote and picking it apart," Merritt says. After Merritt posted a sharply worded critique entitled "Why Evangelicalism Is Failing a New Generation" on the Huffington Post, all hell broke loose.[30] A public campaign of shaming began, with critiques of Merritt from unknown posters taking on sexually charged terms—with "whore of Babylon" and "whore of Satan" taking top billing.

The rising tide of the human flesh attack culminated in a call to Merritt's husband, also a Presbyterian minister, with the unknown caller "starting out the conversation saying, 'You don't want to get your child hurt.'" To Merritt's surprise, online attacks come from even like-minded ministers interested in the progressive "emerging church" movement that conducts much of its dialogue via technology and blogs. "You're in conversation with these people, then all the sudden you'll say things they don't like," she says. "And this has happened with colleagues. Other ministers, they'll start attacking you. This emerging movement is kind of bad about that."

There seems, she says something about the terseness of Twitter that encourages misunderstanding and vicious group attacks. The attacks don't come, as you might imagine, on elevated terms about the nature of the Trinity or the relevance of the Westminster Confession of Faith. They are more along the lines of calling on targeted ministers to "suck a bag of dicks."

> Human flesh attacks on Twitter or other social media can rapidly transform bloggers with singular messages into human piñatas.

Global Opposition Research

When the board of Hewlett-Packard attempted to use a private detective to track a corporate leaker, it wound up costing CEO Patricia Dunn her job in the pretexting scandal. The private investigations used Evil Clone techniques to fish for information. These actions also resulted in a new federal law against using many phony pretexts to fish for confidential information. Even though Dunn was legitimately acting to protect corporate information, and was ultimately found to have committed no crime, the stigma attached to private detective work—no matter how legal—is daunting.[31]

Dirt diggers, however, no longer have to take such risks. Private investigation and its political sibling, opposition research, have moved out of the dark alley and onto center stage. Digital assassins can now draw on the power of social media to task the crowd to assemble secrets to ruin a target or force a change in policies.

The Old School method of opposition research, perhaps going back to James T. Callender, included digging through court records, rifling through trash, and scouring old divorce records. It was labor intensive and hit or miss.

The Human Flesh Search Engine crowd-sources intelligence, as it did with candidate O'Donnell, using social media to farm out the work of digging up dirt on people by everyone who has ever known them or who is in a position to obtain knowledge about them. Digital investigators and some PR firms also still use some forms of pretexting and other "social engineering" techniques. This later term involves hacking people, spoofing them into divulging secrets, often to gain access to their computer networks. In this way, they trick the companies that run web-based systems into giving hackers the keys to their private digital kingdoms.

The same techniques are increasingly being used by national intelligence agencies. China's People's Liberation Army (PLA) is a pioneer of the use of crowd-sourcing for espionage. One division of the Chinese military, says Tom Kellermann, who has served on the U.S. Commission on Cybersecurity, employs more than 30,000 computer scientists. But perhaps China's greatest intelligence asset is not in the PLA, but in the regime's ability to farm out espionage to eager freelance armies.[32]

"To be a nationalistic hacker is pretty much the coolest thing you can do as a child in China," Kellermann says. "They have competitions within their provinces for the best hacker. The winners and their families essentially get taken care of for life. They are given somewhere to live, a regular salary, and then they work for a shell company that allows them to do whatever they want, provided that when they find something interesting, they share it with the government.

"We see hacking as evil and we treat good hackers as evil," Kellermann continues. "They nurture them. The Chinese government has only one rule—and that rule is 'Don't hack us.' And if you do find something interesting, like a U.S.-owned system, or you can infiltrate something within the United States, let us know. There is a sense of nationalism around the tradecraft that is cyberespionage . . . The use of non-state actor proxies by regimes like China and Russia is overt."

Of course, if WikiLeaks ever revealed the innermost secrets of Beijing or Moscow, the worst persecution fantasies of Julian Assange would immediately come to pass as he quickly vanished from the Earth.

In the West, however, crowd-sourced intelligence works, and often for more trivial purposes than espionage. ChurchOuting.org, now gone dark, turned to the Human Flesh Search Engine for crowd-sourcing to collect the gay and straight sex secrets of Catholic priests as part of a campaign to nudge the archdiocese of Washington, D.C., to change its policies on gay marriage.[33] This website seemed to take a page out of Saul Alinsky's *Rules for Radicals*: "Make the enemy live up to their own book of rules," and adds, "You can kill them with this, for they can no more obey their own rules than the Christian church can live up to Christianity."

In the face-off between Jerry Brown and Meg Whitman for the governorship of California, a group calling itself "Level the Playing Field 2010" emerged, purporting to be interested in keeping Whitman from "buying the governor's office." It was funded by special interests, including the California Nurses Association PAC Committee. It established a platform called WikiMeg. This open source site asked "everyone and anyone with factual information to share—from laid off eBay workers and those frustrated with Whitman's eBay policies toward sellers to shareholders to regular voters—to help us fully vet Meg Whitman's job application."[34]

This was a clever use of crowd-sourcing to ferret out dirt on a political candidate. Although WikiMeg was just a sideshow (the most damaging event of the campaign was the claim that Whitman had hired an illegal alien, which came from attorney Gloria Allred), the likelihood is that this technique will become a standard tactic in every campaign.

Social media opposition research has even been used to light up targets for physical assassination. In 2010, ten aid workers—six Americans, two Afghans, a Briton, and a German—working with a nonproselytizing Christian aid group called International Assistance Mission, had just returned from a heroic 120-mile crossing by foot and horseback to bring medical relief to a remote Afghan village. While the aid workers were resting, a band of Taliban attacked, killing them with bullets, grenades, and crushing blows from Kalashnikov rifles. Intelligence sources later told the press that Taliban operatives on the Internet seemed to have tracked the group in real time on their Facebook page before they ever set foot in the village.[35]

> Attackers call on human flesh mobs to perform deep dives into personal backgrounds that exceed the best results of expensive detectives or even government "alphabet" agencies.

The 50-Cent Party

What makes the Human Flesh Search Engine such a potent force? It is a dark manifestation of the power of social media, which can organize cross-functional teams within an organization, set up a church picnic, or call up a flash mob. As a form of social media, however, it has enablers.

One enabler of the Human Flesh Search Engine is of course the power of bloggers. A vitriolic blog can provide the initial energy to stimulate and attract other bloggers, winds that swirl until a hurricane is formed. The immediacy and global reach of a blog can let loose the destructive hurricane to rip up governments, companies, and powerful individuals. This same force, however, can be sent spinning in the other direction by those very authorities to isolate their critics and punish them for speaking out.

For example, a Chinese citizen posted a criticism of the local police in the Henan province city of Jiaozuo, whereupon a flood of countercomments followed. Some 120 different bloggers eventually commented, all of them protesting the criticism, some of them attacking the complainer.[36]

Such bloggers are members of the "50-cent party," trained by the PRC and deemed to be ideologically in sync with the Communist Party establishment, paid spinners—legend has it that they are paid the equivalent of 50 cents per post—who are trained to look for criticism of the government and then change the terms of the debate. They are in effect the final defense the PRC employs against internal comments that make it past the "great firewall of China."[37]

In the United States, it is estimated that thousands of paid bloggers also put up phony opinions, mostly for commercial purposes, on a sliding bonus scale that can earn them $30,000 to $70,000 a year. Others provide news for websites such as Gawker Media, which give out retainers and bonuses for highly viewed posts. The competition to be the first to break news about products on technology sites is particularly intense.[38]

Western bloggers, however, have not proved as malleable or as excitable as their Chinese counterparts in using the human flesh engine to crack down on dissent. In the 2010 maritime dispute between China and Japan, a group of Chinese anti-Japanese protesters, perhaps stoked into action by nationalist bloggers paid by the government, made a media show of angrily smashing Japanese products.

A Chinese national, Hua Chunhui, sent a slightly sarcastic message that mocked this staged human flesh attack to his fiancée, Cheng Jianping, who retweeted it. For this, Cheng was sentenced to a year of hard labor.[39]

> Although Human Flesh Search Engines emerge out of anarchy, authoritarian regimes can turn them into a useful tool for repression.

Anonymous and Mirror Sites

A second enabler of the Human Flesh Search Engine is the relentless ability to use technology to disappear before any would-be tracker and perhaps reappear as someone else. In this game of international Whack-a-Mole, the mole rarely gets whacked.

The flesh engine extraordinaire, of course, is WikiLeaks, which managed to undermine, confound, and thwart the world's most powerful government. When the U.S. government pressured Amazon, PayPal, and other Internet sites to cut off server space and payment services for WikiLeaks, members of Anonymous and other informal activist groups created hundreds of mirror sites that cloned the original WikiLeaks site. Next a Swiss-Icelandic company, DataCell, picked up the slack to process donations from PayPal.[40] Like the many-headed

Hydra, WikiLeaks sprouted new sites as the effort to shut it down intensified.

> With no lack of people ideologically committed to thwarting any effort to shut down information, the Human Flesh Search Engine counts on the crowd to keep a hot thing going.

You Have Been Trolled

Being labeled dog-shit girl by one person is insulting. Having that label slapped on you by an entire nation is frightening and debilitating. Condemnation by an entire society and even the world is a punishment that outweighs most crimes. But the Human Flesh Search Engine does at least serve to reinforce social norms, much as public shaming once brought order to village life.

Another type of human flesh attack comes from people who reject all social norms. These commentators are, like the young men of AutoAdmit, firm in the belief that if you react with outrage to the vilest, darkest, racially and sexually charged language, then you really don't get the joke. These are trolls, the vandals of cyberspace, the id of the Internet.

For example, a Facebook page dedicated to being a memorial to teens who committed suicide is often defaced with comments about her being an "obese whore" and "skank who deserved to choke," or him being "a little fag who had it coming." One troll posted a cruel Megan Had It Coming blog. She was, the blogger posted, a "drama queen" who deserved ridicule for pining over a MySpace boy. "I mean yeah your [*sic*] fat so you have to take what you can get but still nobody should kill themselves over it."[41] The blogger falsely claimed to be Lori Drew.

Another troll site is dedicated to the lawsuit over the AutoAdmit case. Click it, and it will direct you to an image that—after you've taken a moment to make it out—is a photo from a car crash scene in which the head of a young woman has been pulverized into a red mush of brains and hair.

Such tricks are meant to elicit "lulz"—derived from the plural of "lol" (laugh out loud). Lulz is really something more. It's savoring other people's consternation, grief, horror, disgust, anger, and bewilderment.

And if the thought of inflicting fresh pain on bereaved parents leaves you livid, then that only shows the extent to which you are still a slave to words and the artificial constructs of society. If anything, some believe, your anguish is an object lesson in expressions that are inherently sentimentalized and therefore unreal.

Goatse Security, a small hacker group that reveals security flaws, stands at the intersection of the gray hacker and the troll. The name comes from a shock site that slaps the viewer with the image of a man using his fingers to open his rectum to full view (hence the group's slogan, "Gaping Holes Exposed"). One Goatse leader, "weev" (known in the straight world as Andrew Auernheimer, twenty-six), was arrested in 2010 when an FBI raid allegedly uncovered a stash of cocaine, ecstasy, LSD, and controlled pharmaceuticals.[42]

Some of the Goatse members seem to intersect with the small clique of trolls that calls itself the Gay Nigger Association of America, or GNAA. If the name offends you to the core, then YHBT: "You Have Been Trolled."

Why do they do it?

Again, for the lulz, which means the sheer joy of ruining your day. "Griefers" are a related, less sophisticated tribe, people who get their jollies from disrupting online multiplayer games.

If you are so clueless as to actually respond to such an attack with a lawsuit or with an editorial, as John Seigenthaler did, you will find yourself slashed by the piranhas in a human flesh attack of trolls, ideologues who believe that no one anywhere at any time should ever be held to account for what they say, write, or post.

Encyclopedia Dramatica, which is the Bizarro World troll version of Wikipedia ("In lulz we trust"), quotes Jon Postel, one of the architects of the Internet, who offered a Robustness Principle: "Be conservative in what you send; be liberal in what you accept." Postel's law, originally meant for technological application, has become the unstated attitude of wide tolerance most people bring to the Internet.

The troll's rule posted on Encyclopedia Dramatica overturns tolerance with anarchy, declaring, "You are not worthy of my understanding; I, therefore, will do everything I can to confound you."[43]

Jarret Cohen, the insurance broker who created AutoAdmit, took the time to write to Eugene Volokh, an eminent professor of law at UCLA. "One finds," Cohen wrote, "a much deeper and much more mature level of insight in a community where the ugliest depths of human opinion are confronted, rather than ignored."[44]

> Trolls lurk at the place where extreme libertarianism meets the evil heart of fascism.

Takeaway—Standing Up to the Crowd

The terror campaign against HLS left it with worthless stock and no creditworthiness. The company would have closed had it not been for the bold intervention of Prime Minister Tony Blair, who stepped in to uphold science and the rule of law. The government gave HLS a bank account, a large grant to the local police in Cambridgeshire to manage a gauntlet of protection that HLS employees had to endure every day to get to work.[45]

Huntingdon Life Sciences had become this vulnerable only in the aftermath of *It's a Dog's Life,* a documentary that left it with no reservoir of public goodwill.

In the age of Little Snitch, good behavior will not ensure goodwill. But it helps. As the authors advise their clients, companies need to enforce ethical behavior and "build a reputational cushion"[46]—seeding your search results in advance of any attack with credible demonstrations of the value of one's work. Ethical operating principles and proclaiming good deeds from the rooftops remain the best defense against demonization on the Internet.

Most victims are not as controversial as HLS, or the target of such well-orchestrated campaigns of terror. Most targets are somewhat like Reverend Merritt's church, which got a one-star review on Google maps. "Those who posted it had never been to our church, but they didn't like our stance on certain issues," she says. "So they left one star, commenting, 'I wish I could leave no stars in the review.'"

The danger here was that this review would attract likeminded heresy hunters, making the church the focus of a barrage of attacks. Merritt knew, however, that the same power of social media to turn a crowd against her could be used to create a crowd to come to her defense. She got on Facebook and asked all of her friends and followers to post. Naturally they posted praise for the church, postings that, she says, "drowned out the nastiness."

And how to respond to the vicious attacks? A little humor helps.

"Wow, don't drink and Twitter!" is one of Reverend Merritt's more effective responses.

And if your bad behavior, like dog-shit girl, lands you in the cross-hairs of a human flesh attack? What if you become your very own wiki? The survivors apologize, explain what happened, point out the inequity of the punishment to crime, and draw on the power of social media to elicit friends to come to their defense.

It is intimidating to face an angry crowd. With some initiative, you can work up a crowd of your own to stand behind you.

7:// The Fifth Sword

Jihad by Proxy

> Most of the errors of public life . . . come not because men are morally bad, but because they are afraid of somebody.
>
> **—Woodrow Wilson**

WHEN CAMPAIGNS ARE LAUNCHED against a brand, business, or individual, digital assassins often attack through a front organization. The cutout or front can be Nongovernmental organizations (NGOs), a reasonable-sounding blog on the Internet, or a vendetta website masquerading as a high-minded news source. When these attacks from fronts are organized against a target, you have the fifth sword of digital assassination, jihad by proxy.

This chapter also will examine several nondigital and predigital uses of proxy groups. Why? Just as West Point still teaches lessons for future warfare drawn from the Napoleonic era, so too in this Internet age, you must understand how these groups form and work so you can grasp how they now facilitate digital attacks.

Mothers Opposing Pollution

Jihad by proxy was exemplified in Australia in the 1990s with Mothers Opposing Pollution (MOP), which billed itself as "the largest women's environmental group in Australia with thousands of supporters across the country." MOP presented an impressive facade. For an annual subscription of AU $39.95, supporters could get an environmental awareness certificate, tree-growing instructions and seeds, and 10 percent off MOP products such as soap or facial cleanser. The truly conscientious could buy MOP badges through supermarkets to raise funds for turtle research.[1]

MOP's spokeswoman, Alana Maloney, also waged a public awareness campaign against plastic milk bottles for their supposed carcinogenic properties. She raised additional concerns about the degradation of milk by UV rays that can penetrate the plastic.

MOP operated for several years until investigative journalists for Brisbane's *Courier-Mail*, unable to locate the armies of outraged Australian women united against plastic milk bottles, unraveled its identity. They found that Alana Maloney did not exist. She was a cutout, a stand-in for someone else and some other interest.

So who was behind Mothers Opposing Pollution? The Australian press traced it back to a PR professional, who while waging a phony environmental campaign against *plastic* milk cartons was found by journalists to have business links to a firm that consulted for the *paper* milk-carton industry.[2]

Of course, in a digital age, creating a respectable facade to assassinate need not be elaborate. It can be done for a few shillings and keystrokes. "These tactics have filtered down to the bumpkin level," says one digital hound, who points to a website dedicated to local politics in one suburban county in the Deep South run by a 501(c)(4), a nonprofit that is allowed to engage in issue and lobbying activities. Handsomely designed with heartwarming images of families and green landscapes, this site uses an image of earnest, public-spirited people to send out e-mails defaming local county and school board candidates, often with grotesque financial, personal, and ethical charges.[3]

The law does not require that this site disclose its donors, and it does not. "This is small potatoes in a small potatoes field," says the investigator, who was called in when victims sought out the identities of their anonymous attackers. "Yet they find money to do this. It tracks back to some of the richest families and one of the most successful politicians doing business in that state. So it's not just Washington.

"You think it's just the big players," he says. "It has infiltrated all the way down to county elections. You look at this and scratch your head. That's a lot of money for a whole lot of nothing. Proxy attacks are really now just part of the fabric of this country."

They are certainly part of the fabric of university life, where plazas are chock-full of proxy groups pushing petition drives. One of them is an old familiar, SHAC—Stop Huntingdon Animal Cruelty—the "animal rights" group members of which the British government prosecuted for terrorist activities, which presents perhaps the most sinister form of the laundering of motives to the extent it's terrorism masked behind a benign and compassionate public face.

SHAC's alleged association with the Animal Liberation Front (ALF), which is classified by the FBI as a domestic terrorist group, is a dichotomy that would allow it to raise money with a humanitarian facade while allowing the ALF brand to take credit for acts of violence, much as Sinn Féin once operated in public while leaving the violence to the Provisional Irish Republican Army.

Journalist and novelist Jo-Ann Goodwin, in an investigative piece for the London *Daily Mail,* described the benign public face of a particularly vicious motive launderer:

> [A]n unobtrusive stand—a trestle table, covered perhaps with a green blanket—manned by a well-meaning volunteer, sometimes an elderly lady.
>
> On display are pictures which are deliberately upsetting, pictures of miserable monkeys and suffering beagles destined to grab both the heart and the purse strings. Many of us have willingly signed petitions and given cash to the "worthy cause" which pledges to stamp out the torment animals endure because of needless scientific experimentation.[4]

Many of the photos on SHAC's tables are old and do not represent the actions of any current research organization. Nevertheless, the images are sufficiently powerful to open purses and wallets from Bristol to Edinburgh.

British police report that while these stands can take in tens of thousands of pounds, the petitions are typically discarded.[5] The money itself goes to a secretive organization with no published accounts or records.[6]

In short, the money seems to have been used for purposes that have nothing to do with the poor little monkeys and dogs bedeviled by needles and electrodes portrayed in SHAC's pictures. Similar shams exist all over the Internet today, from Haiti relief to orphans, puppies, and whales, because digital technology creates cutout groups with a few keystrokes.

Seemingly motherhood-and-apple-pie organizations may have hidden agendas.

Motive Laundering

Jihad by proxy occurs when a front group launches a publicity campaign of character assassination on behalf of an unidentified special interest for a purpose beyond its stated concerns and public charter. Cutouts such as Mothers Opposing Pollution exist precisely for this purpose of laundering the motive of kneecapping a competitor under the guise of concern for health and the environment. In some cases, organizations with well-deserved reputations for independent thinking or whistle-blowing sometimes cash out by allowing their hard-won credibility to be misused.

Why disguise motives? Jihad by proxy attacks can create or raise phony health or environmental issues to set the precedent for trial lawyers to launch class-action lawsuits. They can be attacks on behalf of a political operator whose real clients have interests too squalid to be publicly acknowledged. Or they can come from companies looking to heap regulatory burdens on their rivals.

As the national conversation goes digital, the lines between these planned shadow campaigns and spontaneous movements will inevitably blur. With social media, after all, all it takes is one tweet to enough followers to generate a spontaneous organization of people willing to send a coordinated message. Is that group spontaneous? Or is it organized? With billions of messages roiling around in cyberspace, does it really matter who starts a particular cascade of messaging?

Organizing like-minded people to convey a shared message is not jihad by proxy. If anything, this is the essence of democracy, even when the organizing begins with a corporation or union.

Both sides create phony grassroots campaigns, or "Astroturf." But not all efforts are phony. "With voters split fairly evenly down the middle on health care reform," blogger and op-ed contributor Ryan Sager wrote in *The New York Times,* "it seems presumptuous to label your side 'real' and the other synthetic. Considering today's 24-hour cable news babbling, down-and-dirty blog activism, and talk-radio-rabble rousing, it's worth asking if the Astroturf epithet still has meaning."[7]

In a social media world, there is often no need to pay people to feign interest in phony campaigns when many issues have a built-in following that can be inspired through Facebook or Twitter. When big organizations find their interests under challenge, they often use a digital thread to locate and activate people who are already in passionate agreement with them—the grassroots.

"You go back to the original Boston Tea Party, and I find it highly unlikely that you had 50 guys dress up like Indians, show up at a boat, bring the right tools, and then leave in an orderly fashion without any kind of organization," Adam Brandon, a spokesman for the conservative organization FreedomWorks, told Politico's Ben Smith.[8]

All true.

The Boston Tea Party would have been an example of motive laundering only if colonial Americans had been led to believe that the attack came from real Mohawks—and that the purpose of the raid was not to manifestly protest British tax policy, but to start a war with Native Americans.

Today many groups are willing to don war paint and engage in precisely that sort of motive laundering. And, there will be no lack of money to fund them or human resources to propel them.

In the political sphere, as a result of the U.S. Supreme Court's 2010 *Citizens United* decision, corporations and unions can fund independent political campaigns, with no legal limits on how much cash can enter into political wars. The court's decision will promote free speech and the First Amendment rights of organized groups. It will bring about more robust discussion of the issues. But this decision will also, as a side effect, inspire the creation of more front organizations.

How much more money will be available?

During the 2004 presidential race, the Swift Boat Veterans for Truth, the group that detracted from Senator John Kerry's war record and critized his protest statements, raised perhaps more than a few tens of millions of dollars in private donations.[9] Technology aided their coming together just for one election cycle. Their group ran a few ads, but mostly relied on the echo chamber of the media and the Internet.

After the U.S. Supreme Court lifted the cap on corporate and union funding of independent expenditures in *Citizens United,* the U.S. Chamber of Commerce raised and spent close to $75 million on congressional races in the 2010 midterm elections—on top of $190 million spent on lobbying in the first two years of the Obama administration.[10]

Not to be left behind, in November 2010 the top hundred donors to causes of the left held a private meeting at the lavish Mandarin Oriental hotel in Washington, D.C. Led by billionaires George Soros and Peter B. Lewis, they are bringing partners of the left-of-center Democracy Alliance to match the U.S. Chamber of Commerce and the conservative American Crossroads GPS advised by Karl Rove.[11]

As the floodgates of corporate, union, and foundation spending are opened, most of the money on both sides will go into ads in which the donors' intent is obvious. But with so much money sloshing around, a lot of corporate and union money is bound to find its way into independent-expenditure groups with facetious public agendas. "If you think that they're shoveling shit now, they're really going to be fertilizing the planet next year with that stuff," says one longtime political consultant looking ahead to the 2012 election.[12]

> Some groups use the new freedom to spend political money to enhance the digital debate. Others will hide behind digital cutouts in the age-old human quest for money and power.

Jack Be Nimble

One August day in 1998, former House majority whip Tom DeLay appeared on *Fox News Sunday* to launch a blistering critique of the International Monetary Fund, denouncing the global lending institution for running the fledgling Russian economy into the ground. "They are trying to force Russia to raise taxes at a time when they ought to be cutting taxes in order to get a loan from the IMF," DeLay said. "That's just outrageous."

DeLay was delighted to be known by his nickname, the Hammer. DeLay's meddling in Russian politics was supported by the U.S. Family Network (USFN), a public advocacy organization headed by DeLay's former chief of staff Edwin Buckham.

This story behind USFN and its related proxy groups, though not a digital example, reveals the hidden life of proxy groups now so prominent in the digital debate. The USFN was an excellent example of motive laundering. Founded in 1996, USFN set a goal of being an advocate for policies that would serve "economic growth and prosperity, social improvement, moral fitness, and the general well-being of the United

States." Tom DeLay called it "a powerful nationwide organization dedicated to restoring our government to citizen control." In fact, the tiny U.S. Family Network did little more than fund a Capitol Hill "safe house" for DeLay, employ DeLay's wife Christine, and pay Buckham a gigantic salary.

In a series of investigative pieces, *The Washington Post* in 2005 revealed that the U.S. Family Network received $1 million from a London law firm. The money, it was reported, originated from two oil and gas oligarchs with links to Gazprom, men described as being always surrounded by armed guards with machine guns, who wanted DeLay to attack the IMF in order to pressure it to bail out wealthy investors.

When DeLay's spokesman was asked about the trip, he said DeLay had gone to Moscow "to meet with religious leaders."[13] The facilitator in this and many other front organizations associated with DeLay was of course his friend Jack Abramoff.

As it turned out, Russia got the loan it wanted, without the strings it really didn't want.

The U.S. Family Network aided the moral fitness and well-being of the United States in other ways. It received half a million dollars from textile companies to stiff-arm Democratic investigations into the maltreatment of immigrant workers in the U.S. protectorate of the Mariana Islands, where products are tagged with a "Made in the USA" label. The U.S. Family Network also received about $250,000 from the Mississippi Band of Choctaw Indians to pressure conservatives in Congress to fight taxation of Indian gaming.[14]

The spider at the center of this web, Jack Abramoff, displayed a genius for creating front groups that waged proxy jihads on behalf of a number of clients. The bulk of Abramoff's manipulation of front groups came from the $45 million he received for lobbying and public affairs work over three years from four Indian tribes to support Indian gaming.[15] The operation, stunningly cynical, even by Washington standards, was well portrayed in the movie *Casino Jack*.

In lining up support concerning state measures on Indian casinos, Abramoff tapped evangelical Christians, including Ralph Reed, whose PR consultancy had on tap powerful networks Reed had developed as executive director of the Christian Coalition under Pat Robertson. Reed, with his eye on a possible future in electoral politics, ensured that his front organization be paid with money laundered through yet another front organization. One of them was the American International Center, a "premiere think tank" dedicated to "bringing great minds together from all over the globe." It was directed by a yoga instructor and a lifeguard.[16]

Abramoff also made adept use of existing organizations with real missions, transforming them into his front groups. He mobilized the Traditional Values Coalition, led by Reverend Louis P. Sheldon, a powerful evangelical in Orange County, California. This group attacked vulnerable Republican politicians for being soft on gambling, when in fact they were being attacked for supporting the Internet Gambling Prohibition Act.

Claiming to represent 43,000 churches coast to coast and in Puerto Rico, the Traditional Values Coalition is concerned with "religious liberties, marriage, the right to life, the homosexual agenda, pornography, family tax relief and education."[17] And apparently its concerns include helping an Abramoff client named eLottery defeat the Internet Gambling Prohibition Act so it could sell lottery tickets on the Internet.[18]

Abramoff served on the board of a think tank, the National Center for Public Policy Research, whose sponsorship he evoked when using clients' money to send DeLay and other powerful Washington officials on lavish golf outings in Scotland.[19] Another trip was paid for with money funneled through the Capital Athletic Foundation, which ostensibly used sports to instill character in inner-city youth.[20] And Abramoff used the Council of Republicans for Environmental Advocacy to seek help from the U.S. Department of the Interior to scuttle an Indian casino in Louisiana that would compete with Abramoff clients.[21]

In sum, the Abramoff machine shows that skillful motive laundering can channel concern for the environment, inner-city kids, the free market, and the Christian evangelical agenda to advance the interests of casinos and sweatshops.

> On digital platforms today, motive launderers similarly enlist the idealistic and the naive to serve squalid interests in the name of God and country.

Romanian Run-Around

Jihad by proxy is not just the domain of the right wing and business interests. It is also a favorite tool of foundations that pursue their agendas—sometimes hidden—through environmental and other activist organizations.

Gabriel Resources, a Toronto-based mining company, was at the receiving end of an NGO-based, social media campaign. The company thought it had made a sure bet when Gabriel invested in what promised to be one of the largest gold-mining operations in Europe located in the remote, mountainous Transylvania region of Romania.*

The site Gabriel settled on is near the village of Rosia Montana, or Red Mountain, whose name derives from the local rivers and streams turned into slurries of reddish-brown mud from centuries of careless mining that began under the Roman emperor Trajan. The Alburnus Maior mine, an archaeological site, still displays the chisel marks of slaves and the remains of wooden wheels used to pump out water.[22]

Rosia Montana today is a backwoods village in which Gabriel saw a golden opportunity to do well by doing good. The old state-run enterprise under the Communist government had left Rosia Montana hideously polluted, laden with heavy metals, including arsenic. So Gabriel promised the Romanian government it would take responsibility for this historic pollution by investing an estimated 35 million Euros to clean up the area.[23]

Though gold had been mined there from the Caesars to Ceauşescu, the gold never bothered to stay. Local unemployment is 80 percent.[24] Due to the area's pollution, a frigid climate, and forest-covered mountains, only potatoes grow well in the rocky soil between Rosia Montana's mountains. Half of the town's ramshackle dwellings have no running water. Two-thirds have outhouses.[25]

With vast deposits of gold to exploit, Gabriel came in with an offer it considered more than generous. To get to the land, it needed to clear away many houses. So it offered locals the once-in-a-lifetime chance to sell their homes at above-market rates, and relocate them to middle-class housing with all the modern amenities. People lined up to sell. By

* Disclosure: One of the authors provided about six hours of consultation for Gabriel Resources in 2007.

2007, 70 percent had sold and 98 percent of residents had their property surveyed.[26]

As envisioned by Gabriel, the project ultimately promised to infuse at least $4 billion into the Romanian economy and create 2,300 direct jobs during the construction phase of the mine, 800 of them high-wage jobs over the almost twenty-year-life of the project, leading to an indirect contribution of 3,000 jobs in the area.[27]

Gabriel also planned to provide the historic restoration that the government could not afford. As a show of good faith, it provided $10 million to fund a hundred-person team led by the best research archaeologists. It worked with the Romanian National History Museum to coordinate with leading experts. And it promised to restore the small historic center of Rosia Montana.[28]

Finally, the company promised that its use of cyanide—a necessary evil in most gold extraction—would be at levels below the rigorous standards of the European Union. This was a vital assurance. In 2000, an Australian-Romanian company reportedly allowed cyanide-laced water to flow out of a tailings dam into the Danube, destroying 1,200 metric tons of fish.[29]

Gabriel also developed a plan for the end of the project to restore the landscape to pristine condition, a state that this land hasn't known for many generations.

Gabriel set out its plans for the economic, environmental, and cultural rehabilitation of Rosia Montana and waited for the applause. The sound it heard instead was that of rocks hitting the windows.

Beginning in 2002, the Internet began to buzz with accusations and opposition from foreign environmentalists. Foremost among them was Stephanie Danielle Roth, a Swiss-French activist.[30] "Imagine yourself living in a small town surrounded by small farms," Roth told an adoring audience in San Francisco as she accepted the $150,000 Goldman Environmental Prize in 2005 for her work opposing Rosia Montana, in a speech now posted online. "Then one day a foreign mining company comes to your doorstep and tells you that you have to leave your home because it will be bulldozed over to make way for a commercial mine. And with it your neighborhood, where your best friends live . . . it will all be gone."[31]

When critical material began to spread throughout the web, Gabriel was puzzled. Most people were lining up to sell their shacks and live in modern housing.

Roth was also quoted as saying that foreign mining companies like Gabriel are "modern-day vampires; who in the name of progress aim to bleed Rosia Montana to death. Their lust for gold has already given rise to flagrant and crying injustices."[32]

Much was also made of the fact that Gabriel intended to use cyanide. Again, Gabriel was puzzled. The CEO, Alan Hill, claimed that more than four hundred other mines around the world use cyanide safely.[33] Gabriel said it would be setting a new standard in its use. Why were they being singled out?

Gabriel had many other questions. What about the pollution that no one else can afford to clean up? What about the archaeological artifacts no one else could afford to preserve?

What about the poor, desperate people of this hardscrabble region?

They would be fine, the project's opponents said. "It is part of the charm of Rosia Montana and this lifestyle," said Belgian environmentalist Françoise Heidebroek. "You know, people will use their horse and cart instead of using a car. They are proud to have a horse."[34]

It wasn't long before the campaign went viral, with Vanessa Redgrave and other celebrities from Los Angeles to London chiming in.[35]

With social media organizing activists and spreading every speech, quote, and protest online, the effect was to panic politicians in the Romanian capital of Bucharest against Gabriel. The campaign against the Rosia Montana mine accelerated, with a bewildering array of NGOs competing to top each other on the Internet with charges, some of them wild, even xenophobic. As the exacting environmental impact process for the project was under way, many Romanian politicians—who were originally ecstatic to have had such attention aimed at one of their poorest regions—began to talk of driving a stake through the heart of this foreign vampire.

Gabriel's executives were staggered because the attacks made little sense. This is not to say that the project was entirely immune to criticism: For example, the project included an open-pit mine, never something to put in a travel brochure, Still, to many observers the charges inverted any reasonable concern for the community and its environment. And the attacks appeared to be highly coordinated, including a network of new NGOs that seemed to enjoy lavish funding for what became a social media crusade.

The result was a win for the opponents, with the suspension of the environmental review process in 2007. Gabriel's stock plunged to a fifth of its former value.[36] The whole project and future of Rosia Montana was in danger.

In September 2007, then-CEO Alan Hill asked why the project was faced "with a persistent disinformation campaign that paints" the Rosia Montana project as a disaster for Romania? He wanted to know who was behind this opposition.[37]

Many of the NGOs were secretive about the sources of their funding. But there were hints. Hill claimed that in 2007 the local NGO, Alburnus Maior, which had indeed been set up by locals, had a website that was not registered in Romania. It was reportedly registered out of Budapest by a Hungarian NGO with ties to the Soros Foundation.[38]

Soon everywhere Gabriel looked, it saw connections to entities funded by George Soros, the Hungarian-American who had made a vast fortune in commodity and currency deals. Hill said he found that Alburnus Maior had the support of at least seventeen non-Romanian sources of support. He said that many of the NGO lawsuits designed to slow down the project were filed by lawyers from a center that also received funds from the Soros Foundation. When local anger began to grow at Alburnus because of alleged misrepresentations, the NGO turned to—where else?—the Soros Foundation to open an information center.[39]

While Soros-funded entities were allegedly exerting enormous pressure to slow down the political and regulatory approval of the Rosia Montana gold mine, the New York–based Soros Fund Management disclosed that it had substantial holdings in Freeport-McMoRan Copper & Gold, AngloGold Ashanti, Barrick Gold, and Newmont Mining, as well as Gammon Gold, Goldcorp, Imagold, Kinross, Northern Orion Resources, and NovaGold.[40]

Hill responded to the attacks with an angry speech in September 2007 that, if true, exposed the deeper motives behind what he claimed to be NGO and online proxy assaults.

"Mr. Soros, founder and funder of the Soros Foundation Romania and the Open Society network of NGOs, is not against mining," Hill said. "How could he be? He's made millions and millions investing [in] mining companies. He has made millions in a company that has moved a village and church to exploit a mine. He has made tens of millions investing in gold-mining companies that use cyanide . . . Yet Mr. Soros opposes our gold mine in Rosia Montana."[41]

Some cynics speculated George Soros funded an NGO-social media campaign against Gabriel's proposed gold-mining operation for the same reason that the fictional Auric Goldfinger wanted to detonate an atom bomb in Fort Knox—to make the value of his holdings soar. But others point out that the Soros gold investments, though large by most standards, are but a fraction of his holdings.

To skeptics, however, the spectacle of environmentalists mounting a social media campaign against a gold mine with money provided to them by a large investor in gold mines does at the very least bring to mind an old term from the ideological wars of the last century—the "useful idiot."

Gabriel pointed to another possible motivation: Hungarian nationalism. Gabriel accused its opposition of using environmental front groups to advance a secret agenda of irredentist claims over national borders. As proof, it circulated photos of protesters' signs that referred not to Rosia Montana, but to Verespatak—the Hungarian name for that area. Others, Gabriel noted, have gone to Rosia Montana to shout, "Keep Hungary's gold for Hungary!"[42]

Whatever the motivation of the project's opponents, or of George Soros—if indeed he was personally involved—it could well be something he regards as noble—Gabriel's project would not have excited as much social media opposition had it not been for the largesse of NGOs and foundations supported by the billionaire.

Soros is justly celebrated as a philanthropist who has done much good in the world. In the case of Rosia Montana, however, questions about undisclosed motives remain for claims made by environmental organizations his foundation funds.

Environmental concern, empowered by social media, may be sincere but it can also be a cloak for other agendas.

Access to the Proxy

The U.S. Securities and Exchange Commission (SEC) is setting rules to bring more openness and access to proxy rules. This rite of spring requires shareholders to nominate and elect candidates for public company boards at annual meetings. The widening access to corporate proxies is a move many hail as a victory for shareholder democracy. No doubt, if it survives legal challenges, some good will come of it.[43] But many executives tell us they are bracing for a fight. They believe that this rule—at this writing it faces a court test—will create a Venetian ball of masked candidates representing groups with shadow agendas.

In years past, every annual meeting had a few obvious gadflies at the microphone who could be counted on for comic relief, before being dismissed with a witticism by the CEO. The authors have advised corporate insiders to prepare for months' long, perhaps year-long political campaigns against a new and different threat—attractive, business-savvy candidates who are publicly concerned about profitability, executive compensation, or dividends, but privately interested in something else. While few violins will be played on behalf of overpaid executives, there is a lot at stake. Such "shareholder democracy" could undermine the prime social function that corporations play—producing profits that fund taxes, salaries, and pensions.

In fact, many of these proxy candidates will be Trojan horses whose secret goal will be to open companies to unionization or to control by environmental or social organizers who could care less about shareholder value. If the rule is enacted, no matter how well they run their business, corporations will be forced to mount demonstrably different and difficult countercampaigns to fend off a range of well-funded players with ideological concerns, not business concerns. They will be besieged by institutional investors with grudges, union pension funds with political agendas, as well as powerful and perhaps extreme special interest groups.

Of course, the discussion will be about say on pay or global warming disclosure or sustainability reporting. The underlying substance—and the critical change in corporate governance—is about proxy groups placing people on boards who answer to constituents, not investors.

> "Shareholder democracy" means the waters of Washington's Potomac River will mingle with New York's Hudson, making for turbulent sailing.

Takeaway—Do Your Own NGO CSI

Over time, the job of exposing front organizations and their real motives will likely become more difficult. Why? Because social media is going to spontaneously generate new organizations across the ideological spectrum; and, they will not be brick-and-mortar concerns that report their income on Form 990. They will be loose social media coalitions that may be genuine advocates one day and somebody's proxy the next.

For now, however, there are about a hundred major brick-and-mortar think tanks in America, not to mention legions of coalitions and associations, some of which will be willing to act as front groups. Starting a new one is largely a matter of a little legal paperwork.

When you are the digital victim of such a proxy attack, how can you identify their sponsors? How can you X-ray their motives?

Start with Cicero, who made famous the great question "Cui bono?" Who benefits?

Then ask: Who supports? It can be difficult to unravel support for front groups, even if you have the resources of a large organization at your disposal. Left-wing investigative hit pieces on corporations from The Huffington Post, or cancer-scare broadsides by the National Resources Defense Council could credibly be said to be sponsored by liberal foundations. On the other side of the ideological spectrum, proxy attacks by empty-shell "family" and "religious" conservative organizations of the sort evident in the Abramoff scandals have not gone away either.

Since many cutout organizations fall on the ideological left or right, you can use the resources of liberal and conservative muckrakers to expose proxy attackers from the other side.

- On the left, the Center for Media and Democracy's SourceWatch and PR Watch offers a "how to research front groups" web page that leads you to the various databases that can reveal the links, membership, and funding sources of conservative front groups.[44]
- On the right, former left-wing activist turned conservative David Horowitz runs DiscoverTheNetworks.org, which has detailed information on left-of-center groups, their funding, activities, and history. Another good source from the right is ActivistCash.com.

In most cases, you can also use public sources to find documentation from the national and state/provincial tax authority that leads back to at least a middleman. If that fails, you can put together clues—an IP address, the country location of websites, the affiliations of board members—and peel that back, from one front organization to another, to reveal the ultimate sponsor.

You can then challenge your attacker to match your transparency. Gabriel is a case in point. Armed with knowledge of their opponent, the CEO was able to issue a challenge: "Play by the same rules we do. Tell us the truth about why you oppose our project—because it cannot be based on the reasons you state publicly. Tell us who funds you. Do not demand transparency of everyone else—and operate from secrecy yourselves. And why won't you meet with us to debate the issue in public in a fair and transparent way? What do you have to hide?"[45]

Finally, once you know whom you are facing, expose the opposition. Gabriel asked a Northern Ireland journalist, Phelim McAleer, who had covered Eastern Europe for *The Financial Times* to write a brochure. McAleer replied that as a journalist he didn't do that kind of work. But he did say that he would take Gabriel's money to produce a documentary with his wife, Ann McElhinney, with the proviso that Gabriel would have no editorial control whatsoever.

If the story turned out to make the company look bad, so be it. With nowhere else to turn, Gabriel took a risk and gave McAleer the money, with no strings attached. McAleer also raised money from nonprofit foundations.[46]

The result was a critically acclaimed film, *Mine Your Own Business,* that demolished the claims of NGOs about local support with man-on-the-street interviews of Rosia Montana residents. One young man told McAleer that "without jobs, we would be dead here." A local doctor told him, "People from Rosia Montana don't need foreign advocates. We are smart enough to take our own fate in our hands." When McAleer relayed the notion promoted by NGOs that local residents were happier riding horses, the residents of Rosia Montana stared back, slack-jawed with incredulity.

In short, Gabriel's challenge and *Mine Your Own Business* began to change the uncritical nature of media reporting. The pushback had an even bigger impact in the blogosphere. As a result, as of early 2011,

Gabriel's project appears to be back on track, with renewed enthusiasm by Romanian leaders.

> When faced with a disingenuous attacker, unmask their motive and put them in the spotlight of transparency.

8:// The Sixth Sword

Truth Remix

All photographs are accurate. None of them is the truth.

—**Richard Avedon**

TRUTH REMIX OCCURS when a fact about a target—often a mistake, shortcoming, or outright sin—has been exaggerated, distorted, and pulled into a direction that makes truth the basis of untruth. A new kind of truth emerges out of this remix—a gray truth that cannot be accepted or dismissed.

Therefore, truth remix.

Truth remix exists because some lies require a pedestal of truth to perch upon. "Man," the Huey Longish character in Robert Penn Warren's classic *All the King's Men* famously observed, "is conceived in sin and born in corruption and he passeth from the stink of the didie to the stench of the shroud. There is always something."

The problem with that something is that increasingly Google or some other search engine knows about it and promises never to forget it. Google's Eric Schmidt, later moved from CEO to executive chairman, famously observed that, "If you have something that you don't want anyone to know, maybe you shouldn't be doing it in the first place."[1]

The memory of the Internet ensures that digital assassins have no lack of material. Witness the AutoAdmit case. In addition to the base slander and juvenile sex talk, someone posted an old *Washington Post* article about the father of one of the targeted women, a World Bank official who had reportedly written forged checks to buy her a Thoroughbred horse when she was ten years old.[2]

The Internet's retention of any facts—especially negative ones—enables remixing of the truth, a slander that has some basis in reality. The loss of context that occurs when a negative fact is indiscriminately mixed in with the good—truth remix—is a tactic that occurs in Yelp reviews, in sexual harassment accusations, and in the premature release of information about technology products.

> It is no longer good enough to be truthful just in the eyes of God. You now have to be acceptable in the eye of Google.

Truth remix is helped along by the arbitrary and often inaccurate nature of search engine results pages, biased aggregator websites, and our own viral rants. Efforts at "social forgetting" and name-changing will always be defeated by technology and the human will to remember the worst about people. The result can be falsehood—polluting politics, distorting history, and perhaps inciting violent philippics that instigate real violence.

Stepping on the Dog

By April 2011, 50 million people a month were accessing Yelp's 17 million reviews of small businesses—restaurants and cafés, beauty shops and spas, veterinary clinics, dentists and doctors—all written by an army of volunteer contributors.[3] These reviews by people identified by their Yelp account profiles—"Molly T, Manhattan," and "Kevin C., New York"—give 83 percent of the businesses rated on Yelp three-star ratings or higher on its five-star scale.[4]

Simply put, Yelp is a social network that aggregates reviews of local business with search functions. If you are visiting San Francisco and looking for a French bistro near Nob Hill, Yelp will find it for you, tell you all about the place, and likely give you a few images. In almost all cases for businesses that are widely reviewed, the judgment that emerges from reading a wide sample of reviews gives a reliable portrait of their service.

To achieve this, Yelp necessarily relies on the trustworthiness of reviewers and the wisdom of crowds. For owners of small businesses, however, Yelp dishes out the good with the bad. The price of a three-star rating and glowing comments is the exposure to occasional snarky reviews.

For example, one Washington, D.C., dentist reports that a bad review came from a patient who claimed to have been given an unnecessary root canal at great cost and pain. When the dentist checked Yelp, she found that this same person had also posted many negative comments about dozens of other businesses.[5]

In response to such serial complainers, Yelp has instituted algorithms to screen out "suspicious" reviews, presumably those from competitors or the permanently and profanely disgruntled.[6] For some businesses, however, this is not enough. It is for that reason that 2010 was the year that made Yelp . . . yelp.

A class-action lawsuit centered around a Long Beach, California, veterinary clinic alleged that Yelp demanded the plaintiff pony up cash for Yelp ads to remove negative posts.[7] A pseudonymous comment on the message board of TechCrunch.com by one small business owner, johnny in baltimore, is typical of small businesses' worst suspicions that quitting an ad campaign on Yelp will automatically result in a rash of bad reviews: "The negative reviews didn't even make any sense. For example, one review said that 'the pool sucked.' Funny. Our gym doesn't have a pool."

According to the post, a Yelp representative contacted the gym owner "and said very cryptically if we ran an ad campaign they could talk to the 'person in charge of the algorithm' and see if the positive reviews could be spotlighted a little more. Honestly, I thought I was talking to a Tony Soprano in training."[8]

Yelp defenders say that the extortion charge is a misunderstanding. Many small businesses first notice bad reviews only after hearing from a Yelp representative selling ads, conflating the pitch with the review process. To improve the process, Yelp developed a category of "Elite" reviewers who provide their photos and real names, who are affirmed that the Yelp community trusts their "personal pizazz" and "Yelptitude."[9] Yelp now buries low-scoring reviews that get flagged by its "quality" algorithm. Since 2009, Yelp has allowed businesses to respond to negative reviews.[10]

> Review sites will always leave small business in fear that one bad interaction—a sandwich with too little cheese, a salesperson with a bad day, an off-color dye job—will overshadow years of great customer service and dedication.

Hurd on the Street

Charges of sexual harassment are breeding grounds for truth remix because they cover a multitude of sins, from the venal to the mortal. At its worst, many consider sexual harassment borderline rape, as it was in the Minnesota Iron Range mine portrayed in the movie *North Country*. At its crassest, it is like the nineties chief executive of a Fortune 500 company who was forced out of his job for his alleged unwanted nibbling of female employees' ears, his patting of their butts, and his atrocious habit of licking his fingers and inserting them in women's ears.[11]

The term might also, however, encompass misdemeanors, an off-color joke, or a thoughtless comment. More often than not, charges of sexual harassment leave us with some distasteful details but no real knowledge of what actually happened, as with Anita Hill, Clarence Thomas, and the misused Coke can, or Jenn Sterger, Bret Favre, and the sexting photo. Those Coke cans and digital photos will always haunt, fairly or not.

Consider the case of Mark V. Hurd, former CEO of Hewlett-Packard, a low-key but driven executive, who rises without an alarm clock every morning in Silicon Valley at 4:45 A.M. to get a jump on the East Coast.[12] He was brought in by the board to bring values and focus to HP after perceived strategic missteps under Carly Fiorina, and the pretexting scandal that forced Patricia Dunn to face down multiple felony charges.

Fix the company he did. Under Hurd's steady management, HP elbowed Dell out of PC leadership and generated revenues that passed those of IBM in 2008.[13] Just as HP investors were settling down to what they hoped was a return to normalcy, Hurd was fired in August 2010.

Facts began to emerge from the firing like the dots in a pointillist image. But the dots never amounted to a coherent portrait. Though digital technology was secondary in the reporting of this case, it clearly demonstrates the kind of mixed truth that is coming to the fore in our Internet age.

Hurd had been accused of sexual harassment by an HP marketing consultant and sometime actress named Jodie Fisher (*Intimate Obsession* and *Body of Influence 2*). Fisher hired Gloria Allred, the country's foremost klieg light litigator. There had been a personal settlement between Hurd and Fisher, but for what it is not exactly clear.[14]

When the HP board investigated, it reportedly found little evidence that sexual harassment had occurred. Fisher herself had publicly affirmed that she never had an "affair or intimate sexual relationship" with the married Hurd. In fact, she said, "I was surprised and saddened that Mark lost his job over this."[15]

There were meal, travel, and other receipts in the thousands of dollars over two years, which the board judged to be personal items improperly expensed.[16] But these expenses seemed to be related to CEO summits with top customers in which Fisher seemed to have acted as a corporate Vanna White.

Oracle chief Larry Ellison, a passionate defender of Hurd, told *The New York Times,* "The HP board just made the worst personnel decision since the idiots on the Apple board fired Steve Jobs many years ago."[17] The HP board acted on advice about disclosure from Washington-based APCO, a PR company that *The New York Times* reported "does not have a particularly strong reputation for crisis management or technology expertise."[18]

So one of the best CEOs in the country was fired for spending money on retreats for elite customers and a corporate hostess, against whom Hurd's own board believes that no sexual harassment occurred? "There is a missing piece here because it doesn't make sense," Shane Greenstein, a professor at Northwestern University's Kellogg School of Management, told a reporter.[19]

Next, to the amusement and consternation of Silicon Valley, Hurd accepted Ellison's offer to become president of Oracle, although he did have to relinquish $14 million in HP stock in response to what Ellison called a "vindictive" lawsuit by HP over trade secrets.[20]

Clearly something happened for the board to fire Hurd. But what was it?

> In the absence of information, rumor will fill the void with the most salacious details, especially in cases of sexual harassment. New facts are remixed in everyone's imagination.

Rumors in Motion

When an Apple engineer left the prototype of the next generation iPhone 4 by a bar stool in the Gourmet Haus Staudt in Redwood City, California, a patron took it home, realized what it was, and sold it to Gizmodo .com for $5,000.[21] The result was the reporting, months in advance, of the characteristics of a prototype that was far from being ready for public release. The mistake also blew Apple's chance to reap the benefit of shaping the release of its information, worth millions of marketing dollars.

More deliberate leaks—those not involving beer—occur all the time for technology companies. When it is time to unveil a new consumer technology product, companies strive for the big reveal. With a vast colony of tech bloggers vying for a scoop and no lack of insiders willing to leak details, the big reveal is more often the long—and inaccurate—tease.

Witness the trouble Research In Motion has had in unveiling new permutations of its BlackBerry. Another site for premature releases months in advance through "unofficial sources" was Engadget, which sparked criticism of the device's perceived shortcomings in one new detail or another, without the context of the overall device. Cranky bloggers pick apart every new function and stylistic detail.

Or consider the Boy Genius Report. Founded in 2006 by a high school dropout, BGR managed to report on the BlackBerry Storm 2 months before RIM officially announced it.[22] BGR has provided lengthy reviews chock-full of technical minutiae of the second-generation Amazon Kindle, Palm Pre, and Nokia products before anyone else, as well as screen shots of Google's Android 2.0 while it was still in development. Given BGR's prominence, some of these leaks are no doubt authorized teases. Many are not, coming from inside tipsters who release details about mobile devices—like the changing interface of the Storm—before the company is ready to debut the product or make an announcement.

In this way, prematurely released facts about the product get remixed by the exaggeration of sour critics.[23]

> Secret snapshots of a new product while still developing in the technological womb often mislead the media, investors, and customers.

Google Groping

Not all mixed truth is created as an intentional smear. Sometimes it is a matter of how the Internet perceives you. Eric Schmidt predicted that the search engine will know "roughly who you are, roughly what you care about, roughly who your friends are."[24] This will likely be true someday, but is not true now.

One problem with any search engine is that its algorithmic mind, lacking common sense and a proper respect for the nuances of human behavior, often assembles raw facts to automatically remix the truth. For example, television writer Seth Freeman received a Gmail from someone about "Holocaust deniers," only to later get an ad pitch for a holistic dentist.[25]

When journalist Jessica Rose Bennett, twenty-nine, performed an online search for herself for *Newsweek*, she found that her profile would tell a prospective employer that she "spends 30 hours a week on social-networking sites—while at work. She is an excessive drinker, a drug user, and sexually promiscuous. She swears a lot, and spends way beyond her means shopping online." The negatives here come not from her lifestyle, but from her reporting projects on drugs, polyamory, and social networking. "The irony, of course, is that if this were a real job search, none of this would matter—I'd have already lost the job," Bennett writes.[26]

Of course Bennett is a bold journalist who deliberately traffics in outré topics. The skewed view of the Internet could be a big problem for someone else. Seventy-five percent of recruiters and human-resource professionals responded to a Microsoft-sponsored poll that the companies they serve require them to research their candidates online.[27]

Consider how search affected Stacy Snyder, a twenty-five-year-old in Lancaster, Pennsylvania, when she was on the verge of graduating from the Millersville University School of Education. College administrators had come across a photo of her from a MySpace page wearing a pirate hat with a drink in her hand. The caption under her photo, "Drunken Pirate," was enough for the school to deny her a teaching degree, though she was awarded an English degree. Snyder sued but lost. The courts found Snyder, as an apprentice teacher who did unpaid classroom work, fell under more stringent employment regulations. So she lost her ability to become a teacher.[28]

And "drunken pirate" is the really tame stuff. So much more negative information is available on social media—especially that posted by youth in their wilder moments—that Schmidt mused that it might make sense to allow young people to change their identity.[29]

Harvard's Viktor Mayer-Schönberger argues exactly for this—a deliberate sunsetting of information in his intriguing 2009 book, *Delete: The Virtue of Forgetting in the Digital Age.* Most information, Mayer-Schönberger points out, is not timeless, but rooted to a certain time, place, and situation, like Stacy Snyder's costume party.

What some call social forgetting is a fine idea. But is it realistic to imagine that someone won't find a way to get around a data expiration date? Who is going to sunset the Wayback Machine? And how?

Eric Schmidt's suggestion that young people should be allowed to change their identity to escape the misadventures of their youth might not be technically feasible. (Although Spain's data Protection Agency is attempting to wipe out negative links on at least ninety people in an effort to enforce a "right to be forgotten.")[30] As facial recognition software develops, won't any effort at identity change be easily defeated for any post with a picture in it?

It is easy to imagine that the Internet, though not an organism and not sentient, acts as if it had a malevolent will of its own. The fact is, it is humans who bring all the will to do harm. Someone will always use technology to keep whatever can be kept. It is hard to imagine any law or technology that could make the Internet forget.

Meanwhile, we are set up to pay a price for e-mails or posts that could last a lifetime. There have been many examples of e-mails exploding months or years later, not unlike the Wall Street analysts who flogged financial products while privately writing about them in company e-mails as pigs with expensive lipstick.

Consider what may result from the blog of one prominent technical writer who created a stir when she reported that she was sexually assaulted at an Atlanta tech conference that began in a crowded room. She wrote of a wild evening of beer pong and networking laced with flirting. "I lay across the bed, sat on laps, generally tried to squish in to any available space and get time to talk to all the fabulous people thronging the place."[31]

When the party moved to an Irish pub, the blogger reports she went to the bathroom, where a young engineer tried to kiss and fondle her. She just didn't just tell the conference administrators and the Atlanta police and warn her friends. She did something that gave pause to many in her online community. She named the guy in her post.

"The real issue is that we have a baseless allegation in a very public place," writes one Reddit commenter. "And once that gun is fired, there's no pulling the bullet back."[32] The young man named in the blog has not been convicted of a crime, and indeed he may have done nothing wrong, but he may pay a subtle price for the allegation until he is an old man.

> Everyone using the Internet needs to think and pause before writing something just because it is "true." And think and pause again before pressing the send button.

Lightning and Lightning Bugs

On a winter's evening in 1912, boys from a local military academy in Bloomington, Illinois, put on a drill to entertain a party of friends in the home of a prominent family. They found an old repeating rifle, took out—they thought—all of the cartridges, and began to show how they could march and twirl the weapon. One twelve-year-old boy was showing off to an older girl, sixteen-year-old Ruth Merwin, when the gun went off, shooting her straight through the forehead.

The boy, Adlai Stevenson, grandson of a vice president, later to run for president himself, was described by *The New York Times* as "overcome with grief."[33] Had Stevenson been a political candidate in the twenty-first century, he would have been expected to repeatedly dissect the tragedy in media interviews and in broadcast. Though Stevenson did not discuss the incident as governor of Illinois and two-time presidential candidate, his biographers believe that it shaped his life—that from that moment on, Stevenson felt that he had an obligation "to live for two." So it came as news to the American people when leaflets began to appear in the 1952 presidential election informing the voters about the incident—and telling them that the Democratic nominee had killed the girl "in a jealous rage."[34]

A digital remixing of the truth was used in the 2010 midterm elections, when Representative Alan Grayson released an ad on TV and YouTube depicting his Republican opponent, state senator and former Florida House speaker Daniel Webster, as a religious fanatic whose Christian views made him "*Taliban* Dan." The ad devastatingly showed a video of Webster saying—four times—that the Bible orders wives to submit to their husbands.

When the independent FactCheck.org looked at the original video, however, it reported that he had been edited to sound as if he were saying the exact opposite of what he was saying: "In fact, Webster was cautioning husbands to avoid taking that passage as their own," and that husbands should *not* pick Bible verses that conveniently allow them to dominate their wives.[35]

In both cases, there was a degree of truth. It is a literal fact that Adlai Stevenson killed a girl. It is also a fact that Daniel Webster is the kind of Bible Belt politician prone to say things that make more secular voters squirm.

In both instances, these existing facts were used as platforms to sell a lie.

> Remixing the truth is a growing feature of our digital age, in which facts are often conditional, partial, and in varying shades of gray.

Deeper Capture, Wider Apertures

For many users, the pitiless gaze of a search engine is a catalog of human flaws. Some 46 percent of men reported that they would be embarrassed if someone saw their browsing history. And someone may well see it. A 2010 study by Stanford and Carnegie Mellon Universities finds that the privacy mode of the four major browsers is no absolute defense against having one's searches exposed from within the house or from without.[36]

Increasing exposure to embarrassment is a technological development that has been scaling up for more than a century. In 1890, jurists Louis Brandeis and Samuel Warren worried that "instantaneous photographs and newspaper enterprise have invaded the sacred precincts of private and domestic life; and numerous mechanical devices threaten to make good the prediction that 'what is whispered in the closet shall be proclaimed from the house-tops.'"[37]

The world moved on. Media that was once so alarming now seems quaint. In the twenty-first century, facial recognition software is advancing toward a state in which users will be able to snap a cell phone image of someone they pass by on the street, subject the image to a Google search, and receive all photos of that person on the Web.

The digital world is also acquiring hardware and extensions to actually follow us around. Personal drones are coming to market, small hovering UAVs that can carry onboard cameras and thermal imaging technology to track and record your every move. "If the Israelis can use them to find terrorists, certainly a husband is going to be able to track a wife who goes out at eleven o'clock at night and follow her," a New York divorce lawyer told a journalist.[38]

A similar compromise of privacy occurred when a Google Street View camera caught any number of men coming out of porn shops—not to mention the inexplicable shot of a naked German man rising out of the trunk of his Mercedes.

> Technology captures and immortalizes embarrassing facts, so truths are often remixed to look far worse.

Candid Camera Blackmail

A thirty-one-year-old man in Santa Ana, California, was arrested in 2010 for hacking into the computers of about 230 people, 44 of them minors. He had managed the difficult task of secretly viewing girls and women through their web cameras. The case affidavit states that he also offered audio files of in-demand songs on peer-to-peer networks that contained malware.

He hacked into the women's e-mail accounts in order to impersonate their boyfriends. He pleaded for the victims to send erotic pictures for his personal enjoyment. Once he was armed with videos of girls and young women performing sexually explicit acts, his Evil Clone impersonation of the boyfriends contacted them with an alias to demand more explicit videos, or else he would release the ones he had.[39] In this way, one questionable act—downloading free songs—led to a chain of ever more embarrassing exposures. These girls found themselves in a gray zone, compromised and therefore compromisable.

In the 2010 Nevada Senate race, the Tea Party candidate was upended when she tried make an insider Washington deal with a marginal candidate ("whatever juice I have, you have as well") who recorded their thirty-eight-minute conversation. It wound up in the hands of a journalist and then online.[40]

> The most common exposure to blackmail is from your own computer, or perhaps the person you are confiding in who has set an iPhone or other PDA to record.

True Lies

All across the Internet, phantom websites wink in and out of existence, like so many Cheshire cats. They often aggregate legitimate news—but selectively, in a way that is always negative to their targets.

Corporations often have surrogates create anonymous websites that aggregate real news stories on an issue of interest that, while fairly done by reputable sources, offer only one slant on a competitive or regulatory issue. The cumulative effect is to overwhelm the visitor with the sense that there is only one side to the case.

The vendetta website of HKLaw Investigation is an exemplar of what appears to be a high-minded investigative news site. It is complete with an inset picture of Sherlock Holmes in silhouette, when in fact it is the get-even tactic of a disgruntled insider or competitor who anonymously aggregates mixed-truth dirty laundry of a global law firm, Holland & Knight, its alleged internal disputes, sexual harassment claims, and personal gossip.[41]

Or take jewwatch.com. Beneath its ugly overlay of anti-Semitic agitprop, this site does the same thing in a much more disturbing way—aggregating many legitimate news stories in which the perpetrators just happen to be Jewish or Israeli citizens.

> The aggregation of a slanted selection of news creates an effective calumny. Selection bias, taken to the extreme, can enlist truth into a monstrous gray truth smear.

Viral Rants

Remixing the truth can be most damaging when you are captured in a moment of anger. When actress Lily Tomlin was filming *I ♥ Huckabees,* she got into several fights with her director, David O. Russell. During a moment of frustration over a scene, Tomlin expressed her exasperation over last-minute script changes. "I'm not as brilliant as you," she told Russell with unmistakable sarcasm. "I can't keep up with you."

The argument escalated, with Russell letting loose foul epithets, raking papers off a desk and kicking them. "Yeah, fuck yourself!" he screams.

"Why don't you fuck your whole movie," Tomlin says in a memorable retort. "Why don't you fuck your whole movie because that's what you're doing."

There was, of course, a video camera catching the whole scene, a scene posted by someone to become a TubeBomb for the amusement and mirth of millions.

The digital capturing of celebrities at their worst is now as common as the regularly televised car chases down the LA Freeway. The most devastating example, of course, is Mel Gibson's meltdown on the phone with the mother of his child, Oksana Grigorieva. Before that, there was Christian Bale's rant against a crew member who stepped into his scene, a rant later turned into a rhythmic song by DJ RevoLucian, with a splice-in of Barbra Streisand's voice on stage saying "Shut the fuck up—shut up if you can't take a joke" as a refrain. And of course before that was Alec Baldwin and his voice mail tirade at his daughter.

In most cases, it is not just the vehemence of the celebrities' anger, but the length of their diatribes that takes one aback. What is not captured on tape is the context—what pushed their button, who else was responsible, what they are like the rest of the time.

In the case of Christian Bale, he is now endlessly TubeBombed with images from *American Psycho* of his crazed, blood-splattered face to accompany his tirade. Alec Baldwin's screaming at his daughter is accompanied on one popular post with studio photos of him holding a gun, a baseball, and a blood-splattered axe.

It is likely that those who feast on these images would not recognize themselves if their worst moments were replayed with disturbing images. What most people don't realize is that the devices that captured Lily Tomlin, Mel Gibson, Christian Bale, and Alec Baldwin, not to mention South Korea's dog-shit girl, can mix the truth about you.

> Technology instantly immortalizes your worst moment into a tombstone epitaph.

Defining the Other Guy Down

Truth remix, more than any other of the seven swords of digital assassination, is the weapon of choice in politics. Truth remix does not include outright inventions, like the story that circulated to newspapers in the election of 1876 that Rutherford B. Hayes had shot his mother while insane from a night of drinking.[42] It does not include outright forgeries like the Morey letter, a phony missive leaked to the press that roiled the 1880 election by purporting to show that James A. Garfield secretly conspired to swell corporate profits by undercutting American workers with poorly paid Chinese immigrants.[43]

It does include the bigamy charge leveled against President Andrew Jackson, one so hurtful that it cut a man called Old Hickory to the core. Jackson's wife, Rachel, had been previously married to a violent man who promised to obtain a divorce but did not. This left the Jacksons to wander ignorantly, but temporarily, into a state of bigamy—a paperwork blunder the Jacksons fixed as soon as they could (even to the point of remarrying).

Enemies ran with this, calling Rachel a "whore" who was known for "open and notorious lewdness." One Republican paper asked if a "convicted adulteress and her paramour husband should be placed in the highest office of this free and Christian land?"[44]

For General Jackson's earlier signing of the execution warrants of six leaders of a militiamen mutiny, Republicans circulated a "Coffin Handbill" in the 1828 election, complete with a graphic of six coffins. When Jackson supporters learned that John Quincy Adams, as minister to the court of Czar Alexander I, had introduced his wife's servant girl to the court, they portrayed the diplomat as pimping American women to the Russian emperor.

By the late twentieth century, these tactics migrated to telephone "push polls"—phony polls that wrap smears in a facetious question about the opposition candidate. In the South Carolina 2000 Republican primary, operatives favoring George W. Bush used just such a tactic to plant the idea that rival John McCain had an illegitimate "black baby"—(the baby in question, now Bridget McCain, was a seriously ill Bangladeshi child adopted by the McCains from Mother Teresa's orphanage in Dhaka).[45]

Of all these cases, there is an element of truth to make the lie palatable. The fact of the matter is, the Jacksons were technically bigamists. Jackson had signed execution warrants. John Quincy Adams had introduced a young woman to the czar. The McCains had adopted a child of color, a remarkable act of love.

Concerning the latter, if such a fact can be turned into a weapon, almost any fact is subject to weaponization.

> In this century's second decade, the digital arena is the prime ground for this form of assassination . . . and nowhere is it used more viciously than in politics.

The Queen of Bithynia

The remixing of facts is such a constant in politics that it makes much of what we call history questionable. What do we really know for sure about, say, Julius Caesar? We know that as a young man, Caesar distinguished himself as a solider, winning the Roman equivalent of the Congressional Medal of Honor. He was also a young diplomat assigned to the court of Nicomedes IV, the Roman client king of Bithynia.

The king, recognizing something special in the young Roman, brought Caesar into his confidence and showed him the ins and outs of being a ruler, an experience that may explain the mature Caesar's appetite for kingly power. Caesar stayed so long under the king's mentorship that gossip began to spread.

So when he returned to Rome, Caesar was openly ridiculed as the "Queen of Bithynia." Years later, even after his conquest of Gaul, Caesar's soldiers, who had survived years of battle under their beloved commander, marred a triumphal procession through Rome with their ribald humor: "Home we bring our bald whoremonger; / Romans, lock your wives away! / All the bags of gold you lent him / Went his Gallic tarts to pay." It was a colorful if somewhat fair assessment.

But they also proclaimed, "Gaul was brought to shame by Caesar; / By King Nicomedes, he. / Here comes Caesar, wreathed in triumph / For his Gallic victory! / Nicomedes wears no laurels, / Though the greatest of the three."

Most modern historians believe it unlikely that Caesar shared the king's bed. Caesar himself denied the charge under oath. The problem for Caesar—and for us—is that this bit of mixed truth (mixed because the ever-promiscuous Caesar, as a young Roman, was unusually close to a foreign king) remains an indelible part of history, forever clouding the true image of the man (which was racy enough).[46]

Mixed truth permeates Roman history. Caligula and Nero, for example, were both without doubt unusually cruel and strange, even by the standards of Roman emperors. The few fragmentary histories we have of these two emperors are packed with many lurid details, however, that are probably remixed literary creations derived from later historians who had political and ideological biases.

So much of modern scholarship on ancient Rome must forever remain interpretative because we are forced to rely on source material that was poisoned by Rome's permanent atmosphere of character assassination and truth-twisting.

> How much of today's "history" is being distorted in real time by the Internet?

Verbal Violence

In modern America, the shooting of Congresswoman Gabrielle Giffords prompted endless media lectures and soul-searching about the link between caustic language and violence. In this case, there seems to be no connection between political rancor, mainstream or otherwise, to the mad inner dialogue of the Tucson gunman. Jared Lee Loughner's YouTube postings are a poignant and frightening portrayal of the disconnected logic of a sick mind. The fear, however, that personalized politics based on mixed truths can lead to violence should not be casually dismissed by anyone.

Words affect human emotions, which more often than not govern human actions. Nowhere is this social poison of casual character assassination more apparent than in Rome's late Republican era. Cicero, a Roman politician, orator, philosopher, and contemporary of Caesar, was the great litigator of his day. When standing for the prosecution, Cicero lustily employed coarse invective of the sort that thrives on the Internet today, calling his targets "swine," "filth," and "pest."

In one prosecution of a notorious defendant, Cicero said that the accused was "not only a thief, but a wholesale robber; not only an adulterer, but a ravisher of chastity; not only a sacrilegious man, but an open enemy to all sacred things and all religion; not only an assassin, but a most barbarous murderer of both citizens and allies; so that I think him the only criminal in the memory of man so atrocious, that it is even for his own good to be condemned."[47]

Cicero engaged in the orator's old parlor trick of promising not to disturb the sensibilities of his audience by telling them something is too vile, too awful, too stomach-turning for their delicate ears to hear, and then telling them anyway. "Nothing shall be said of his drunken nocturnal revels; no mention shall be made of his pimps, and dicers, and panders; his losses at play, and the licentious transactions."[48]

The man in this case was guilty of many horrendous crimes, including acts of murder. But he was also a prominent citizen well liked by many. The portrait Cicero paints is of a man so vile that it would be remarkable if his fellow citizens allowed him to walk down the street without stoning him to death. Cicero went on to employ his winning invective against the Catilinarian conspirators, many of whom wound up being frog-marched past the Roman Forum, thrown into a state dungeon, and strangled. After Caesar was assassinated, Cicero launched into a series of blistering philippics against Mark Antony.

When Antony came to power, he demanded Cicero's proscription. With all escape routes cut off, Cicero meekly submitted to execution, his orator's head and his writer's hands nailed up on display in the rostrum of the Forum—but not before Fulvia, the wife of Antony, pulled out the tongue of her husband's verbal tormentor to jab it repeatedly with a golden hairpin.

> Character assassins poison a political culture and prompt enemies to impeach, imprison, and even physically exterminate one another.

Unmixing the Facts Without Rancor

Another historical example shows us a better way. It shows how the remixing of truth can be faced down without rancor, much less violence. One of the worst gray truth attacks occurred in the election of 1884, one that sets a model for all time in responding to an embarrassing, complex charge. It all began with a sensational newspaper story:

A TERRIBLE TALE

A DARK CHAPTER IN A PUBLIC

MAN'S HISTORY

THE PITIFUL STORY OF MARIA HALPIN AND GOVERNOR CLEVELAND'S SON*

> A child was born out of wedlock. Now ten years of age, this sturdy lad is named Oscar Folsom Cleveland. He and his mother have been supported in part by our ex-mayor, and now aspires to the White House. Astute readers may put the facts together and draw their own conclusion.[49]

The story depicted Grover Cleveland as fathering an illegitimate child, abandoning mother and child, and then conveniently hiding the poor woman in an insane asylum. Reverend George Ball, a Baptist minister and Republican Party mouthpiece, took it upon himself to spread the story across the East Coast and embellish it with depictions of Cleveland's debauchery.

The accusation of bad behavior went against what Americans thought they knew about the Democratic nominee for president. Cleveland had won a reputation as a tough reformer: first, as Erie County sheriff, who reluctantly pulled the gallows handle on two murderers, mayor of Buffalo; and then as reformist governor of New York. Up until that moment, the election of 1884 was going to be close. Any little thing could tip the margin of victory.

The story of the Cleveland baby was just such a tipping point. The article, which ran on the front page of *The Buffalo Evening Telegraph* that July, added to a portrait of Cleveland—a bachelor who enjoyed fishing and poker and was no stranger to saloons—as an amoral wastrel. It was the perfect way to undermine the case made by Democrats and their allies, Republican Mugwumps, that Cleveland was the reformer the nation needed to cleanse itself of a long Republican rule that had grown corrupt.

The Republicans made sure that a song, whose title made up the famous refrain "Ma! Ma! Where's My Pa?" was distributed by a national song company. "We do not believe that the American people will knowingly elect to the Presidency," wrote the ever-blunt Charles A. Dana of

* For a briskly written and colorful biography of Cleveland, see *An Honest President* by H. Paul Jeffers (New York: William Morrow, 2000).

The New York Sun, "a coarse debauchee who would bring his harlots with him to Washington and hire lodgings for them convenient to the White House."

The story left the Cleveland campaign in a panic. Grover Cleveland sent his instruction to a prominent supporter by telegram:

WHATEVER YOU DO, TELL THE TRUTH[50]

What was the truth?

In 1874, Maria Crofts Halpin had been a respectable widow, holding a position as head of the cloak department at a fashionable Buffalo dry goods store. Educated and fluent in French, Maria was tall, lively, attractive, and popular. She was also discreetly promiscuous, counting a number of suitors that included several married men, many of them friends of Cleveland, then a prominent lawyer. A flutter of fear, then, shot through a circle the city's leading men when she gave birth to a son one September day in 1874.

Halpin named Cleveland the father. Perhaps to protect the others in his circle, he stepped forward and took financial responsibility for the child, who was christened Oscar Folsom (after a friend and law partner who himself may have been a candidate for paternity) Cleveland. Suffering the stigma of being an unwed mother in late nineteenth-century America, Maria Halpin saw her tenuous place in respectable society slip away. She began to drink, neglect the boy, and show signs of mental instability.

Cleveland could have ignored the situation, buying distance from it with money. Instead, he turned to a county judge and friend to investigate. It was the judge on his own instigation who had Maria committed to an asylum run by the Sisters of Charity. Cleveland paid for the boy's commitment to the Protestant Orphan Asylum and paid his board through the judge. He helped Maria start a business in Niagara Falls. She sued to regain custody of her son and even tried to kidnap him. Thanks to Cleveland's network, the boy was adopted into a prominent family in Western New York.

Cleveland's supporters organized a legion of journalists and lawyers to nail down and publicize the facts. Foremost among them was a minister—Reverend Kinsley Twining—who neatly overturned the charges that Cleveland had abandoned Maria and the child, or that he had her sent her to an asylum as a coldhearted matter of convenience. When the facts were laid out, Twining said, it instead revealed that though the bachelor had a culpable irregularity, he had behaved in a way that was "singularly honorable." Twining proved that Maria, as she admitted to her lawyer, had never been led to believe that Cleveland would marry her.

Armed with the facts, Cleveland cultivated ministers with national reputations who could attest to his character. Cleveland turned a truth remix attack to his advantage by separating what was true, using respected third-party allies to painstakingly document those portions of the charges that were false, and deploying these allies to make sure everyone knew the difference. The result was blowback for the Republicans, exposing them as shrill benders of the truth while revealing Cleveland's essential honesty.

Cleveland later summed up his approach to the scandal in a letter to a friend as the policy of "no cringing."[51]

This is good advice today. Even when the charge is embarrassing, it pays to correct the false parts with documented evidence. Alexander Hamilton had done exactly this, but he had worked much of his defense alone with quill by candlelight. Cleveland was much more effective in recruiting friends and developing third-party support from respected people.

> This nineteenth-century example of defense by testimonials is ever more relevant today. The ease with which digital technology assembles crowds encourages like-minded people to go online, preferably on YouTube, to defend you, your brand, your company, or your product.

Takeaway—Pulling Out the Stingers

"Everyone has a break point where they take it personally," says Leo Yakutis. He cites a case he worked on in which the enemies of the head of a hedge fund tried to associate him with embezzlement. "We had to go out and counter this while someone on the other side was making sure that the bad information was being propagated to a couple of dozen websites that conspiracy theorists read, so they would remain very high in the search engine results," he says. "We had to break down those links and knock them off different pages, systematically, and also put correct information at top."[52]

If an Internet search brings up facts that add up to an erroneous portrait of you, then create positive websites, post positive items—your work with charity, your resume, a website with your blog—and then link those items together. Raise the profile of positive material to add to your reputational armor.

What should you do when truth about you is remixed? One way to address this issue comes from Snopes.com, run by the husband-and-wife team of Barbara and David Mikkelson, separates Internet fact, fiction, and urban legend on the Internet on a wide array of topics, including business. Snopes is candid when the facts cannot be nailed down and offers the visitor a color-coded range of reliability, from "true" to "false" "undetermined," and "unclassifiable veracity." One Snopes category, "multiple truth values," is especially useful in unmixing truth remix.

Ideally, Wikipedia's new Biographies of Living Persons policies should do the same for notable individuals. FactCheck.org polices the claims of politicians, and alerts visitors to sources of bad information, like viral e-mail rants.

When it comes to Yelp, businesses should not shrink from participating in the online discussion with customers. Yelp allows business owners who sign up to communicate with customers in public, apologizing for a mistake, explaining a shortcoming, or denying an unfounded comment.

Yelp also gives businesses tools to track how many view their page, add appealing photos, and announce special offers and upcoming events. As much as some businesspeople dislike Yelp, we should be grateful that it aggregates complaints and gives business a single platform on which to respond. Otherwise, businesses would have to contend with a Google soup of complaints.

The hard question about truth remix is how much to disclose. Alexander Hamilton provides the utmost example of providing excruciating detail in order to separate truth from untruth. This is utterly unlike the treatment of a ridiculous rumor in which victims, like McDonald's, avoid repeating lurid charges.

And perhaps we would all do well to set a better example, if not for Eric Schmidt, then for ourselves.

Grover Cleveland set an example when he was given a delicious chance at payback. He was presented with proof about problems in the marriage of his opponent. He purchased the evidence.

"Are all the papers here?" Cleveland asked.

Yes, he was told.

Cleveland slowly drew up a wastebasket, tore the sheets to pieces, and asked a servant to burn them in the fireplace.[53]

> In truth remix, the worst details to our portraits are often added by ourselves. Whenever you speak, the person sitting across from you can easily be recording you on his PDA; whenever you send a message, the person receiving may post it in a public place.

9:// The Seventh Sword—Clandestine Combat

> In the twenty-first century it's not just about tanks and artillery.
>
> —**NATO spokesman,** after cyber attack on Estonia[1]

THE KNOWLEDGE that our devices and data are insecure nags at us. Day by day we move forward, believing that there will be no adverse consequences to our exposure. Day by day, we live . . . in a fool's paradise?

We live, in fact, with the seventh sword of clandestine combat—the ease with which enemies or competitors can simply purloin secrets. "The head of one of the most profitable law firms in the country knows that his office, his house, and his mistress's apartment are all bugged," says one digital hound. "He doesn't care."

More often than not, however, even the most nonchalant victim of spying eventually discovers a breaking point.

The authors learned that the head of one national hotel chain knew that his office was bugged by another corporate interest reading his e-mail. He didn't get upset until he hired a firm to do an inventory of the intercepts and was told that his daughter's college dorm room had been bugged. Up until that time, he just said, "That's how we do business." When the competitor went after his daughter, it suddenly became very personal—and unacceptable.

He asked Leo Yakutis for protection. Yakutis is a bit of an anomaly in the IT world. With two master's degrees, one in history from the University of North Carolina at Charlotte and another in information science from the University of North Carolina at Chapel Hill, Yakutis has a combination of technical and human skills that make him popular with corporations in need of an investigator to trace a digital thread.

He often finds himself working for his clients to protect them from hackers and hacking firms paid to commit acts of corporate espionage and mayhem. "I only white-hat," he says. "I do not gray-hat. I do not black-hat. I can pass top secret with poly. That doesn't mean I don't know how the opposition works. In fact I *have* to know how the opposition works."[2]

> Corporations and special interest groups resort to digital technology to undermine, blackmail, or demonize.

Tracking the Joker

In one assignment, Leo Yakutis came up against the most formidable group he has ever faced—"an intelligent group of fanatics" backed by a corporate interest that waged a wide-ranging digital war on a premier law firm in Washington, D.C. This confrontation demonstrates the lengths to which ideologically or financially driven people will go to in order to get the right information. That the firm was under assault became apparent after a senior partner sat down to type out draft legislation on a laptop to present to a U.S. senator friendly to a major client. This in itself was not unusual. Law firms routinely offer draft legislation on behalf of clients for Capitol Hill. The draft legislation was on nothing but the lawyer's laptop. "He didn't tell his wife, he didn't tell his son, he didn't tell his dog," Yakutis says. "It was only in his machine."

The day before the law partner was to present the legislation, he made a visit to the Hill on other business. A senior aide to another U.S. senator, known to be a leading opponent of the draft legislation, walked up to the law partner and asked him not to pass his draft bill on to any of his colleagues. The staffer for the opposition senator knew legislative details he could have learned of only by being informed by someone who had actually read the draft document.

"This guy [the law partner] just about strokes out on us," Yakutis says. "He doesn't understand what happened. He had a company come in and do a conventional sweep for wiretaps and bugs. Nothing. He checked the office access codes, and this guy has some nice equipment—nothing. He has months of videotape of his office to review that proved that no unauthorized person had gone into his office and taken anything. Nothing like that. That left the last vector—electronic."

When Yakutis investigated, he found that the law firm had a sophisticated firewall. As with all systems, however, it had a back door that was discovered after numerous probes by the intruders. The nature of the back door was simple. The law firm's software connected his phone and computer so voice mail messages would register in the partner's e-mail inbox. This link created a digital opening that the intruders were able to enter to place a payload on one such message. Once the payload detonated, the intruders were in the system, then had the means to take control of the partner's machine. And once in that machine, they spread malware from his laptop to other computers throughout the office.

"It allowed the opposition remote access to this guy's computer," Yakutis said. "Then they managed to go on his computer and other computers in the office and put more malware on there in order to destroy things and randomize things in an effort to make the attack look messy so that we wouldn't be able to track it back. Their hope was that there would be so much malware in the system that we wouldn't be able to see how they got in."

Once Yakutis learned the nature of the breach, he deployed sniffers to trace the traffic coming in and going out of the system. He found something even more disturbing. The intruder had not only broken into the system but had left the door wide open so that unrelated and less sophisticated hackers, "script kiddies," could embed malicious code that would propagate from machine to machine to commit random acts of digital mischief.

The intruder's strategy was akin to that of the Joker, Batman's nemesis, who often covers his tracks by throwing heaps of stolen cash into the air in order to escape through the confusion of a money-frenzied mob.

Only this Joker instigated a digital riot.

After a lot of painstaking work cleaning up the workplace, computer by computer, Yakutis was able to uncover the pathway by which the Joker was able to access the partner's laptop.

A funny thing happened in the hours Yakutis spent monitoring the digital code streaming in front of his face. An anomaly appeared, deliberate and in real time—too obvious, in fact, to be a covert effort. The

Joker had recognized that he was being watched, and he gave Yakutis a sort of digital wink. "We saw that it was somebody on a wireless network," Yakutis says. "We knew the approximate range of this network and knew that it was without amplification. And we knew that the only public wireless network around was coming from a Starbucks several stories below our office on the ground floor."

The Joker could be caught physically in the act.

Downstairs, there was only a coffeehouse on a workday in a busy downtown, a good dozen men and women standing in the coffee line or sitting on plush, overstuffed furniture, earnestly staring into laptops. All were dressed casually but had the look of well-groomed professionals.

The Joker might as well have been in a football stadium.

"So at least one of them was the perpetrator sitting downstairs three stories below in a coffeehouse laughing at us," Yakutis says. "It became obvious that this person was freakingly cheeky. He knew I was in there and he knew what I was doing, and he was having a little fun at my expense . . . I remember saying, 'Great, all right, we've got somebody with a sense of humor.' "

While the Joker hid among the coffeehouse crowd, a go-between who was paid to set up the hack was ultimately caught. He had once worked in the data center of a Fortune 500 IT company and used its equipment surreptitiously to create the platform for the intruder to use.

He was eventually exposed—not through technical means, but through his own greed and stupidity. "We found out when the hacker tried to generate more business for himself by boasting on hacker blog sites that he had gotten into this particular law firm using this methodology," Yakutis says. "We caught that. We validated it. If he hadn't had boasted, we probably wouldn't have known that last detail."

No one was arrested. There simply was not enough evidence for a prosecution. Eventually, however, enough information was compiled to confront the opposition and persuade them to call off the Joker's attacks, although the opposition intensified their efforts by other means.

For some competitors and ideological groups, hacking is a blood sport taken up with relish.

Everyone Pays

It's called "insurance.aes256."

It is a 1.4-gigabyte file large enough to hold hundreds of thousands of pages worth of information. It is protected by a 256-bit key encryption code. And perhaps by the time you have read this, the Anonymous friends of Julian Assange may have followed through on their threat to open it to the world with the push of a button.[3]

At this writing, what it contains is anybody's guess. The claim is that it is something so damaging to the United States that its leaders will back down before pursuing charges against Assange.

Insurance.aes256 may be a hoax. But the suggestion that it might be a credible threat represents a monumental change in our civilization—the ability of loosely, self-organized hackers to intimidate governments and large corporations. And yet the WikiLeaks phenomenon is only the public manifestation of the extreme vulnerability of personal, business, and governmental systems to the seventh sword of clandestine combat.

WikiLeaks' hundreds of thousands of purloined files are but a trickle compared to the Mississippi of data diverted by spies, black hats, and unscrupulous competitors. McAfee reported at the World Economic Forum that cybertheft cost people and businesses $1 trillion in 2009.[4] Organizations that suffered one or more data breaches in the United States in 2009, according to a Ponemon Institute study, lost an average of $6.75 million per incident, not including long-term litigation costs and possible penalties. Perhaps worst of all, these organizations lost on average 3.7 percent of their customer base. For pharmaceuticals, communications, and health care, the loss of customers was even worse—6 percent.[5] Heartland Payment Systems, a payment processor, disclosed what might have been the largest data breach on record in early 2009—losing at least 100 million credit and debit card records a month. [6]

Cybercrime continues to morph into ever more creative imitations of legitimate business. Long-discredited spam has become "spim," or instant messaging spam, used to trick you to clicking to a fraudulent phishing website for your personal or financial details. "Malvertising" camouflages malicious code as online ads. Now that more people are on to the legitimate-looking phisher websites, criminals have moved to "spear-phishing," e-mails with malicious payloads. The FBI reports that spear-phishing attacks are increasingly aimed at getting at corporations through their law firms and PR firms.[7]

> Criminals are not just looking for credit card numbers. They wish to do harm to reputations or commit informational blackmail.

Scraping Society

We accept an implicit bargain when we use web-based platforms. The various sites at our fingertips—our search engine, the sites we visit—offer an array of powerful services for free in exchange for the ability to track our wants and desires and report them to advertisers. For most people, this deal is acceptable, even if it does make one a little queasy, thanks to the use of pseudonymous identifiers. It allows Google and other big players to attach details about our interests and demographic information to a particular cookie, without correlating it with information that identifies us as individuals.

We have learned to delete our cookies, so companies now track computers' "fingerprints"—the unique time stamps and other settings that identify them, effectively, as you. So increasingly advertisers are following our devices, whether computers or cell phones, giving them "reputations" based on our searches, the things we buy, and matching them to our demographic information.

Even the apps in our cell phones can also follow us, telling advertisers which stores we visit in real time. In April 2011, it was revealed that Apple's iPhone and Google's Android are building massive databases on consumers' information by pinpointing cell phone locations and movements. Representative Edward Markey, Democrat from Massachusetts, issued a statement: "Apple needs to safeguard the personal location information of its users to ensure that an iPhone doesn't become an iTrack."[8] Tracking companies are also looking into "deep packet inspection," a peering into the actual data we send through the network. Again, the promise here is that any information gleaned won't be correlated with our real-world identities.[9]

The problem is that given the billions of dollars at stake, industry will be continually tempted to make the connection not to the device or to the unique identifier, but to the actual person.

A groundbreaking *Wall Street Journal* investigative series on online advertising found that many popular games like FarmVille (59 million users) and other apps on Facebook have been negligent at best in safeguarding consumers' identities, even those who choose the strictest privacy settings. About 70 percent of Facebook users enjoy one such app or another. The *Journal* reporters found that all of the ten most popular apps on Facebook were transmitting users' IDs to outside companies.[10] One of them, RapLeaf, uses its possession of real names to "build extraordinarily intimate databases on people by tapping voter-registration files, shopping histories, social-networking activities and real estate records, among other things."[11]

The technique of "scraping" personal information is so powerful that one Democratic political consultant used RapLeaf to target a key group of swing voters, 200,000 suburban women in Southern California over the age of forty. It helped him defeat a state ballot initiative on auto insurance rates.[12]

Facebook and companies that supply its apps are not devious. Many of the app developers seem not to have known that they were correlating this information, which after all was contrary to Facebook policy. Two weeks before the story broke, Facebook created a control panel that allows users to see "which apps are accessing which categories of information about them."[13]

The problem is that one way or another, what can be done will be done. And what can be done is a lot.

The *Journal* reported that the problem goes far beyond Facebook, which is at least transparent about making your Facebook user name and identifier searchable. In fact "the nation's 50 top websites on average installed 64 pieces of tracking technology onto the computers of visitors, usually with no warning. A dozen sites each installed more than a hundred."[14]

Tracking tools—cookies, "flash cookies" that reinstall, and "beacons" that can follow what you do on a website, including what you type—scan what you are doing on a website in real time, matching your activity to your location, income, shopping interests, and even medical conditions. "Some tools," the *Journal* reported, "surreptitiously re-spawn themselves even after users try to delete them."[15]

In a social network, of course, the compromise of one might mean the compromise of all. "If I have access to your Facebook profile password, I not only have access to your information, I have access to all your friends' information," says social media expert James Lee. Speaking of the thousands of followers of one digital guru, Lee says, "I could get all their birthdays, phone numbers, e-mail addresses, hometowns, anything that they made available to you under the privacy setting of friends. That's a huge treasure trove of data you're not able to get anywhere else. Same for LinkedIn, MySpace, all of those different sites . . . Mark Zuckerberg was right, though it may not have been good PR to say it—privacy as we know it is a dead concept on the Internet."*

Consider the finding of a joint team from Microsoft and Germany's Max Planck Institute that algorithms can intuit a person's sexuality and then effectively out them if they click on a gay- or lesbian-oriented ad, many perhaps still under the illusion that they were doing so in complete privacy. Any advertisers who collect data such as Facebook IDs could match a person's sexual preference with their unique ID and their name.[16]

While Facebook earnestly works to discipline its app providers and clarify its privacy policies, the evolving capability of the technology itself will continually outrace our ability to contain it. Already exchanges resembling stock markets are buying and selling masses of humanity's personal information by the gigabyte.[17]

> Eight out of ten children under the age of two in ten Western countries have their pictures online. They will be the first humans to be digitally tracked from cradle to grave.[18]

Street Stalkers

Breaches in our personal security can come from the street. When Google dispatched its vans around the world with 360-degree cameras for its Street View project (which matches local images to Google Maps), it picked up unencrypted information from Wi-Fi networks, including e-mail addresses, web page URLs, and passwords. Google, which promised it had not stored the data, apologized in 2010.[19] The scooping up of all this private data was in fact inadvertent, an example of robust technology outstripping customer relations. Again, what can be done will

* In a TechCrunch interview in the fall of 2010, when asked, "Where is privacy on the Web going?" Zuckerberg replied that Facebook would innovate to keep up as "social norms" evolved over time.

be done, if not by Google then by some other entity, competitor, or government.

There are other street dangers. Keep in mind that we might be tracked from the sky by that first generation of personal camera-equipped drones already on the market—indeed, tracked by means of gadgets in our own pockets. Cell towers have long allowed police to triangulate the position of a cell phone and its owner, solving kidnappings and finding missing children. GPS is now a standard feature of cell phones, helping with emergency services, enabling social mapping and other location-based services, including services that allow parents to use the phone to track their kids.

After *The News of the World* voicemail hacking scandal a lot of urban legends arose about how easy it is to "hack and track" through a cell phone. While it is unclear how easily cell phone hacking actually is, there is always the possibility of an inside job or those misrepresenting their right to know to use social engineering techniques to spoof phone companies or to persuade law enforcement to use your cell phone to follow you. "This is not uncommon with domestic disputes," one telecom executive told us.

An easier and more direct approach for eavesdropping is for a hacker to build, for about $1,500, a directional antenna of the sort already used by law enforcement to spoof a cell tower to collect outbound calls and data from callers.[20] This would in effect suck up all the calls and data in a local area for exploitation.

Even city speed cameras may be spying on you. In Great Britain, speed cameras check for speeding, tailgating, and seatbelts. They can also correlate with databases to ensure that you are up-to-date on your car insurance and taxes.[21]

Getting tracked and hacked is no longer just an indoor sport.

The Burglar Sitting on Your Lap

A former National Security Agency (NSA) cyber expert has demonstrated that he can exploit security flaws in common web browsers to remotely gain control of a computer in under ten seconds. In one test, he opened the target's e-mail, activated his laptop's built-in camera, and took his picture.[22]

What do Scarlett Johansson, Miley Cyrus, Vanessa Hudgens, Emma Caufield, Addison Timlin, Busy Philipps, Renee Olstead, and Ali Larter have in common? TMZ broke the story that they're among fifty celebrities who've had compromising video and images taken from their mobile devices and computers by hackers.[23] Or consider what happened to the MySpace pages of Alicia Keys and two dozen other performers. Chinese hacking groups embedded malicious code in video software downloads on these celebrity pages that enabled the theft of credit card information.[24]

Of course your computer may itself already be enlisted as a soldier in a vast army of botnet cyber-thieves. By 2008, the FBI's Operation Botroast estimated that at least 1 million U.S. computers were infected.[25] The defense contractor's experiment with the quick infection rate and zombification of a plain vanilla computer described in chapter 3 suggests that the number of computers being used by unauthorized persons is by now likely much larger.

Another portal to turn Internet users into victims is through their embarrassment and guilt over downloading copyrighted material over file-sharing networks. Those who enjoy hentai—Japanese illustrated pornography—are sometimes encouraged to download what the user is led to believe is an illegal copy from a file-sharing network. Malware is also downloaded; it steals the victim's domain and computer name, software, search history and favorites, clipboard content and screen shots, all of which is posted on a website. Soon the victim receives an e-mail from a self-styled consumer defender warning the victim he is guilty of copyright infringement, not to mention the loss of privacy. This can all be fixed, of course, for a fee.[26]

> There are many ways into computers, some physical, some through emotional blackmail.

Corporate Info Wars

Elite hackers are winning enormous victories at the commanding heights of the world economy. Consider what happened to General Motors. In the first decade of the century, GM was crashing in the U.S. market but enjoying robust growth in Asia. The GM Daewoo brand in South Korea introduced the Spark, a car new to the Chinese market. As the Spark was being unveiled, China's Chery Automobile unveiled a new car of its own, the QQ.

GM executives were flabbergasted at what they saw in the showrooms. Chery hadn't bothered to make even a minor cosmetic disguise of its wholesale theft of the Spark. When examined by independent experts, the Spark and the QQ were found to be identical in body structure, exterior design, interior design, and key components. The two cars were so similar that parts were perfectly interchangeable. "This incident defies an innocent explanation," the U.S. secretary of commerce said in 2005.[27]

It seems apparent that the precise mathematical description of the Spark was taken by hacking into GM Daewoo's computers. Confronted with irrefutable evidence of intellectual property theft, Chery agreed to an undisclosed settlement between the two companies.[28]

In July 2010, a former GM worker, Shanshan Du, and her husband, Yu Qin, of Troy, Michigan, were charged with the unauthorized possession of trade secrets concerning hybrid car designs. They allegedly made an offer of design secrets, downloaded onto a hard drive, to . . . Chery Automobile (which denies knowing anything about the scheme).[29]

Other high-profile cases of alleged Chinese espionage involve Dow Chemical, DuPont, and Motorola, alleged inside jobs in which the alleged perpetrator often had to only download the data and hit send.[30]

Similar breaches are apt to happen in lawsuits in which nine or ten figures are on the table. One law firm involved in a major class-action lawsuit discovered that not only were its computers compromised but bugs had been installed in each office and in the homes of each partner involved in the lawsuit. A digital hound was able to source the attack back to an Asian firm owned by an American company in the lawsuit, making effective legal action all but impossible.[31]

> Hackers are more than just thieves or trolls. They can be effective strategic competitor-intelligence agents.

The Roots of Insecurity

No other system in human history has so quickly pervaded all aspects of our lives as computing while creating so much vulnerability. But *why* are we so vulnerable?

Most American industries and government agencies rely on COTS, commercial off-the-shelf technology designed to meet the Internet's high standard of interoperability, not security. Only banks and hospitals have devised their own closed loop systems that are reasonably secure.

"Banks get it because they have credit cards," Yakutis says. Despite the 2011 hacking of Citigroup credit card information, all the cyber experts interviewed for this book agree that if the rest of the U.S. infrastructure had the security protocols and secure links as strong as those of banks and other financial institutions, the nation's commerce would be much more secure. But they do not.

A good demonstration of the dark side of openness is regularly revealed by gray hats who purport to expose security flaws, usually in the commercial space, as a public service. A leader in this space in 2010 was Goatse Security. After exposing holes in the Mozilla and Apple Safari browsers, Goatse—of "Gaping Holes Exposed" fame—handed over to Gawker 114,000 e-mail addresses of early adopters of iPad 3G; these included Diane Sawyer of ABC News, movie producer Harvey Weinstein, and New York mayor Michael Bloomberg.[32] Clearly, the amorphous group of hackers who identify with Goatse have fun aiming their best shots at new security. What they reveal is just the tip of the iceberg of espionage, subterfuge, and theft that takes place in the corporate space.

Stealing can also be done physically. Slip into a hotel room or promise to guard someone's laptop while he or she goes to the airport restroom, and the quick insertion of a memory stick is enough to do the job.

Turning off a computer is no safeguard against expert thieves. When a computer is turned off or put into sleep mode, recent actions exist for a short time in its random access memory. Researchers at Princeton University, the Electronic Frontier Foundation, and Wind River Systems have demonstrated that with a can of compressed air or liquid nitrogen, a thief can mount a "cool boot attack" to restore residual data from a computer, including the decryption keys of disk-based encryption products.[33] One digital hound we interviewed practiced this technique and got it down to under five minutes.

Such elaborate, labor-intensive techniques are too dangerous for high-stakes corporate espionage. But there are far easier ways and legal ways to get high-level corporate information. For example, we learned that one senior executive at a top technology company regularly shares his digital calendar with employees in a way that outsiders can readily view. Whom he visits and when is proprietary information of the highest caliber, revealing potential customers to competitors. Despite repeated warnings by security consultants, he has yet to change his habits.[34]

> The Internet, spun out of a Cold War era research project, was given an open architecture to provide resiliency. Today the Internet's openness is our vulnerability.

The Hardware Store

In the early days of the Internet, anyone who wanted to use it had to master a certain amount of code. As information technology evolves toward an easy user interface, hacking is becoming user-friendly. This is good news for corporate spies, usually deployed by an upper mid-level executive under intense pressure to meet numbers. Such an executive can go to the online bazaar of hackers' websites and find illicit hacking firms for hire. For cyberespionage, the best can easily be recruited.

"There are websites where hacking is reduced to a tool chest, like being in a hardware store," security expert Bill Livingstone says. "All these different tools you can apply to hack into something. One might be a software program to break passwords. You don't have to write the program. You just take it off the shelf and apply it."[35]

More and more, cybercrime is organized by people who themselves are not hackers. This nefarious world works because there is a certain necessary amount of honor among thieves. Clients enter into a marketplace for services and software in which hackers are rated by their dependability in providing a product and clients are rated for paying on a full and timely basis, much like sellers are rated on eBay. As long as you don't get a reputation for being a "ripper," someone who does bad deals, you can choose from among an astonishing array of products.

"The way it will be done is that they will say, 'I need a Zero-Day exploit for Juniper routers,'" says Tom Kellermann. "And 'I need someone else who can give me the scanner that produces that exploit.' And then 'I need someone else to lease me a botnet so when I launch the attack, no one will know that it came from me.' And then 'I need someone else to datamine the information of whatever the code has gotten into and then find what it touches that is not me.' And lastly, 'I need someone else to be the command and control.'"[36] Thus an anonymous organizer can assemble a virtual army out of people who don't know each other, will never meet each other, and do not know—and do not want to know—the ultimate purpose of their work.

What can you buy on this market? For starters, you can buy the software to mount a Zero-Day attack.

"Zero-Day is an invincible weapon, it cannot be stopped by anything," Kellermann says. "It works when there's a vulnerability in the operating system itself that has never been seen before, so there's no patch or cure for it. And if you can hit the operating system with a Zero-Day, all of the security, firewalls, virus scanners, encryption, intrusion-protection devices, and forensics means jack shit because I literally own the foundation of your house."

The going rate for Zero-Day exploit for Windows 7, the latest Microsoft Operating System, is $75,000. A Zero-Day for Apple's Snow Leopard operating system goes for $25,000. To purchase a system rivaling the Stuxnet virus (which contains at least four Zero-Day applications), be prepared to pay a couple of hundred thousand dollars.

When you do a cost-benefit analysis, a system that can allow you to hack a bank's database in minutes could pay for your Zero-Day in the first thirty seconds of access.

It is for this reason that gifted hackers are like smash-and-grab artists who break the glass tops of jewelry store counters so they can run off with the biggest diamonds. Most hackers would rather get in and get out, hacking into a system and swiping the numbers of, say, 50,000 credit cards or stealing a priceless trade secret. They are often too impatient for the delayed satisfactions of a well-orchestrated smear campaign.

"For that reason, many corporate attacks are more direct," Yakutis says, explaining that many hackers won't take on corporate reputation smears unless the employer can show it will pay a lot of money. "But if someone has deep enough pockets, the hacker will do it."

When it comes to reputational warfare, one way to operate is to import material gleaned by hackers abroad. "I as an American cannot start hacking into a company website," says one digital investigator who wishes not to be named. "That is against the law. However, if someone from another part of the world hacks in to that site, and that illegally gathered information is brought into the United States and I use it, that is not against the law. And you have a lot of talented people outside of the United States who are doing a lot of interesting things."[37]

The good news is that once an attacker from a rival company is informed that he has been unmasked, he almost always backs down.

And what about the hackers themselves? One of the best ways for security experts to defeat hackers is to read their blogs. Being a successful hacker, after all, is somewhat like being Clark Kent. You may have flown to the ends of the Earth to defeat Lex Luthor, but as far as anyone around you can see, you're just another schlub with thick glasses. A hacker might have broken into the sanctum sanctorum of the CIA. But what good is it if no one knows?

So hackers need to brag. And they do, telling the world of their exploits. For example, we learned that at least one hacker actually did succeed in exploiting the penetration of a computer asset of the CIA. He did not go in directly. Instead, he followed a popular botnet that wormed inside the CIA-owned computer. Rather than follow it all the way in, the hacker waited outside the agency's digital firewall to catch the botnet as it exited. "He robbed the highway robber," someone close to this case says. It was a neat trick. It might have continued to work, except for the fact that the hacker bragged about it—and the agency noticed.

Harder to catch are the environmental and ideological groups that have begun, since 2009, to enlist millions of computers into botnets to mount data-flooding attacks to swamp sites, knocking companies offline. Perfume companies have been a particularly high-profile target for animal-rights activists.[38]

> Hackers hire their services like jobbers. Their weapons can be seen and purchased by anyone.

Cockroaches in the Cloud

The original Internet was, as Tom Kellermann says, a "giant, aquatic environment," a vast open ocean of information. It was not originally conceived to be a network that business, government, and the military could securely operate within. "So whoever the thought leaders were who said, 'Let's use this giant aquatic environment and put everything important on it,' kudos to them—because they're paying my salary right now," Kellermann, a highly paid security adviser, says with a wink.

Military and defense contractors worry about "trapdoors" built into the COTS hardware of our machines by the Chinese—tiny hard-to-notice anomalies in the design that can be remotely activated to turn over control. Kellermann says, "That's actually not the scariest part of supply chain. There is a virtual supply chain that makes it even more horrifying . . . the thing that everyone's talking about who wants to be hip, and that's the cloud—cloud computing." He calls cloud computing "giant apartment buildings in the sky."

Cloud computing is the practice of locating software applications and data in off-site, often distant data centers that store and manage your data. Its scalability brings powerful new efficiencies to computing. A prime feature of cloud computing is virtualization—using abstract computing platforms, with no need to immediately interact with a physical computer. The cloud is used to store data that we once stored in our machine or on backup memory or on a stick.

Why do this? The cloud gives us access to vastly more computing power at a reduced (or in some cases, almost no) cost. Microsoft raises three important questions every person and business should ask about a cloud host:

> —Are hosted data and applications within the cloud protected by suitably robust privacy policies?
> —Are the cloud computing provider's technical infrastructure, applications, and processes secure?
> —Are processes in place to support appropriate action in the event of an incident that affects privacy or security?[39]

In short, do we know where our organization's computer assets begin and end?

These are good questions, to which most people who are not chief information officers would answer, "I dunno." And yet we live in the clouds, even though we also know that breaches often come through third-party systems.

"Think of the national security and economic security implications of more than 50 percent of the Fortune 1000 and more than 50 percent of the federal government agencies that will be in a cohosted, multitenanted cloud environment by the end of 2011," Kellermann says. "What is the significance of polluting that supply chain and/or infiltrating that supply chain? Because in the cloud if your neighbor has cockroaches, so do you."

Kellermann says we should not be overconfident about the protection afforded us by encryption. "Encryption can and will be defeated, by technical innovation and human error," he says.

Most companies and people who use cloud computing enjoy significant levels of security. The benefits of cloud computing should not be underestimated.

> The cloud creates economy of scale for hackers as well as for clients.

Baking the Grid

Senate minority leader Mitch McConnell received a lot of criticism for rhetorical overkill for calling Julian Assange as "a high-tech terrorist." In fact, among the many secret State Department cables revealed by WikiLeaks is one that offers a helpful terrorist road map of overseas factories and infrastructure, from cables to pipelines, vital to the physical security of the United States.[40]

These are greater dangers from the cyberworld than damage to our reputation or bank accounts. Actions by hackers—whether by a group of lunatics, Al Qaeda, or a hostile nation-state—can kill. With Stuxnet-like viruses, an attacker can turn a power plant, in the words of one former U.S. national security official, "into a useless lump of metal," prompt the combustion chambers of chemical plants to fatally overheat, or ruin the turbines of a hydroelectric plant.[41] In a survey released in 2011, of two hundred IT executives in charge of oil, gas, and water utilities in fourteen countries reported that 80 percent of them had experienced large-scale denial of service attacks.[42]

Or an attacker could follow the example of Vitek Boden, a Queensland technician who commanded 300 systems governing sewage and drinking water from a stolen computer and radio transmitter in his car. He sluiced 800,000 liters of raw sewage into local parks, rivers, and the grounds of a luxury hotel.[43]

Aside from the closed systems of U.S. banks, the rest of the American infrastructure relies on public and easily accessed Internet connections. "The CEO likes to have the big shiny panel in his office he can show visitors by which he can track and control his facilities second by second," one security expert told us. "The problem is, any number of other people can reproduce that control panel on their laptop."

When most people think of a cyberattack on the electrical power grid, they think of blackouts. Less well known is the potential for push-button destruction. "Why think one direction here?" Kellermann asks. "Imagine if I were to cause a power surge. And instead of knocking out power, I were to pump too much power through the system. What happens then?" It might look something like the Aurora Project test at the Idaho National Labs, now on YouTube, of a hack attack on a twenty-seven-ton generator. In a few seconds, malicious code prompts the massive machine to destroy itself, sending bolts flying and smoke belching out. It would take months to replace such a generator, which would have to be ordered from overseas.[44] A smart grid of the sort touted by the Obama administration would only make the electrical system even more a creature of the vulnerable Internet.

Experts say that as much as 85 percent of all system relays in our electrical grid are digital. Kellermann says that a single exploitation of a vulnerability could be propagated across a cyber or power system network and potentially affect an entire class of assets at once. With a smart grid, an attacker wouldn't have to hack into a bay station. He could act from a house, causing a cascade of damage from relays to substations.

Most pernicious would be man-in-the-middle attacks, which operate within networks to attack central control rooms and push bad firmware out to remote field devices that won't be able to reboot or be recovered. "You can also actually hack into the system and maintain a presence within the system so you can cause surges at will by having remote access to command-and-control SCADA systems within it," Kellermann says. SCADA, or supervisory control and data acquisition systems, are controls that can be accessed over the Internet or phone lines.

In his 2010 book, *Cyber War,* former NSC official Richard Clarke writes that not only have both Russia and China deeply penetrated the U.S. electricity grid, but that the Chinese have "laced" the U.S. infrastructure with "logic bombs" capable of causing havoc on a similar scale of the Stuxnet attack on Iranian nuclear facilities.[45]

The Stuxnet worm is the first cyber weapon to demonstrate mass effects in the physical world. Its success against Iran's uranium enrichment facility and its nuclear reactor and elsewhere heralds things to come.

"When something succeeds spectacularly twice, it is ready for wider application," one cyber expert says.

Stuxnet can make robot arms go berserk, elevator doors close, and HVAC systems shut off.[46] It can open the valves of refineries, chemical plants, and water treatment facilities. "What keeps me up at night," Kellermann says, "is the fact that you no longer need to be there in person to kill or to maim or destroy."

One scenario he worries about is a pax mafioso between, say, former Soviet bloc mercenaries and terrorists or a hostile state to launch a two-prong attack. "The first prong is to play with the integrity of the information on which first responders rely," Kellermann says. "I don't mean turning it off. I mean playing with time, switching GPS coordinates, things like that. And then coupling that with a physical attack. There are so many ways you can kill a lot of Americans through cyberattacks on the infrastructure, it is unbelievable. And I don't just mean poisoning the water or turning off the electrical grid. Just look at the pharmaceutical industry." Kellermann worries that a hacker might turn off safety controls in an automated manufacturing facility to deliberately change computer formulas to mismeasure the amount of drug that goes into each capsule or pill.

Some cyber experts we interviewed believe that the nation's chemical plants are unconscionably vulnerable. Kellermann sees holes in plant security. "The problem is that the guys who run security at chemical plants are former FBI or Secret Service guys, not the cyber guys," Kellermann says. "They understand perimeter and physical security and . . . their generation was trained to believe that technology helps improve security, not that technology exacerbates security.

"And so these guys go wireless on everything, they use video everywhere, they connect those video camera systems into their primary systems, and they have all these wonderful widgets to protect themselves in a physical sense," Kellermann says. "But all those wonderful technological solutions meant to improve physical security actually create an Achilles' heel from a cybersecurity perspective."

Another set of worries is the hacking of the SCADA systems of chemical plants. A security expert who works with chemical companies told us that growing public awareness and the threat of fines have prompted the leading chemical companies to make big strides in security. In fact, several executives of large chemical companies told us that they have installed redundant physical systems that would use mechanical means to defeat an attempt to wreck a chemical plant over the Internet. Industry sources also conveyed that smaller companies have been less diligent and are more vulnerable.

Softer targets can also be attacked, including the results of an election. In the fall of 2010, the District of Columbia Board of Elections and Ethics opened an Internet-based voting system to the public for one week, inviting experts to mount exploitations to see what would happen. One University of Michigan professor did just that, unleashing his students on the system. Within days, rather than report the right election results, the system was playing, "The Victors," the fight song of the University of Michigan.[47]

What about the financial markets? Kellermann worries about hackers playing with the time stamps on trades in the New York central equities depository. If that could be done, it could cause serious disruption. Others question what would happen if a black hat got into large trading companies and started generating mass volumes of buy and sell orders.

When attacks happen, who is the most likely perpetrator? Two years ago, the eight major criminal syndicates of the world passed a major threshold. They derived 50 percent of their revenues from cybercrime, Kellermann reports. So in Kellermann's pax mafioso scenario, the actual work of committing cyberterrorism might be commissioned among any of a hundred criminal organizations, from the Japanese Yakuza to the Chinese Triads.

This is happening as the gang bosses, who are in their fifties or sixties, are increasingly turning to protégés in their thirties for advice. "If they are not tech savvy themselves, they are appreciative of it enough that they are going to coerce someone to work for them who does it really well," Kellermann says. "Or they are going to hire someone to do it really well. Or they are going to find someone who can barter online to get the capabilities they need, because in the end, who doesn't want to be omniscient?"

And the sweetest part is that for those who commission cybercrime, there is almost zero risk. "Only 1 percent of cases of hacking banks—cybercrime against financial institutions—are successfully prosecuted by either the Secret Service or FBI," Kellermann says.

Then there are attacks that have the unmistakable imprimatur of a state actor. Russia in 2007 launched a wave of cyberattacks on the

Estonian parliament and other institutions in a fit of anger over the removal of a Soviet-era war memorial. In 2008, Russia launched a cyber offensive against Georgia's Internet infrastructure in coordination with physical war.

The nation with the greatest demonstrated capability to attack the United States is of course the People's Republic of China. During an eighteen-minute period in April 2010, a state-owned Chinese firm hoovered the Internet, redirecting 15 percent of the Internet through Chinese servers, sweeping up U.S. government and military data. It caught data sent between the "dot.mil" branches of the U.S. armed services, as well as data from the U.S. Senate and Fortune 500 companies.[48]

Thanks to WikiLeaks, we now know that an inside source informed the U.S. embassy that the deep penetration of Google and the theft of its proprietary codes was ordered by the highest levels of the Chinese government, coordinated by the State Council Information Office, which reports directly to the PRC's Politburo Standing Committee.[49] It is rumored, but unconfirmed, that a senior Chinese official ordered the hack after seeing criticism of himself on sites that came up in a Google search result of his name.[50]

While launching these attacks, China also unveiled the creation of the world's most powerful supercomputer, the Tianhe-1A, which can manage 2,507 trillion calculations a second. Some experts see a connection between these two events, as if China is saying, "Not only do we have access to what you know, we can parse and distribute what you know with exceptional speed."

The greatest immediate source of physical danger is of course terrorists. While state-sponsored attacks can often be traced back to their source, terrorists are the most obvious candidates to mount a physical attack. Given their rootlessness and nihilism, they cannot be dissuaded or easily deterred. Al Qaeda offers an interesting example of how a hunted group, if it chooses to become a cyber-hunter, could mount attacks with attendant propaganda, without being found. Jihadists maintain online libraries in Egypt and Great Britain, resources for inspiration, propaganda, and fundraising. Those who are actually operational terrorists, however, have to be on the move. "Terrorists cannot openly operate a website for long without attracting the attention of government authorities," says Bill Livingstone. "So their sites are perpetually going up and coming down, changing addresses, locations."

We tend to think of cyber-warriors as sitting in a chair in front of a computer. Most of the developing world, however, doesn't use PCs. It communicates with mobile devices. The network for a terrorist act can be coordinated by cheap disposable cell phones. Terrorist videos and messages are sent in daisy-chain bursts, from cell phone to cell phone, from device to device.

While Al Qaeda doesn't have the sophistication of state-sponsored actors, it does have the will and the malice to carry out terror operations by remote control. Given the shifting topology of its network, it is hard to track and counter. Some experts believe, however, that Al Qaeda is currently too busy financing old-fashioned terrorist attacks with bombs and guns to use digital technology to mount digital attacks on critical infrastructure.

Besides criminals, nation-states, and terrorists, there is another source of deadly attacks against the United States—the individual, someone who might inflict on American infrastructure the same level of damage that twenty-three-year-old PFC Bradley Manning is accused of inflicting on American diplomacy by collecting secrets by the truckload before offloading them on WikiLeaks. For months, Manning is believed to have sat at a terminal surrounded by fellow soldier/technicians, pretending to listen to a CD, lip-synching to Lady Gaga's "Telephone" while filling the disk with compressed files containing secrets by the gigabyte. In thinking of the damage he was going to inflict, Manning reportedly told hacker Adrian Lamo, "It's beautiful and horrifying."[51]

> Like PFC Manning, some strange antisocial young person might mutter to himself "beautiful, horrifying" while watching smoke rise from the carnage of a city.

The Jesus Bar

We are dependent as never before on the digital devices that copy, store, and enact almost every transaction. An exabyte is a billion billion, or 1 followed by 18 zeros. By 2010, humanity required 40.8 exabytes of storage space for new data, or 2.7 gigabytes for every man, woman, and child on the planet.[52] And yet our deep and growing dependence is on systems that are utterly insecure. More than 221 million records containing individuals' personal data were compromised in 608 incidents in 2009.[53]

Tom Kellermann believes that the penetration of Internet and computer-enabled devices is pervasive in the United States. "From Grandma's computer at home to so many university computer systems that on a heat map it looks like it's all coming from here, but that just means the hackers have actually colonized more of our cyber infrastructure than anywhere else on the planet," he says.

Another expert with deep experience in national security systems invokes a simple handgrip in the cockpit that test pilots call the Jesus bar. It has a precise purpose. The Jesus bar allows a test pilot to do nothing. There are times in a stall in which anything a test pilot does will only worsen his predicament. He is better off toughing it out for a few seconds to see if the plane eases out on its own. In moments like these the Jesus bar allows the pilot to hang on for dear life and call out to Jesus.

The Jesus bar is a favorite metaphor of Dr. Eric Haseltine, who after he served as director of engineering at Hughes Aircraft managed technology projects and the virtual reality studio at Walt Disney Imagineering, then was recruited to be director of research for the National Security Agency. From 2005 to 2007, Haseltine was also associate director for science and technology, Office of the Director of National Intelligence (ODNI), a position he described to a journalist as "the CTO [chief technology officer] of the intelligence community." He oversaw the most sensitive computer systems of the CIA and much of the alphabet soup of intelligence agencies. He is now an author and a much sought after consultant and lecturer.

While at ODNI, Haseltine helped the federal government hone its offensive capabilities to deter and attack foreign governments and hacker clubs, as well as sharpen the government's means to defend its own systems. Through his experiences, Haseltine has had the world's best education in what could be achieved by offense and what was possible in the way of defense. His conclusion? "I think we're screwed," Haseltine says. "We're never going to be safe—and the situation is getting worse quickly."

How much worse can it get? According to some IT industry sources, there are more people in the world today devising malware than there are people writing software. Alarmed by the extent of penetration into federal systems and the vulnerability of major infrastructure, the Obama administration is pushing its own version of a Bush-era policy called the Comprehensive National Cybersecurity Initiative (CNCI), a federal program to unify the fragmented approach of federal agencies' approach to cybersecurity. Although it is a "black" budget program, journalists estimate CNCI's five-year budget at $40 billion.

While in government service, Dr. Haseltine was so impressed by the openness of federal systems and U.S. infrastructure to attack and was so discouraged about the prospects of defense that he believes that CNCI's colossal budget may be worse than a total waste of money. He wonders if federal cybersecurity efforts might actually be making us less safe, in much the same way a pilot's instant response might send a plane into a spiral, so that the best course of action for federal cyber administrators at this moment in history would be to grasp the Jesus bar, hang on for dear life, and do nothing at all—except perhaps scream.

> Governments are still sorting responses to cyberattacks at the most basic conceptual levels.

The Best and Brightest

The U.S. government is in action to restore cybersecurity. And when the government flies into action, new agencies are formed, each with their own shiny new emblems and shields. At the apex of cybersecurity is the newly formed U.S. Cyber Command, part of the U.S. Strategic Command and located at National Security Agency headquarters in Fort Meade, Maryland.

Although not charged with protecting commercial infrastructure, Cybercom is lending its expertise to the U.S. Department of Homeland Security, which has primary responsibility to protect critical private-sector networks in the United States. However, the head of Cybercom, General Keith Alexander, told Congress that "it is not my mission to defend today the entire nation."[54] He said that any defense of the power grid, for example, would have to rely on industry.

Industry is being asked to lead, but without clear guidelines to follow one has little reason to feel more secure. In May 2011, the Pentagon became so alarmed by the vulnerability of the United States that it announced that it would leave open the possibility that it might consider a large-scale cyber attack "an act of war," worthy of physical retaliation. Perhaps the most realistic, if fatalistic action being taken in 2011 is debate over a so-called Internet kill switch, legislation that would give the president the executive authority in a cyber emergency to shut down broad portions of the Internet that deal with critical infrastructure.

There is also a lot of emphasis on resiliency, which Kellermann fears is a sign that we learned the wrong lesson after 9/11. The problem with resiliency—hooking up remote users, putting up wireless LAN over fiber optics, setting up a backup data center—is that they "expand the target" for potential hackers. "I can now hack into that remote user, I can hack the wireless transmission wire, I can hack the backup data center, [there are] so many points by which I can ingress myself into your system," Kellermann says.

Dr. Eric Haseltine worries about an opposite problem, that cybersecurity efforts to reduce the federal government's "attack surface"—the external face of the system through which an attacker can enter—will simplify the attacker's path into our systems. He believes we should confess our ignorance of the laws that govern the cyberworld, a new realm whose fundamental laws we do not yet understand. Wouldn't it make sense to understand how the cyberworld evolves before trying to shape that evolution?

Biological metaphors come naturally to Haseltine, who has an eclectic background for a cyber geek. By training, Haseltine is a neuroscientist who believes "we understand the natural world, we understand the Newtonian world, but we don't understand the laws that govern the cyberworld, even though we act like we do." If he had his way, Haseltine would stop spending billions to defend cybersystems we imperfectly understand and instead begin with a pure science effort at mastering the rules of this cyberworld we've created.

Just as bacteria will eventually become resistant to an antibiotic, so too might CNCI's quest for a unified federal approach to cybersecurity breed the cyber equivalent of a superbug. Instead of one software platform with a preferred antiviral vendor, the federal government might do better to emulate Heinz's 57 varieties.

Another fallacy Haseltine sees in the federal approach to cybersecurity is an unshakable faith in "airgapping" computers—the belief that a computer system that is not connected to any other computer or to the Internet is safe. If evolution teaches us anything, it is that intelligent systems like to network.

Of course no computer is going to extend its own cable and plug itself in. But a computer doesn't have to network itself, because every computer comes complete with a parasite called a human, a creature with an irrepressible desire to network.

Federal chief technology officers design such airgapped systems for as many as 100,000 users, acting as if it is reasonable to believe that each individual will always act as he is supposed to act. If just one human inserts a stick drive into one computer, however, the entire plan is instantly compromised. With large numbers of people, Haseltine asks, how reasonable is it to suppose that not one of them will insert that drive? Such plans, Haseltine says, are "very precise and have zero validity."

In comparing natural laws from biology and physics to try to unearth the hidden principles of the digital world, Haseltine says that we need to also consider "unnatural law" (meaning natural laws of the cyberworld we do not yet fully understand). Dr. Haseltine borrows a phrase that originated in social planning circles to call the challenge of cybersecurity a "wicked problem," one that is difficult to solve because of incomplete, contradictory, and changing boundaries that are hard to recognize. Afghanistan is a wicked problem, as are health care and global warming. Cybersecurity is a wicked problem par excellence. What can we do when we know enough to let go of the Jesus bar?

In lacking a clear definition of the laws that govern the cyberworld, we are obliged to begin to solve the problem in order to discover what the problem is.

The best way to do that? Haseltine says, "Go on the offense." Take the fight to the hackers. Disrupt their systems, find their assets, rock their world. It is only when we acquire the agility and exploitative capabilities of the world's legions of hackers—some sponsored by malevolent states, some by gangsters, some by Mom's cooking—that we will have a fighting chance.

Cyber theorists often borrow from their intellectual predecessors in the defense community, applying the well-worn theories of nuclear deterrence to this new world. This, Kellermann believes, is a mistake.

"This is not nuclear destruction, there is no endgame, there is no second or third strike," he says, taking issue with a famous prediction of former White House cyber chief Richard Clarke, who predicted that a digital "Pearl Harbor" could decimate the country in fifteen minutes.

"The enemy doesn't want to conduct a cyber Pearl Harbor," Kellermann says. "In his [Clarke's] evangelism of this issue in coining that term, he made everyone focus on denial of service and disruption of service as the number one dangerous thing that could happen. And it's not. Your enemy would rather take you over, essentially take over your nervous system and turn you into their puppet . . . The name of the game is colonization."

Kellermann sees us less like the U.S. Navy on the morning of December 7, 1941, and more like the Maya awaiting the conquistadors. "How are we actually going to create shared risk and elevate and create the level of discomfort not just technologically but through hard and soft power of those adversaries who seek to colonize us in cyberspace?" Kellermann says. "How do you incentivize the developing world, most of which doesn't see cybercrime as illegal, away from institutionalizing the problem of organized hacking?"

Kellermann envisions a public policy response with three legs.

Nation-states that institutionalize cyberattack and employ nonstate actors as proxies constitute one leg. Kellermann would directly tie foreign assistance through the World Bank, USAID, and IMF to incentivize state actors to change behavior.

Second, Kellermann would "increase the level of discomfort" for alternative payment channels that launder the funds. "The reality is that the money is not moving through the financial sector," he says. "It is moving through these alternative payment channels. I am not going to name them in this interview, because I don't want to be a dead man walking when you print this book. I will tell you that there are more than two hundred of these alternative payment channels out there."

He praises PayPal for having a standard of care and due diligence that sets a global standard. "If everyone were to act like PayPal, we wouldn't have this monstrosity of a trillion-dollar shadow economy," he says.

The third leg of his approach would be to address the larger hosting economy, the server farms, which lack standards of due diligence and regulation. "They are hosting the child porn, the hacker services, the malware, the stolen financial credentials, the stolen national secrets," he says. "And if you don't tackle these three legs through soft and hard power, then you don't stand a chance of dealing with this issue. You are never going to build a Fortress America in cyberspace unless you create a brand-new protocol."

He agrees with Haseltine that offensive measures are needed. "It is functionally important that we begin to appreciate that nation-state adversaries are in our systems to stay, and that being the case, if they are in your capital, then you need to build a better dungeon, and create better torture equipment in that dungeon."

> Compare the science of cybersecurity today to the U.S. space program, and it is clear we are not yet even in the Project Mercury phase.

Takeaway—Basic Protection

Given the vulnerability of computers, you might be tempted to throw your hands in the air in helpless frustration. That is an understandable response, one that many adopt. But that is the wrong response.

It is possible, bordering on likely, that criminals will enlist the unused capacity of your computer to mount botnet attacks. This is creepy, but it need not shut you down. Every computer is wide open to hacking. But in every herd, there are some cagey animals that are less vulnerable than others.

Or think of it in terms of home security. For your home and family, you already do the logical things necessary to protect them. You might reinforce windows and doors. You might install sophisticated locks and burglar, fire, and smoke alarms. You might time lights to go on and off at different nights and different days. You might ask neighbors to watch or check your house when you are traveling. Some have a dog or an automated dog-barker so people approaching your home will take heed.

None of these measures could possibly keep a world-class cat burglar from getting into your house. But these measures work well enough to discourage the greater threat—that you will be targeted by the garden-variety house burglar. In a similar way, everyone should adopt the full measure of practices and systems available to discourage the likely attack.

- Defend your personal and small business computers with the latest version of three layers of defense—the best firewall, the best antivirus, and the best antispyware software products. Evaluate leaders like Symantec and McAfee. Microsoft Security Essentials is one of the best free antivirus softwares. If you are a more sophisticated user and a more likely target, however, you might use quality but lesser known security products, since "firewall killers" are most frequently built for the most popular programs.
- Set your software security settings to automatic update.
- Keep up with automatic updates to keep your software and web browsers current.
- If you have a wireless connection at home, reset the router password with your passcode, a robust series of numbers, letters, and ASCII code (the funky little symbols on your keyboard). Enable wireless encryption so you won't be an open store to your neighbors and anyone passing by on the street.
- You cannot secure a home wireless network. If this is intolerable, then go with a hardwire. But if you do use a router, guard it with that elaborate passcode to make it more secure.

A good way to set a passcode is to hark back to a favorite childhood memory, perhaps a beach vacation, that not even someone who knows you would necessarily think of—and certainly not something anyone who studies you from afar could discover. If, for example, you still relish the memory of the day your parents took you to, say, Rehoboth Beach, your passcode might be:

R#h@b@thB#@ch!

All you have to do is remember to capitalize the "R" and the second "B," replace the "o's" and "a" with an ampersand, and the "e's" with hash marks, and end it with an exclamation point, then add in numbers—but not your birthday or that of anyone in your family. Such a passcode is not unbreakable. But it would be enough work to discourage all but the most sophisticated hacker.

Once you've created your passcodes, share them only with your spouse—and then only if you are reasonably certain that you are not headed to divorce court.

- Configure your webmail account—Yahoo! Hotmail, Google—to use "https" (the "s" is for "secure") instead of "http." Shop on https websites, and look for the lock icon in your browser frame. You might consider the Electronic Frontier Foundation's "HTTPS Everywhere" plug-in. It forces websites wherever possible to use the https standard.
- If you use an e-mail client, configure the client to use "SSL" and "TLS," cryptographic protocols, according to the vendor recommendations.
- Study and select the most appropriate privacy settings when you use social networks services like Facebook. Be cautious. Don't be like the vast majority of people who automatically accept "friend" requests from beautiful strangers.
- Never click on an e-mail attachment or link without knowing or verifying the source.
- Sensitive business and credit card transactions must never be made on public computers or on a public Wi-Fi networks. Turn off your Wi-Fi when you are not using it. Bluetooth security is pretty strong, but to avoid getting "bluesnarfed," use your device's "hidden" mode instead of leaving it "discoverable."
- Never open an e-mail offering you a solution to a new "monster virus." That is likely the monster itself. Go straight to your preferred vendor.
- If you still use a desktop with a dedicated hardline, you might unplug the line to the Internet when not in use. If your house has Wi-Fi, you might want to that off when not in use.
- To stay current, go to the "Alerts and Security Tips" section of U.S.-CERT, the United States Computer Emergency Readiness Team.

Postscript: The Most Unpredictable Factor

In the last minutes of the twentieth century, a group of U.S. generals assembled deep in the headquarters in the Cheyenne Mountain Complex in Colorado Springs. They sipped coffee and nervously watched the second hand turn on the clock. An air of quiet tension rose until midnight. At the stroke of the new year, the generals anxiously sprang into action, contacting the commanders of the prime strategic systems of the United States.

One of the authors was briefed on this incident, in which the issue at hand was Y2K. There was a fear among the brass and military CIOs that software, computers, and information systems used in military operations, which like their civilian counterparts were not built to accommodate date changes to the twenty-first century, would go haywire.

Patches were installed, but it was far from certain how well they would work. Insiders say that the greatest source of worry was of course how the transition might affect strategic systems.

Even since the fall of the Soviet Union, Moscow and the United States had on several occasions been spooked by bad data from satellites, radars, and computer systems. The world had come close to nuclear war before because of computer misinterpretations of solar reflection, a Norwegian scientific rocket, and a "go-to-war" missile test tape that was inadvertently injected into the main operating systems.[55]

Could Y2K cause a glitch that would cause a strategic miscalculation by either power? Russia dispatched military and political leaders to sit next to their American counterparts inside the Cheyenne Mountain complex, a sure sign of how serious the issue was. When it was clear that nothing significant would happen, they joined their American colleagues in breathing a sigh of relief. Everyone relaxed as morning came.

Then came some Y2K surprises no one had envisioned. At the stroke of midnight, Russian President Boris Yeltsin stepped down, to be replaced by Vladimir Putin—a stark surprise for the generals. Not long after, U.S. spy satellites caught the unmistakable glint of rocket engines igniting in the Russian interior. Russia was launching missiles.

Was Y2K causing accidental launches? Or had Putin inaugurated his administration by launching World War III?

Once it was determined that the glints were from intermediate-range missiles, could they represent an attack on U.S. forward-deployed bases in the Middle East? A retired military officer one of the authors spoke to was there in the Cheyenne Mountain control room. He recalls, "We had done everything technically right. And still we had a moment of surprise."

Sensors determined that these missiles were actually tactical SCUDS, heading on a trajectory against Moscow's opponents in Chechnya and not against U.S. forces in the Middle East, Mediterranean, or Europe. The Russians present soon assured their American colleagues that these missiles were not launched because of any Y2K-related computer glitch.

"Still, for a few tense moments, we knew what it felt like to be on the brink," the retired officer says.

> The greatest surprises will always come from humans, not from technology.

10:// Swimming in the Silicon Sea

> We have to abandon the idea that schooling is something restricted to youth. How can it be, in a world where half the things a man knows at 20 are no longer true at 40—and half the things he knows at 40 hadn't been discovered when he was 20?
>
> **—Arthur C. Clarke**

INFORMATION TECHNOLOGY AMPLIFIES and globally distributes every human want, answer, whim, and foible. As it changes in the near few years, how might technology change us? How might it reshape society? How will technology affect our concerns about security, reputation, and privacy? Above all, what fresh challenges will we be grappling with in a few years that will be as unexpected as those we are grappling with now?

We should first take a step back and assess the changing technology and media landscape. It is actually more of a combat space, one in which Facebook and Google struggle for dominance, cyber insecurity will grow, reputational wars will open up in the new space of combat marketing, and reformers will look more and more to the best practices of the commercial world for answers.

The Window and the Mirror

Google is our great window on the world. Facebook is the mirror in which humanity sees its reflection. These are two distinct models of the Internet, and like two robust plants in the same pot, they are slowly trying to strangle each other.

The insight of Google was revolutionary—the notion that a page's value is determined by how many inbound links there are to that page. In contrast, Facebook is working to deliver search results based on a different proxy for popularity, on what you and your friends have liked in the past. In 2011, the window and the mirror are starting to look a little more alike. Google Social Search lets you see what your friends "like." Googlet is a full rejoinder to Facebook, one that allows for more discrete seperation of friends by categories. Facebook Connect's aggressive promotion is a breach of the walled garden; and some social media watchers are predicting Facebook will open up more of its data to search indexes.

They still remain two fundamentally different ways of approaching the world.

Google is the great democratic leveler that incentivizes the breaking down of all walls so that everyone and everything can be found. This is a transformative technology, though it might be undone to a degree by the proliferation of apps that bypass traditional search to go straight to given transactions.

Facebook, meanwhile, chips away at Google's ideal of unlimited access, threatening to break up the Internet into archipelagos of social groups. Increasingly, we will be tempted to e-mail, exchange videos, buy and sell, make friends, and set up events on Facebook through the "social graph," or nodes of our friends, their recommendations, and shared experiences online without ever venturing out into the wider world.

"Facebook, Tumblr, Twitter give you kind of a sense of what it's going to be like," says Ned Desmond, who has devised strategies and built websites for some of the world's largest media companies. "It's going to be more like the world of Instant Messaging when it comes to connections between people than it is going to be like the world of conventional publishing.

"Google is an older model, which is more intuitive to most of us, at least for my generation, the notion that there is content out there, I can type in some keywords, and I can with that retrieve the content that I'm looking for," Desmond says. "Facebook is not content specific, though it can include content. It has to do more with finding things not through keywords but through frames of reference that are fundamentally about people." And about what they *like.*

How effectively will digital attacks work in the future? In a Google world, an anonymous digital assassin can post an assertion about an individual, product, or company. It seems to arise out of nowhere and hang in cyberspace without any context. In a Facebook world, "an attack on you arising out of nowhere that has no relevance to the established social graph and activity patterns would make it far more suspect," Desmond says. It is the difference between being attacked on the street or attacked in your home, surrounded by twenty of your best friends.

When it comes to search, however, if all searches are somehow suggested by our "social graph," we might stand to lose something valuable—the serendipitous adventure that random web surfing can be.

In a typical surf, for example, you might look for background on the 2010 movie *Inception,* and get caught up in one of its stars, Ellen Page. Where did this wisecracking bright-eyed wonder come from? Then you learn that her character, Ariadne, is named after the character in Greek myth who helped Theseus kill the Minotaur, which leads you to delve into ancient Cretan civilization, something you had always kind of known about, but not much. This of course leads you to thinking about Crete as a good vacation destination. Except that the blogs advise you that the Cyclades or even the Turkish coast may be better for what you're looking for. So you set out to learn more about the making of *Inception* and you wind up booking a summer beach vacation in Ephesus.

Google is like that. You start out looking for one thing and you wind up in a completely different universe of ideas and activities. The sheer randomness of it tends, if you are curious, to fill in gaps in your knowledge.

Before the Internet, such strolls through the informational universe occurred only in libraries and reading rooms, restrained by time and space. In the window world of Google, every fact is Kevin Bacon, ready to skip a few degrees of separation to any other fact.

In a Facebook world, we run the risk of being narrowed by the "likes" of our self-chosen friends.

Vivid, Mobile, Networked, and Smart

Like compound interest, which transforms pennies into fortunes, the exponential growth in computing power continues to create media that promise to be millions of times more powerful than anything we enjoy today. The most obvious shift will be the way in which technology becomes ever more vivid. The vibrant images on today's HDTV sink into the brain in a way that the ghostly shadows of the black-and-white images of the first Philcos or even the flat, pixilated color of conventional television never did. With 3-D without goggles and "telepresence" around the corner, we are fast approaching a time when the term "virtual reality" will no longer be an exaggeration.

While the media experience becomes richer and more tactile, many of the most disruptive technologies will sneak up on us. Take, for example, Bell Labs's Picturephone that dazzled millions at the 1964 World's Fair in New York but never took hold.

Then suddenly, when the idea of a videophone seemed like a relic of a World of the Future exhibit, Skype subversively infiltrated our laptops. Many new technologies will creep in like Skype, especially as television fully converges with the Internet.

Television itself, as with radio and cinema and much of the old media, will not disappear. It will just get subsumed. Those who want to watch a football game or to enjoy the big-screen experience of *Lawrence of Arabia* will turn to the large screen format of something that looks like TV. Those who want to watch *30 Rock* will go to the small screen of a mobile device. "Programming will flow to where it fits in terms of how people use it, and of course the size of the screen and the quality of the resolution they need to enjoy it," says Desmond. "It will be who you are, what stage of life you are at, what is the nature of the programming, just call it down and watch it on the relevant device."[1]

Whatever the device you are using, while you watch *30 Rock* you will be able to buy Tina Fey's scarf or Alec Baldwin's tie, or search for the bio of that squirrely character actor whose name you can't quite remember.

Mobile devices, of course, will be smaller, thinner, faster, and less expensive, with stronger batteries. Dumb appliances will be smarter and networked, and most content will be "device agnostic."

Some of our devices—and perhaps our house and car—will acquire simulated human voices. And these won't be the monotone of automatons like your GPS. Machines of the near future will cut through the ambiguity of human speech to converse with us in a way that will finally meet the requirements of the Turing test—that is to say, will be indistinguishable from a human being. The rub may be, as Jaron Lanier wrote in his master polemic, *You Are Not a Gadget,* that the Turing test may cut both ways. "You can't tell if a machine has gotten smarter or if you've just lowered your own standards of intelligence to such a degree that the machine seems smart."[2]

New, New Media

The Twitter mode of bite-sized chews is going to drive old media leaders like *The Wall Street Journal, Bloomberg Businessweek,* and many others toward punchier and shorter stories. Already the web-based sites of the major TV networks break up the nightly news and other programs into similarly bite-sized pieces, as shows formatted to the half-hour and hour slots are disaggregated into YouTube-like clips. Stories lose clear boundaries as they are expanded by multiple links to other sources, perspectives, and visual media. Our shorter attention span will be well served by media, although sites will be able to back up their reporting with unprecedented depth of written, video, and audio material that once would have been edited out and lost to posterity.

Another trend will be the blurring of media categories. If you look at nytimes.com or abcnews.com or your local TV, radio, and newspaper websites, you will see in each case a combination of video, downloads, slide shows, and text. As these media channels become more and more distant from their physical origins, the distinction between a newspaper, a radio show, and a television show—already blurred—will be more a matter of emphasis and legacy.

Social media will continue to erode the ability of columnists and critics to act as the gatekeepers of politics and culture. Already, celebrities and movie stars find more value in their Facebook and Twitter followings than in the obligatory and more dangerous round of interviews with journalists. There will always be a latent demand for quality and exclusiveness. So Rotten Tomatoes aggregates critics' judgments in its Tomatometer. But the critic Hollywood cares about most is the judgment of the crowd in Rotten Tomatoes' Audience meter.

Claire McCaskill, a Democrat from Missouri, is still a relative newcomer to the U.S. Senate. But she has built up a hugely influential following among the press and blogging community with her frequent, pithy tweets. Chris Christie, the iconoclastic Republican governor of New Jersey, has perfected the art of the verbal slapdown with what amounts to his YouTube channel. Barack Obama is the first politician to fully utilize the Internet to organize and fund-raise. Sarah Palin will be remembered as the first politician to brand her social media outlets as if she were a social media Oprah. And, of course, Representative

Anthony Weiner of New York will forever be remembered as an opposite example of a politician who let a Twitter controversy wreck his image and turn him into an object of ridicule.

While new media creates dedicated channels for people and movements, the traditional media—led by Rupert Murdoch's paywalled *Wall Street Journal* and iPad-enabled *The Daily*—will be in a slugfest against Google's drive to live out the dictum of Stewart Brand, of *Whole Earth Catalog* fame, that "information wants to be free."

Actually, Brand said at the first convention of hackers (meaning programmers) in the decidedly non-Orwellian year of 1984: "On the one hand information wants to be expensive, because it's so valuable. The right information in the right place just changes your life. On the other hand, information wants to be free, because the cost of getting it out is getting lower and lower all the time. So you have these two fighting against each other."[3]

Brand's formulation will define the polarities of the media wars of the second decade of the twenty-first century. And while the giants slug it out in this war, pygmies will conquer. Consider *The Cove*, which won Best Documentary Feature at the 2010 Academy Awards. It was an amateur effort led in part by Ric O'Barry, Flipper's trainer, to expose the slaughter of dolphins that turned an idyllic cove next to a Japanese village blood red. It was directed by a former *National Geographic* photographer, Louis Psihoyos. What is telling about *The Cove* is that the dolphin movement was a poor stepchild of the mainstream antiwhaling efforts of Greenpeace. It had little formal publicity and no celebrity endorsement or support.

The Cove was funded by a dotcom billionaire, a documentary filmmaker, and O'Barry, with help from experts once with Industrial Light and Magic to create rock sculptures to hide HD cameras that the crew seeded around the cove, *Mission: Impossible* style.[4] *The Cove* went viral when Facebook users started replacing their photo with the movie poster, with O'Barry giving Skype webinars from Japan. This happened without all the traditional celebrity-driven heft of the mainstream environmental movement.

"The Japanese didn't really know what hit them when this film came out and went viral," James Lee says. "Sure, they were used to American reporters coming over, the odd celebrity, the antiwhaling stuff, and the

Greenpeace guys. They were used to that. They weren't used to this international wave of people cutting, pasting, sharing, tagging, liking, and promoting this film."[5]

From Michael Moore to James O'Keefe's phony Muslim donor sting of NPR, documentaries and exposés from small, ideologically driven groups, marketed by social media, will increasingly edge out even edgy organizations such as Greenpeace, MoveOn.org, and the Tea Party. The edgiest of all, in the mode of the Yes Men and BPGlobalPR, will wrap their *Saturday Night Live*–style webisodes against corporate targets under the banner of political commentary and satire, bulletproofing themselves for now under the First Amendment. Imitators will proliferate.

Similar attacks could easily become viral political ads in corporate politics as "access to the proxy" campaigns heat up. Expect to also see a raft of "Lonely Girl"–style phony testimonials and mashed-up imagery to fill up the screens of 4G mobile devices.

As satirists and documentary filmmakers explore ways to mau-mau targeted institutions, trial lawyers will be working to erode Section 230 protections of interactive computer services providers. All they need is an opening. Internet companies and foundations may give it to them.

The leaders of Google acted decently but perhaps unwisely when they briefly moved against the offensive Michelle Obama image, citing malware concerns.[6] Online services are going to be increasingly challenged by other cases that cry out for correction. What will they do?

An act of favoritism or even compassion by Google or Wikipedia as well as Internet service providers could open a loophole through which a runaway jury could drive a Mack truck to treat these technology platforms as content providers.

We should at the least expect renewed assaults on Section 230 protections by lawsuits trying to piggyback off discrimination and copyright law.

The Coming Cyber Crisis

As we become more networked, the nodes and networks themselves will become ever more insecure. "At least in the short term—three years to five years—hacking is going to get easier," Yakutis says. "The number of organizations that have the funding to put in true intrusion detection systems and implement them at the level at they are intended to be used, with the correct monitoring, the correct auditing, the correct penetration testing, are very few."[7]

Identity theft will remain rampant. You can expect the steady boil of personal and business cyber insecurity to continue. Governments and large and small businesses will be assaulted by the wholesale theft and compromise of secrets by groups and their mirror sites that will be far more shadowy than WikiLeaks.

"The thing that I don't think the world has fully comprehended that it is not just the Citibanks that will be attacked," says Rich Daly, chief executive of the giant technology services firm Broadridge Financial. "It's going to be the guy selling gazebo parts by mail order, patients' records—you name it, that will be vulnerable."[8]

We may or may not see Richard Clarke's predicted full-scale cyber 9/11, but there will almost certainly be such attempts at mass mayhem. Some Stuxnet-like cyberattacks will go physical, with the attempt to inflict injury and death, either as a result of a cyberattack in tandem with a terrorist attack or the skillful hacking and sabotage of a critical part of our national infrastructure.

Cyberattacks, stolen data, and the seven swords of digital assassination will lead to ever more persistent cries for authentication—so that only the right people can access the right facility or data, and that those who make accusations on the Internet have to stand by them with their real identities. As the crisis deepens, many will turn to biometrics as the answer—retinal scans, voiceprints, thumbprints.

Biometrics, however, is probably at best a stopgap solution. Why? Biometrics ultimately reduces physical characteristics to algorithms. And such algorithms, once stored, can be reproduced infinitely at will. The first company that maintains a database of retinal scans for its customers is going to be a prime target for the world's best hackers.

How bad will cyber insecurity become? Having no history to turn to, we look to our imagination and science fiction for lessons for the future, where many of the consequences of cyberwars have already been explored. In the reimagined TV series *Battlestar Galactica,* the only humans who survived a combined physical and digital attack by cyborgs were stationed on a decommissioned starship that was being turned into a museum. The ship was the only one in the fleet to survive because its systems had never been integrated into the fleet's network.[9]

More and more real-world institutions are going to be tempted to become Battlestar Galacticas. Some are going to forgo the advantages of the digital age in order to be more secure. There will be more closed loops, more virtual private networks, more walled gardens.

In short, the digital city of the future will still have freeways, but with more guards and gated communities. A few eccentrics will try, as much as possible, to live off the grid altogether.

The Death of Privacy . . .

At the end of his life, the great science-fiction writer Arthur C. Clarke collaborated with author Stephen Baxter to write a novel, *The Light of Other Days.*[10] It was not a masterpiece. The characters are a bit thin and the plot is stuffed with filler scenes that don't amount to much. None of this keeps the book from being a great read, because the book's premise is startling.

In this futuristic novel, scientists develop an invisible microscopic "wormhole camera" that allows them to see anything happening anywhere on Earth. Over time, the technology becomes as cheap and commoditized as cell phones. Soon anyone can open a wormhole to learn what anyone else is doing.

The result is the WikiLeaks vision taken to the extreme, the utter and immediate loss of all privacy, the figurative dropping of all walls. There is no discussion inside the White House, CIA, or any other governmental or corporate entity in the world that cannot be seen and overheard by millions of people. There is no love affair, no payoff or bribe, no minor vice, that can be performed without instant discovery and public observation.

After a number of years, the loss of privacy begins to alter the essence of what it means to be human. Some people walk around in the nude and shamelessly perform every bodily function imaginable in public. Others who once had disgraceful secrets to protect carry on as they did before, only now without apology or shame. But many people conform to the standards of the society that is watching them, slavishly mugging for the cameras and making anodyne statements about virtue. In this novel, Robin Williams's Little Snitch finally makes the full transition to becoming Big Brother.

While a right to privacy is found nowhere explicitly in our Constitution, most Americans feel they have one. A famous 1890 *Harvard Law*

Review article by Louis Brandeis and Samuel D. Warren enunciated this right to privacy, which is now seen today as a modern necessity. Arthur C. Clarke and Baxter showed us that the expectation of privacy is essential to being human. Without it, we would all go a little bit nuts.

And, as we have seen throughout these pages, that is exactly what is beginning to happen.

. . . And the Ascension of Anonymity

The strange fact of the Internet, however, is that while it strips away privacy from victims, it readily bestows anonymity on the attackers. Facebook Connect provides a partial answer by encouraging us to log on to third-party websites, mobile devices, and gaming systems with our Facebook identity. If this is a trend, if everyone actually did go without a mask on the Internet, would that really be a good thing?

Think of the unanimous decision by the U.S. Supreme Court in 1958 to prevent the State of Alabama from forcing the NAACP from revealing its membership list. Had the NAACP been forced to do so, individual members would have been subjected to state retribution, and the NAACP itself subjected to fines as an out-of-state ("foreign") corporation.

The court found a constitutional principle, related to free association, that allowed the NAACP to keep its membership list private. But the same principle invoked to protect the membership of the NAACP was also invoked to defend the confidentiality of another organization prominent in Alabama at that time—the members of the Ku Klux Klan (though the courts later upheld state laws unmasking them).[11]

Identification makes people take responsibility for their assertions and actions. But it would also be a victory for conformity and for those who would persecute whistle-blowers and the outspoken.

One proposal often bandied about is to make pseudonymity a social standard. The idea is that if users were encouraged to have one consistent virtual identity, they would still be more open than their analog selves, but they would have enough reputational equity in that secondary identity so that they would be more careful about what they post, an incrementally better standard.

If we could know who everyone was—or if they had a consistent pseudonym—then the crowd could regulate the digital conversation. This self-regulation is already a long-held practice in the commercial space. Many commercial sites shine a spotlight on reviewers who use their real names. Amazon and eBay were among the first companies to start to regulate the conversation, with Yelp recently having taken steps in this direction. Broadridge Financial is doing the same in the shareholder arena. Commercial companies now routinely give more weight to commentators with a history, people who had engaged in commerce, who dealt honestly at both ends of the transaction, whose posted commentary was fair and accurate, and who generated more results and more of a following.

Commercial space lets crowds regulate themselves. When people are malicious or obstreperous or have no history and therefore no standing to make sweeping pronouncements, the crowd drowns them out.

But how do we keep track of who's who in the vast Venetian ball of the greater Internet? How do we manage the fine balance between the protections of anonymity and the need to know who is making an accusation?

There might be a way to automate the cleaning up of digital assassinations by search engines. Steven J. Horowitz, while still at the Harvard Law School in 2007, proposed an interesting approach to search. His proposal "would require search engines to remove a web page from their indexes when an individual notifies them that the page contains defamatory content, while allowing those who post the content to respond with counter notices or other legal action," he wrote in the Yale Law Journal Online.[12]

Horowitz's plan might create reciprocity—the poster could maintain his accusation on search results, but only if he pulls off his mask and steps forward. This would neatly defuse many Google bombs while allowing the current regime of unfettered, free, and anonymous expression to reign on the message boards of the world.

Cass Sunstein, a regulatory czar in the Obama administration and a faculty member at the Harvard Law School, suggests a right to "take down" notices of defamatory material modeled after the Digital Millennium Copyright Act. "It is true that this approach might be burdensome," he acknowledges.[13] In fact, if any such claim would have to be judged and adjudicated, it might require something that not even Google could afford—an army of lawyers the size of India.

Horowitz, while still a student, seems to have the better understanding of what can and cannot be done on the Internet. Unlike other, more chimerical schemes from hallowed legal scholars, Horowitz's proposal would not necessarily require millions of lawyers and millions more for lawyers. In fact, his scheme might be automated.

Social Media Upheaval

What happens to people and society in the next few years?

Some will begin to suffer from "digital depression" caused by "social comparison" when they see on Facebook where the Joneses went for vacation. More dangerous will be the addictive nature of digital activity—call it "virtual confusion"—when users decompress from the vivid, enhanced, exciting virtual worlds into the glum real world of jobs, taxes, and dateless weekends. Like the guide in Mombasa says in *Inception,* the elderly men go to a opium-den-like dream room not to sleep, but to be waked up. "The dream has become their reality."

The troll phenomenon—whether the funeral rants of the Westboro Baptist Church or the hipper precincts of Internet's trolldom—will continue to invade our screens. Jokes about the deaths of children and racist-misogynistic-homophobic rants will continue to be explained by troll apologists as Socratic ironies meant to point to deeper truths, though they never get around to expressing what these deeper truths truly are. One can only hope that the more extreme members of the troll community will one day see their reflections in the Westboro Baptist Church and realize they are at that segment of the ideological wheel where libertarianism touches anarchy and anarchy gives way to fascism.

In the midst of all these challenges, we must struggle to keep in mind that the positives of digital technology will continue to outweigh the negatives. We must never lose sight of the remarkable age of discovery before us.

Scholars of the humanities, for example, are finding ways to use digital technology to map collaborations across the history of jazz. Stanford and Oxford scholars are "Mapping the Republic of Letters" between Voltaire and other eighteenth-century figures to graph the flow of Enlightenment ideas.[14]

Reverend Carol Howard Merritt sees "genius constellations" of new media infused with the intellectual enthusiasm of Parisian cafés in the twenties and the artistic energy of the Harlem Renaissance. In her online chats with other progressive ministers, she says, "There is definitely a kind of electricity that is there that isn't there at regular mainline denominations."[15]

In the political sphere, the limits of social media to organize will be tested. Some have argued that social media breeds weak links—affinity groups centered around soccer or collectibles or some other fascination—but lacks the leadership and resources to effect significant social change. The Egyptian man who named his firstborn daughter Facebook—after the leaderless uprising that overthrew Hosni Mubarak—is a living rebuke to the weak-links argument.[16] It will remain to be seen, however, how effective social media will be in managing the aftermath and the myriad disappointments that will follow revolutionary euphoria.

For business, social media's scale and reach will continue to level the playing field between small and large enterprises, in which boots on the ground will not be nearly important as strategy and the ability to influence markets through new media.

The power of wikis to bring crowd wisdom to tasks will be more fully expressed by new technologies. In institutions of all kinds, chief information officers will become more deeply involved in netcentric management, encouraging workers at all levels of the hierarchy to create spontaneous teams by task.

Deloitte and Booz Allen Hamilton are pioneering social networks that help managers quickly find information inside the institutional human memory. The authors learned of at least one Marine Corps general who is finding that classified blogs are a more efficient way to get a quick answer to his queries than through the traditional military hierarchy.

Technology and the Internet will foment a renaissance of rural communities. High incomes can be accessed by the talented and the educated in less expensive and more wholesome environments. With so many retirees financially unprepared for retirement, many will live on their Social Security payments in scenic places like rural Colorado, or exotic and inexpensive locales like Panama and Thailand, while using vivid online connections to stay close to family and grandkids, perhaps by Skype HD 3D.

Digital Alienation, Conformity, and Conditional Truth

For Ned Desmond, the big question about the near future of social media is "what does it mean to be in real-time contact with so many more people?" He sees especially profound implications in the melding of mobility and constant contact through social media. For younger people born into this way of life, "they have their phones out all the time, and it's not even that they're text-messaging," Desmond says. "They're checking a lot of different things—they're checking posts, organizing to go do things as a group, and when doing things as a group they still have got their phones out, organizing as a group to do things later.

"It's quite impressive, this sort of organization on the fly, mobile computing linked up with Facebook," Desmond continues. "This combination of mobile and social in real time has got to be one of the most profound social developments in human history. I don't know what comes of it, but the behavior by itself is so objectively immense that it can't be innocuous."

Desmond worries that not all of the implications will be healthy. "When you are reporting on everything about yourself, pretty much in real time, and you're organizing for the next crowd in real time . . . there is a certain level of thought that appears to go completely missing," he says. Just as obsessively taking photos of your vacation can put you at a distance from your own vacation, can the full-time tracking, reporting, and comparing of real-time experience alienate you from your own life?

Desmond also worries about digital technology enforcing conformity. He once lived in Japan, where he noted that the ready adoption of mobile apps seems to make it easier for individuals to navigate in Japan's conformist culture. "I can see this same conformity being driven through my kids' lives, whether there's a group that wants to do something and you've got to go along with the group. Because you're either in the group or out of the group—and if you're out of the group, who knows what they might be saying about you?" he concludes.

The strikes of silent slashers, evil clones, and assassins and attackers will be softened by friends coming to one's defense. But will digital attacks present the human brain with a task we are not evolved to manage:

the dilemma of living with conditional truth about people, brands, and businesses?

Internet lies are global and lasting. Will the vividness of online media make lies sink in? And how easily will we be able to dismiss these images and statements when the images are utterly realistic and follow us room to room in full motion 3-D, with statements made to us in the calm, cultivated voice of our house computer?

Skepticism is one thing. To half believe something is another. Will a coming age of conditional truth force us to adopt a kind of Schrödinger's cat attitude toward everything and everyone?

Combat Marketing

"It's always easier to tear something down than to defend it," James Lee says. "But eventually, the defenders catch up." He likens the future of reputation management to the "virus wars" between garden-variety black hats and security companies like Symantec and McAfee. Over a long period of disruption, the security companies gained enough experience to counter ordinary viruses. The struggle soon settled into the equivalent of trench warfare, where defenders and hackers "just lob stuff at one another periodically, but there is no real movement. Everyone is stuck in the Argonne forest, nothing changes."

Now we are fighting the "reputation war," Lee says, and this war is less like the stalemate of World War I than like the early phase of World War II when the Germans blasted through Poland. And make no mistake, in Lee's metaphor, most of us are Poland.

The battle space is not completely without organized resistance. Reputation.com (Reputation Defender's new name) is a first generation company that counters bad information on the Internet. While reputation companies evolve, corporations will turn to marketing and consulting firms that promise not only to help their brand but to damage the other company's brand without fingerprints. It is easy to foresee the emergence of combat marketing companies, and a technological arms race between these combat marketers and a slew of reputation management firms that will attempt to do for reputation management what Symantec and McAfee do in security.

Lee imagines boutique firms that will surreptitiously make and post viral videos that put their clients' competitors in a very bad light. "In the digital reputation arena, you will see companies out there trashing products, trashing people, trashing candidates," he says. "You're going to see similar companies out there trying to set the record straight or erase those comments, or manage that process, or verify who is saying those things."

Much of the business of reputation defense today involves laborious keyword searching, quick evaluation of difficult context, and the penetrating of paywalls and other barriers to get at and counter all the trash on message boards with positive content. It is a complex process requiring contextual judgment that cannot yet be fully automated. "The company that comes up with a way to automate either destroying someone's reputation online or defending and resurrecting their reputation online is the one that is going to win that battle," Lee says. "The automation and the 24/7 ability to do it without human intervention is what separates a company's ability to be successful in this arena—just as it has in the virus wars."

The practices of consumer companies, which pay the highest dollar per user for content and cognitive data mining, are beginning to migrate to the less profitable areas of politics, public affairs, and ideological nonprofits. Witness the successful use of RapLeaf data in that recent California initiative campaign.

In reputational attacks, businesses will be the most frequent targets. "Companies can defend themselves in a court of law," Lee says. "They can't always defend themselves in the court of public opinion. The court of public opinion is more devastating to the brand than what happens litigationwise."

In the meantime, Lee believes that the 2012 election will stimulate "a really unholy year on social media sites," forcing corporations, institutions, and individuals to get realistic about fighting back in the reputation wars. "One of the biggest challenges is for law firms to figure out how to get ready for this next wave of product and brand assassination."

Staying Human

Put off for a few more decades the question of whether or not computers will achieve sentience and what that would mean for humanity. There are already profound philosophical questions emerging now about how digital technology is affecting human nature, from shorter attention spans to a loss of critical thinking skills.

The yeastiest of all debates now under way was sparked by Jaron Lanier, whose *You Are Not a Gadget* raised the humanist objection that we are degrading our culture and allowing ourselves to be treated as "digital peasants," peripheral to the network instead of the reason for the network. In the Web 2.0, the "combination of hive mind and advertising has resulted in a new kind of social contract. The basic idea of this contract is that authors, journalists, musicians, and artists are encouraged to treat the fruits of their intellects and imaginations as fragments to be given without pay to the hive mind. . . . Culture is to become precisely nothing but advertising."[17] When everyone can publish an e-book or offer a song for free, the web pries "culture away from capitalism while the rest of life is still capitalistic," turning culture into a slum.[18]

And in Facebook, Lanier sees us straining to live within trite boxes devised for us by a Harvard sophomore. In the world of the mirror, connections matter more than the content. The result, he says, is the trivialization of culture.

Novelist Zadie Smith, in a tart *New York Review of Books* essay on Lanier's ideas and the movie *The Social Network,* worries about the cultural impact of Facebook. "When a human being becomes a set of data on a website like Facebook, he or she is reduced," Smith writes. "Everything shrinks. Individual character. Friendships. Language. Sensibility. In a way it's a transcendent experience: we lose our bodies, our messy feelings, our desires, our fears. It reminds me that those of us who turn in disgust from what we consider an overinflated liberal-bourgeois sense of self should be careful what we wish for: our denuded networked selves don't look more free, they just look more owned."[19]

Writer Alexis Madrigal pushed back in *The Atlantic*: "But we will never live on the Internet in the way we lived those other places. Let's not reify our online meanderings. The angst of a body slowly dying doesn't go away no matter how many times you type something into a box and then hit return. And that is a good thing. Smith wants to say, 'You are who you appear to be on Facebook.' But who believes that of themselves or anyone else? She makes the drastic overstatement only to serve as her grounds for outright rejection of the service."[20] Madrigal ends the piece with a digital snapshot of cute farm animals sent to him by his girlfriend. The snapshot made him think of *her*—the hands that took the picture, the woman behind the camera.

Our own take is that Facebook and the wider Internet so far seem to move us in both directions. We confess to exchanging platitudes on web-based platforms that, if spoken, would mortify a used-car salesman, as well as clicking on our share of videos of singing dogs and laughing babies.

But we have also heard some of the best poetry, seen environmental images of rare and unearthly beauty, and profited from video posts of some of the most thought-provoking material we have ever encountered shared with us by e-mail and by Facebook friends.

Another debate will be about how the Internet defines deviancy down. How many of the 75 million monthly visitors to porn sites would have ventured into an adult bookstore a generation before? Or how many of the millions who access adult dating sites would have so readily sought sex with strangers?[21]

And with file sharing, one doesn't have to be a hacker to break the eighth commandment (this is stealing, in case you've forgotten). In the days before broadband, consumers turned to file-sharing services that allowed them to get faster downloads, depending on how much music they themselves shared with the network. Given this incentive to stuff the database, many people—who would never dream of lifting a CD from an old-fashioned record store—sought to increase their download speeds by stuffing the system with pirated music.

Finally, how many of us would have so readily, on a daily basis, compromised our privacy twenty years ago as easily and as often as we do now with virtually every free service and platform that we use?

The trade-offs are real, the outcomes unclear. The debates will rage on.

Outsourcing Our Thinking

The average American is flooded by 100,000 words a day from all media—heard on television and radio, and encountered in print and the Internet.

In less than five days, the average American encounters more words than are in *War and Peace*.[22] Over a year, American households consume 3.6 zettabytes of information in all forms, from words to pixels (a zettabyte is equal to 100 billion copies of all the books in the Library of Congress).[23]

But more than information is coming our way. In very real sense, the computer now functions as a part of our brain, serving as our memory and even performing some of our thought processes for us. More than once, we have started to commit a fact, a timeline, a joke, a quote, or a riff to memory—only to stop and realize that it is no longer necessary. The Internet will remember it for us.*

Wiki research on any given topic also allows us to get to the core of a selected issue much faster than we could by ourselves. It is a kind of a SparkNotes for everything. By getting us to the essence of any issue quicker than we could on our own, the crowd is doing much of our thinking for us.

As a peripheral to human intelligence and a companion to our imagination, the computer is undoubtedly a boon. And just as we are tempted to celebrate this fact, we read a quote from Eric Schmidt, who with his gift for Orwellian statements, predicted that Google would one day know so much about us that it will be able to help us plan our lives. "I actually think most people don't want Google to answer their questions," Schmidt said. "They want Google to tell them what they should be doing next."[24]

If that statement fills you with "an intense and crushing feeling of religious terror," as Wally Weaver says in *Watchmen,* "don't be alarmed. That indicates only that you are still sane."[25]

The Final Takeaway—In a Machine World Be More Human

The greatest danger is that what now serves as a useful tool will become a crutch, and the crutch will atrophy those skills that make us most human.

Perhaps the most important response will be to properly educate the first generation of humans to use this technology from infancy. There is immense promise in more deeply integrating technology into teaching. Digital technology lets anyone climb the Ivy wall by downloading Yale's Open Courses lectures, whether it be historian Donald Kagan's descriptions of the Peloponnesian War or philosopher Shelly Kagan's meditations on death.

Software has the infinite patience to expose a student to every conceivable permutation of a math problem, to diagnose the cognitive roadblock, and then to lead that student to the best way to solve it.

* No sooner were these words written than researchers reported in *Science* that online databases do, in fact, affect the way people remember information—"the Google Effect."

Technology will be critical to restoring mastery of the subjects of science, technology, engineering, and mathematics that must be recaptured in the United States and other developed countries, who are failing to graduate sufficient numbers of engineers and scientists. But education must also include the emotional intelligence and social skills that arise from team sports and from team-based, team-building intellectual projects. Every student should be engaged in activities that teach them etiquette and respect for the knowledge of others. We don't want to raise a generation of social outcasts, painfully shy and morbidly obsessed, whose most developed aspects are their thumbs. Education must also include world history and literature to provide perspective for the seemingly new dilemmas of the technological age.

In short, we need the sort of education that will prepare people to function well in the spontaneously forming teams that netcentric organizations will require. They will need to be steeped in Postel's law for both the digital and analog worlds—to be conservative in what they do, liberal in what they accept from others.

In a technological world, the killer apps will belong to the well rounded, to the trustworthy, to those who can communicate well with customers or write a deft response on Yelp. The future will belong to the high touch.

Above all, people who understand human behavior, based on the age-old motives of money, sex, power, and envy, will still have the best grasp on things to come. This insight is needed as never before when our computers will have us relate to them by a familiar name. It will be a world of robots, androids, and intelligent homes and cars.

Will technology degrade our culture or liberate it? Will it devalue individuals or magnify us?

Will it foster so much mixed truth that we will lose our bearings? Or will it be the most powerful instrument in history for separating truth from untruth?

And when the day comes that the unseen computer behind our walls whispers a lie, will we have the presence of mind to keep our own counsel?

11:// The Seven Shields of Digital Assassination

> If you don't know where you are going, you'll wind up somewhere else.
>
> **—Yogi Berra**

THE SEVEN SHIELDS of digital assassination are, the means to prepare against the seven swords of digital assassination. The seventh shield culminates in a game plan on pages 235–36 that must be adapted and personalized.

Even if you are Internet savvy, the first half of this chapter, "Managing Reputation," imparts broad strategic guidance from the seven shields on how to build and maintain a defense. If you are not Internet savvy, the second section of this chapter, "Managing Digital Platforms," provides basic explanations for maintaining a positive image on Facebook, Yelp, Twitter, Wikipedia, and other technology platforms.

Social media is changing all the time. Best practices are always evolving. Visit our website, www.DigitalAssassinationBook.com, to stay current.

Managing Reputation

Think strategically about your defense. But first, what do we mean by "you"? You can be your business, your product, your brand, your celebrity. Even when you just means you, things are not quite so simple.

Appreciate the interaction between your two selves, the self that you know or think you know, and your online self, the public profile that you can shape but never fully own.

This distinction became clear when Yogi Berra sat next to one of the authors at a private dinner a few years ago. When asked about the body of oxymoronic sayings attributed to him, Yogi said with a world-weary sigh, "I'm not sure I said all of those things."

Yogi is a smart, engaging man, an accessible icon whose grit and maneuvers as a catcher, outfielder, and manager are baseball legend. Like all public figures, he has two personas. One is the character—in the ordinary sense of the word—of his private life, the Lawrence Peter "Yogi" Berra who strikes at the truth with a unique and colorful style of expression. The other is the public image of Yogi, which is sometimes that of a goofball whose obtuse sayings have a Zenlike quality.

Like Yogi, each of us has two personas. One is our actual self. The other is our public self, with varying degrees of agreement between the two.

In Yogi's case, his greatness established, he is free to regard the goofier part of his public profile with sardonic humor. For most of us, our digital self is our significant public profile—and how that profile is perceived becomes our personal brand. Perceptions about brand can determine the fate of careers, reputations, products, or businesses. That's why digital profiles are so important.

The difficult truth is that we will never own our digital profile—the Internet owns it. However, this profile is within our power to shape and manage.

Here is where Yogi's advice is again pertinent: If you don't know where you are going, you will wind up somewhere else. And it usually is someplace you really don't want to go.

For that reason, we tell clients that it is absolutely necessary to take control of how you are perceived.[1]

> Whether you are a corporate executive or mid-level manager, entrepreneur, restaurateur, doctor, lawyer, accountant, consultant, a singular sensation or a team leader, celebrity, model or fashion designer, parent or grandparent, you must manage your reputation or others will do it for you.

The First Shield of Digital Assassination: Back to School

If you are Internet savvy, you keep up with changes in cyberspace by reading online sources like Mashable, Ars Technica, Chris Brogan's advice on digital media marketing, Gawker Media's Gizmodo, Boing Boing for amusement, and Wired for the take of the digital establishment. *If you surf these sites without giving them a second thought, proceed to the second shield.* If not, please read on.

If these websites sound like Martian names to you, there are many other places to visit and easily, painlessly expand your knowledge about social media.

Learning social media is like learning to play the piano. To be proficient at it, you need hands-on education, learning through the actual keystrokes. It is easy to find such instruction in public libraries or civic groups, business associations, colleges, and continuing education programs. There are myriad one- or two-day boot camps on the Internet and social media, many offered as webinars, video on demand, or podcasts. SlideShare.net has many slide decks from such presentations. Similar classes are offered by associations in many professions.

Local chambers of commerce, clubs, and business or professional associations organize regular and ongoing lectures about new media. Also, you might seek help from younger office colleagues or relatives, those who are born swimmers in this digital age. Keep in mind, however, that youth may be far behind you in thinking carefully about privacy or exercising good judgment on the Internet.

Read everything possible about platforms or services. Use search engines to find explanations for any information you do not understand. Study question-and-answer sections or discussion areas of search engines, major blogs, and free services. Clear answers in everyday language are at your fingertips.

Don't stop until you understand—*with your fingertips*—how search engines really work, how to start a blog and maintain it with an easy free software like WordPress; how to access the popular social networking services like Facebook, Tumblr, or Jaiku; how a search term can be optimized; how to use Google AdSense.

Whether you take classes, learn online, or explore with your fingertips, you are not equipped to manage your reputation until you can comfortably navigate and post and actively participate on the Internet.

The Second Shield of Digital Assassination: I Am, Therefore Who Do I Think I Am?

After you have developed an understanding of the power and reach of the Internet, now undertake a brutally honest assessment of the first of your two selves—your actual self.

To do this well, act as your own father confessor. It might be necessary to write down everything—*just not on your computer.* Be brutally honest with yourself about your sins, shortcomings, and bad raps.

So how do you begin? Do a brain dump—not a brain freeze—by asking a series of probing questions about your subject.

Who are you—really?

Who are your detractors, and why are they detractors?

Who are your enemies, and how did they become your enemies?

Who wants to get back at you for something you did in high school or college or during your career?

Do your detractors, enemies, and revenge seekers have a point? Would you feel the same way they do if they had treated you the same way?

Why were you once fired? What were the worst customer-relations or product disasters you managed? How did they happen? Have you addressed the problem that led to these failures?

What about that nasty breakup? What is your ex saying about you?

You assessment of yourself should not be a quest for fairness or justification. One digital expert we know is an acknowledged technology leader who was discreetly cashed out of a corporate Fortune 500 job after having his decisions second-guessed by his wayward board. Now a nationally recognized entrepreneur, he is still haunted on Google by a blog from a former colleague that offers excruciating detail on his departure from that old job.

What failing do you have buried in your background, no matter how well papered over, that could be pumped up into stark words in primary colors by a blogger?

Most of all, what have you done in your private life that someone somehow could find out about you? What might people learn about you that you currently believe no one could possibly know?

Consider a female executive who is married, politically well connected, a community leader. A few years ago, she went in for a medical procedure that required anesthesia. Like many patients in the twilight state of moderate sedation, she became disinhibited and recounted a graphic sexual experience. Like others who have done this, she likely has no memory that she said anything.

A few months after her procedure, one of the nurses who was in the operating room committed a gross violation of medical ethics. She related the woman's story to a friend over a glass of wine. This should not have happened, but it did.

Now that friend, whenever she sees this executive, can't help but marvel that he has access to a secret from her unconscious mind that she surely could never suspect he knows.

What secrets do you have that could conceivably come to light?

Be brutal. Be hard on yourself. Think of yourself as the target you aim to destroy and you will have completed this task.

Place yourself on the scale of risk.

Are you like most people, a sometime target?

Are you at moderate risk, a person with some visibility and enemies?

Or are you at high risk, a person with a public presence? Are you an individual—a celebrity, ultrarich, a politically active person—who is very high risk?

Once you've defined vulnerabilities, review the seven swords and imagine all the ways you could be attacked. Write them all down on paper and put them to the side.

The Third Shield of Digital Assassination: Peekaboo, I See Me

You've made a brutally honest personal assessment of your life. Now turn from your actual self to your perceived self, the profile or personal brand as it is perceived on the Internet.

What do people seem to believe about you? What do they likely believe that they might not tell you? What does that biggest brain of all—the web—know about you, and say about you, true or false?

It is easy to stand inside your home or business and look out. Today everyone must stand outside and look in to see what friends, employers, clients, customers, fans, investors, and others see about you.

Look at yourself from the point of view of a digital assassin. What is out there that would make a lethal weapon?

To do this, look beyond the surface search results and into the databases of the "deep web"—sources of personal information not indexed on the major search engines. Before beginning, turn off personalized accounts, like Gmail and other services that could otherwise skew the search results.

- Check out your online profile on iSearch, Pipl, ZabaSearch, and similar "people search" sites that pull data from public sources like from Wikipedia, Facebook, Flickr, Twitter, and government data centers. Check out OpenSecrets.org to see if it reports your campaign donations and political activity.
- If it is a complicated history, consider spending up to about $40 on a background source like Intelius or BackgroundChecks .com to see what pops up.
- Check county or city databases to see if speeding tickets or any other civil or criminal information pops up. The formats differ among jurisdictions, but you can pull up liens, violations, court appearances, and tax issues online. Even if you have never been arrested, check to see if someone with a similar name has. This is very important to know and understand if malefactors are out there with the same name as yours.
- In the United States, check your credit score on AnnualCre ditReport.com, a free credit report you can access once a year.
- Check out how your home or office looks from Google Maps and Street View. Check out your real estate evaluation on sites like Zillow.com.
- If you have a business, you might want to spend a little bit more and do a D&B on it—the Dun & Bradstreet website with access to deep web material on your small business.

The greatest tool at your disposal is the most accessible—Google's exquisitely precise advanced search function, which allows refined searches and eliminates irrelevant results. Search for your name, subject, or key phrases—in as many likely variations as you can think of—to access a 360-degree review.

If you were divorced, arrested, fired from a job, put in every conceivable search term that might pull up a negative thread about that.

Review as many search engine results pages as necessary until the relevance to you completely thins out.

If you have a rare name—Xavier Stoneberry, for example—check for any conflation of your identity with that of a namesake—there could be another among the world's 7 billion people. This could unfortunately lead searchers to conclude that negative information about that other Xavier Stoneberry is about you.

On the other hand, if you have a common name, you will find it is relatively easy to hide among the trees.

While conducting the search, keep in mind that comments posted on message boards or behind paywalls may not show up. Still, you can uncover a lot of data about yourself with free sources.

Here are some key resources to flesh out the self-search.

- *Identity:* KnowEm is a site that can check to see if an evil clone is using your name, or forms of online identity, or if a brandjacker has hijacked your business on social media.
- *Message Boards:* BoardTracker, Boardreader, and Omgili are free services that catch a lot of what might be said about you or your subject on message boards and discussion threads.
- *Social Media:* Google Blog Search is a good place to start to take in what blogs are saying about your area. Social Mention can track what is being said on social networks like Facebook and blogs. IceRocket is another good blog search engine. Technorati indexes blogs, breaks them into helpful categories, and performs searches. BlogPulse tracks blogging trends that might affect you. Addict-o-matic, whose motto is "inhale the web," can collate a load of material from across the social media universe.*
- *Business:* Yelp is the essential self-search for small or consumer business. Search sites specific to sector, such as Revinate, which tracks online reviews of hotels. Use Radian6 and Alterian SM2 to monitor social media conversations about your brand or product.

* Keep in mind that the openness of various social media platforms is not uniform. Even for major sites like Twitter and Facebook, how searchable they are continues to change. How data points from social networking sites are indexed is an ongoing negotiation between data owners and search engines.

- *News:* The Internet is rich with free searches from news organizations. If mentioned or quoted in a story, searches tend to be time sensitive. So be sure to use the correct time parameters if you are searching about news about yourself. To do a robust search, access Factiva or Nexis, or search local news outlets, many of which require payment.
- *Images:* Google, Bing, and Yahoo! image searches are a critical, often overlooked part of any search. Keep in mind that TinEye can perform a reverse search on an image, telling others who you are from an online photo.

Are there any photos, images, or cartoons of you that are accessible on obscure sites? Check out the photo indexes on your friend's Facebook sites. Keep in mind that someone may have posted a college photo of you and that seven-foot bong that you had long forgotten about.

If an image exists, it can go viral. And if it goes viral, your identity can be tracked down, just like the photo that forced a Republican congressman to resign after he posted that shirtless photo of himself as a Craigslist's personal.

Keep in mind that the goal is just to see how the search appears online. Now take look at all this online information—information that is true, not true, or suggestive—and ask:

How could a silent slasher use it?

Could someone use available information to create an evil clone?

Is there anything that could be distorted to ignite public indignation and make you the target of the human flesh search engine?

And the hardest question of all: Is there a bad fact about you that might be remixed to make it look far worse?

Truth remix is the difficult problem. It forces contingency planning, deciding in advance that if push comes to shove, whether to admit to some imperfection, what to disclose, how to explain, and where to explain.

Finally, after all the facts have been inventoried from your brain dump to the web, then inventory the information inside your computer and how it might be used by an assassin practicing clandestine combat.

If you were digitally assassinated, like Steve in chapter 5, do you have pictures, letters, or documents in your computer that would be deeply embarrassing or items that could falsely incriminate you? If you do, either you need great confidence in your security or you need to store it somewhere else—like a cheap, airgapped laptop.

Compare your inventory of real-world vulnerabilities from the second shield against your online profile. What is revealed? What is distorted? What is made up?

In short, match your online profile with your offline life, that other you. What did you find? Then, regularly monitor the online profile of your brand, product, or celebrity for anything new that changes instantaneously on the web.

The Fourth Shield of Digital Assassination: The New and Improved You

The fourth shield protects by creating a new and improved image of you on the web. It involves a set of affirmative, positive actions to build what we call a "reputational cushion"[2] to absorb blows against your public persona.

This concept becomes clear when we compare the fates of two California politicians. The first was a little-known executive who ran for office. Just as he was getting his campaign off the ground, an embarrassing incident surfaced in the media. This man was an avid jogger who had been changing in his office for a run when a female colleague opened the door and caught a glimpse of him naked.

The story spread, making it a staple of drive-time humor.

No matter what the candidate did after that—no matter how qualified he might have been—he was forever more just the "naked guy." His campaign was soon swept away.

Now compare him to Arnold Schwarzenegger, running for governor of California when he was attacked by a *Los Angeles Times* series of stories of sexual excess and even harassment of women in his youth—charges far more serious than inadvertently being spotted naked.

Some of the charges Schwarzenegger laughed off as the folly of his youth. The more serious charges he denied.

An unknown candidate would have been dead then and there. Schwarzenegger survived because after years at the top of the box office, we felt as if we knew him personally. And because his wife, Maria Shriver, unequivocally supported him. Schwarzenegger had a baseline of respect, that cushion, that allowed him to take a reputational beating without folding. Schwarzenegger's reputational armor was only destroyed—and his return to the movies delayed—when substantive proof, in the form of a "love child" caused his wife to walk away from him.

You don't have to be a movie star to build such a cushion. What is needed is a solid, compelling, and attractive online persona that comes to the fore in any search—so that any static, like someone accidentally catching a peek at you naked, is swept into a proper context.

To immunize yourself as much as possible, several pages of positive or neutral hits on search engine results pages are necessary. To create these hits and protect your brand, link your name and business to as much positive content as possible.

Social media engagement is therefore a must to maximize reputation.

First, have a storefront on the web. This site is your controlling digital anchor from which all other efforts radiate and to which they link back. It can be a personal website or blog, your page on your company, business, or product site, or a blog about your celebrity or hobby.

Fill out a Google Profile. It influences search results, and consider opening a Twitter account to tweet to friends or to create a following on a topic in which you have a deep interest or expertise. Namechk.com is a good place to establish a user name or vanity URL across all social media.

Naturally, be careful in choices of images, words, or style. Your posts speak before all audiences: employees and coworkers, family and friends, investors and analysts, clients, customers, the media, and all other constituents. Give a brief autobiographical description of yourself on your website—keep it professional but light.

In this effort, we can learn a lot from how big corporations deepen their relationship with customers through detailed product-related blogs.

- Dialogue is central. The iconic corporate example is Dell's IdeaStorm, which lets customers suggest ideas that Dell engineers evaluate and a community of fans vote up or down on. If you have a small business, having a moderated "suggestion box" that you act on might be one way of enticing customers into a deeper relationship.

- Tone is also vital. Southwest Airlines hosts Nuts About Southwest, a popular corporate blog. It opens a dialogue with customers in the casual, slightly flippant tone that is a hallmark of that airline's culture. For many small firms, such a friendly, open tone is just right.

Whether you are cultivating a brand or business, use this same spirit of openness, responsiveness, and above all, dialogue, to present a positive public profile and image.

Consistent and valuable blogging on areas of expertise will draw a crowd that keeps coming back. If you are passionate about a hobby, offer hints about growing decorative winter cabbage, adopting a shelter dog, or lifting free weights.

Establish a dialogue with other bloggers and link to a host of positive material on sites concerning your subject. But stick to your area of expertise and meet the expectations of visitors by offering consistent information in this area.

If you write a letter to the editor to your local paper, cohost a charity ball, or speak at a PTA meeting, these are all items and images that can be posted and linked to other groups that come up high in search results.

If you own a small business—a bakery, say—you might offer regular advice on cooking, recipes, and seasonal treats. If you are an accountant, you might blog about common tax and payroll pitfalls or common mistakes of recordkeeping.

Post less frequently but with quality advice that has great "nutrient density." Or go in another direction and offer a steady diet of low density, high frequency posts that will raise the prominence of positive material in searches. Visitors are always eager for helpful tips, from cooking to pet grooming.

Another technique is to "pack the database"[3] with plain vanilla information. This means linking to descriptive data—the roster of your high school or college class, professional associations, faith community. Simple vanilla data can be useful in pushing down unwanted results on a search page.

Optimizing Reputation

In posting positive and neutral data, understand the three steps that companies use to maximize search engine optimization (SEO). These steps boost your profile in a search, according to Laszlo Horvath, founder of ActiveMedia, a website optimization company.

- The first SEO step is what Horvath calls "mind reading," the analysis of popular keywords that—without theory or intuition—*tell* you what people are thinking. As in the third shield, think of yourself as a brand and try every permutation of every conceivable keyword about yourself—light, dark, and humorous. Use Google Analytics to see the keywords that brought visitors to your website. Like a compass, this analysis will point to what people are thinking about you, your brand, and business.
- The second SEO step is to make sure that your website has the right architecture—the keywords that link you to your subject ("baking," "tax time," "intellectual property expert") that will help the search engine's spider index your website where you want it. But keep these keywords in context. Overuse them and Google's algorithms might think you are trying to game the search and kick you down the rankings.
- The third SEO step is to link all your websites and social media sites together and to legitimately encourage as many links from others as you can.

This is central. Today links are the currency of the web. The boost in visibility that occurs when one website links to another is called "link juice."

Links are the insertions of hypertext that, when clicked, take the visitor from one site to another. Making such links does not require a deep knowledge of coding. It can easily be found in the "help" part of your toolbar, in free software like WordPress, or in the encoded software of many social media sites.

There are illegitimate ways to generate link juice, which happens when black hats create the equivalent of spam links. Link farms are shady businesses that increase links with content that is high in volume, but with little or no meaning or value. Google adjusts its algorithms daily to catch billions of spamblogs created to game the rankings.

Take the opposite approach by making organic links to valid communities of interest. This includes every club, association, and civic or faith organization in your life. Colleges and universities, for example, are especially highly ranked sites, so any connections of your sites to a higher education site provide some link juice.

Positive content created by individuals is increasingly taking multimedia forms. Now that digital cameras are cheap and it's easy to upload video on free platforms like YouTube, anyone can create his or her own digital "channel" with video blogs, or vlogs, inexpensively and instantly. Your vlog might be a brief talk about a business issue, an interview with a guru in your sector, or a view of a rare aurora borealis from your backyard.

If you are politically minded, and don't mind being open about your views, blog about a hot political topic and link to sites with high search rankings, like the Huffington Post or National Review Online.

Once you have completed this, link all your sites to each other and link as many of them as you can to friends. You might do a friendly "hat tip" to an insight on a popular blogger's post, giving him a reason to link back to you.

A risky but potentially successful strategy arises out of a tendency of human nature: a fight tends to attract a crowd. Taking issue with the position of another blogger—as long as he or she is rational and not prone to personal attacks or derogatory hate speech—can drive both of your rankings.

Whether a major blogger or site wants to pick a bone with you or steer consumers to you for advice, either is link gold. In short, the more positive, neutral, and interesting items you post and link, the more reputational cushion you create on your search engine results against the blows of digital assassins.

The Fifth Shield of Digital Assassination: Regulating the Ether

"The Internet is an odd thing," an analyst for Shore Communications writes. "In some ways it is a medium that acts in essence like radio, but with a nearly infinite number of broadcast channels. Sometimes this 'ether,' as radio was termed in its early days, is used for one-to-many communications, as in websites and feeds; sometimes it's used for one-to-one communications, as in email, instant messaging, and IP telephony."[4]

How do we regulate something as amorphous as the ether?

On the broadcast side—Facebook and the other social media platforms—find one or two, but not three or four, specific themes to promote about yourself and stick to them. Few bloggers are so interesting or so well positioned by television or celebrity that visitors will keep coming back to hear their views on everything. If you are a butcher known with a huge following among foodies for maintaining a deep, informative blog about quality meats, your visitors will be put off if they come to your landing page and see that you've written about the crisis in Syria.

If you think about it, the most famous people are essentially known for one or two things. You will attract a following by offering deep information on a handful of areas of expertise germane to your profession, business, or personal passion. A simple but deep profile is a manageable profile likely to attract a community of followers.

This is true as well for business. One of the authors saw a Fortune 500 client lose the impact of months of communications planning for the company's CEO succession. The goal was to regulate the ether in the announcement of the new CEO, using his wide name recognition and sterling credentials, by keeping him at the top of the headlines for several days after the announcement.

The announcement was released at 7:00 A.M. EST, well before the market opened in New York. It was to be followed by transatlantic news conferences and key employee and constituent calls. The whole company was told by the general counsel's office not to release anything. At just after 11:00 A.M. on that very day, a division of that same company released a four-page product news release on the wires. An hour later, another division announced a new midlevel manager.

The story about the new CEO sank out of sight.

Businesses of all sorts should take note when they "broadcast" across the ether. Good news, special sales, and new products should be released in a disciplined, staggered way, even if you operate a neighborhood bakery. We all know people who compulsively post the most anodyne material about themselves—like that ancient Pompeian in chapter 4 who "posted" the graffito, "On April 19th, I made bread." What was true in the days of the Caesars is true today. It is for people like this that Facebook created a "hide" function that lets you eliminate chatty friends from your news feed.

In narrowing one-to-one communications, you can be as chatty or as intimate as you like. Remember that any message you send to any one person can be resent by malice or by accident with a single click and posted for the world to see.

We all write things we don't want the world to see. *Never* ever write anything that would actually make a bad news story, would get you in trouble with regulators or law enforcement, or would mean you lose the respect of your profession, employer, future employer, or family.

Be careful even about what you say, how you say it, and where you say it in the offline world in this age of Little Snitch. A friend of one of the authors was mortified to learn how close he came to being surreptitiously video-recorded while making an irreverent joke at a public hearing by a man slowly panning the room with his PDA.

Strategic Advice for Businesses, Corporations, and Celebrities

Almost all corporations, brands, or high-profile people are not ready to handle the instantaneous blow of digital assassins. Few would look to such an attack as an opportunity. But never lose sight of the profound effects a digital attack will have on you, your brand, or your business.

Over the past few years, one of the authors developed a strategy manual, some secret sauce, for his corporate clients to use when they are digitally attacked. Here is a distillation of the topline points from this manual, elements of which can be adapted to small businesses and even individuals.

Before a Digital Attack Occurs

Have at the ready response plans that include a fairly elaborate decision tree, a set of "if this . . . then that" set of responses. Playing out realistic scenarios based on likely events is also useful. War-gaming and role-playing offer the visceral learning people need to be ready to launch into instant action.

While future steps should not be cast in concrete, you should have some sense of whether your response to a given attack will be to defend, to counterattack . . . or both. Ask ahead: What is the strategy? What are the messages?

What tactics should be employed? Think through these questions, and make key decisions in advance. Planning will help you to remember: ready, aim, fire. Not: ready, fire, aim.

Once attacked, an organization should take the following action steps:

- Create a war room and a war room environment. Who is in that war room? Different points of view are needed: operations, legal, communications, sales, marketing, and human resources. Are business line heads included so you have realistic assessments of what can and cannot be done?
- CEOs should not run the war room or the crisis team. One corporate head has to have ownership of the war room—usually PR, marketing, or the general counsel. But no one discipline should dominate. The CEO needs to hear all points of view—legal, sales, investor relations, communications, etc.
- Legal and logistical considerations may delay the actual (as opposed to the promised) response. But the real issue is, *could* you react in a digital day if you had to? Could you post a YouTube response within two to four hours? Could you get a statement through legal, PR, and the C-suite in an hour? Remember, a digital day is at most eight hours long.
- More important than having the camera and technology in place for a YouTube upload, does top management understand the need to have such a capability? Is management willing to rearrange sacrosanct schedules?

Responding to an Attack

As soon as an assassin attacks, continually monitor and analyze blogs and video posts. Where is the chatter spreading from? What keywords are driving it?

- Define, if you can, who is attacking and why. Is it a disgruntled customer or employee? A competitor? Uninformed investors panicked by a rumor? A special interest, activist, or extremist group? Or just someone, to again quote *The Dark Knight*'s Alfred Pennyworth, who just wants to watch the world burn?

- List constituencies affected by the attack. Immediately set up short-term and long-term responses to address each constituency's concerns.
- Understand that attacks do not just go away—never, ever. If you ignore them, they get worse very quickly.
- A digital attack often cannot be handled internally. Staff is often constrained by corporate culture, turf, and personalities. Professional outside objective counsel is often necessary, though its advice is sometimes difficult to digest.
- For a variety of legal, logistical, and regulatory reasons, an instant business response—a rebate, a recall, the setting up of a call center—may be the worst thing to do when the facts are unclear or the organizational response will take time. *But at the very least some kind of responsive message must be issued, one that shows a willingness to listen, to be in dialogue, not monologue.*
- With an eight-hour digital day, a response forty-eight hours later is five digital days late. Aim to respond within a two- to four-hour window. Your initial response can always be enriched and sharpened as you move along. Remember: In today's digital world, if you are silent or even just late, you are guilty.
- Identify which media platforms are being used to promote the attack. Can you use the same platforms to defend yourself . . . and perhaps punch back? Can you activate friends who have an organic interest in backing up your response?
- When the values of a company or product are called into question, a personal response on YouTube is often called for. Don't forget the immense usefulness of the posting and targeted distribution of a news release. Once wastepaper sent scattershot to a thousand uninterested reporters, the humble news release is now an indexable response that can be searched by all interested constituencies instantly, globally, without filters on a twenty-four hour basis. This is for media and digital pundits, all constituents—customers, employees, vendors, investors, government officials, and other stakeholders.

- The tone of the statement should be appropriate to the facts. Have you been smeared? Show outrage. Has someone made too much of a legitimate mistake? Show some contrition, while setting out the facts. Define in simple language what happened, perhaps why it happened, and most important, what you are doing about it. This will be repeated many times to many constituencies in the days ahead. Don't get caught up with who is at fault or legal issues at this time unless this is necessary. Show how you are solving the problem and address those issues later.

- Deploy your spokesperson. Media interviews must be planned to reach strategic opinion gatekeepers. Work all media to tell your story and get your messages in the public arena.

- Top executives must demonstrate leadership first, then management. These are not the same. Leadership creates a vision to inspire people to rise to challenges they could not normally meet. Management is the deployment of the resources of finance, operations, and people.

- Be visible, communicative, and responsive.

- The CEO and top executives must make wise judgments that can be communicated in simple language, that creates a balance with those immediately affected by the attack as well as the company's stakeholders.

- Never lie. Never fib. Admit what you don't yet know, and promise to get back with an answer. Correct any factual inaccuracies immediately. Understand that a difference of opinion is not a factual inaccuracy.

Human Resources (HR) officers report a particularly nasty crisis arising in social media—the tendency of a few employees or ex-employees to run down the reputation of their company, its products, or its leaders. Even some large companies do not have a solid policy governing employee social media communications. Many seem unaware that their employees are putting up such posts in real time from the office through their mobile devices on Facebook, Linkedln, Twitter, and other platforms.

This is a multidisciplinary problem that involves HR, legal, sales, and communications. Companies need to formulate policies, make those policies clear in their hiring, constantly monitor what is being said about them, and have consultants at the ready to counter an inside or outside job by a digital assassin.

On the other hand, companies need to distinguish legitimate—if harsh—criticism from digital assassins. When the neck of musician Dave Carroll's $3,500 Taylor guitar was broken by baggage handlers while Carroll and his band were connecting from one United flight to another and the airline refused to reimburse him, Carroll retaliated by posting a catchy song on YouTube, "United Breaks Guitars," that received more than 10 million hits in less than two years. Taylor Guitars stepped in and offered Carroll guitars for his next YouTube song. United's embarrassment was Taylor Guitars' opportunity, though United later apologized, belatedly offered Carroll compensation, and asked to use his video in its employee training.[5]

On the other hand, if you are being attacked unfairly, can you distinguish whether the charge is being intentionally driven or if it is organic? Is the story naturally snowballing or does it appear that someone is purposefully accelerating it? If you see the same charged words being repetitively echoed across multiple blog sites, from detractors who link to each other, then you can surmise that the attack is deliberate.

An attack can come at you without warning, on holidays, weekends, in the middle of the night. And it can happen to anyone. Ask Domino's, Dow Chemical, or Apple. You can't control how a story breaks, but you can manage how a story spins.

The Sixth Shield of Digital Assassination: Lean on Me

In the future, which is now, we will all have our fifteen minutes of shame. The Internet can be a cold, black, indefinite place. When the moment comes, there will be no authority to which you can appeal for fairness. This does not mean that you are completely powerless, but it does mean that the Internet is not like most other social situations. In the digital era, the buck stops . . . nowhere.

In order to level the playing field you cannot depend on appeals to justice or fairness to ultimately vindicate yourself. But you can call on friends, both real and virtual, to help. Being actively connected to a community of friends is the greatest resource in the face of a digital assassin. They can also alert you when you are making a digital mistake.

An old Italian proverb holds that, loosely translated, only your real friends will tell you that your face is dirty. Friends are not only helpful when you need to be warned about your dirty face. They can defend when you, your business, or your brand come under attack, with a credible counter.

Some trolls, flamers, or just angry individuals are best ignored. But if you choose to respond, quickly provide as much relevant data as you can to get your digital friends' support. Their support may be strictly internal, within the discussion board of an organization. They may just let everyone they know on their Facebook pages that you are the victim of an unjust attack.

Or they might, as the friends of Reverend Merritt's church did, add stars to a rating or come to your defense on blogs indexed by the search engines.

What people actually do with what you tell them will be beyond your control. Your part is to send them an accurate, dispassionate brief that lets the facts drive their response. If the facts are outrageous enough, those facts will inspire campaigns that grow organically.

And if there is an element of ideology to your case, more "friends" will appear than you know you had.

- On the left, this happened when USDA official Shirley Sherrod was forced to resign after conservative blogger Andrew Breitbart released an excerpt of her speech that made her sound like a racist. When the full import of her speech was made public—Sherrod was describing how she overcame her own racial biases—the NAACP reversed its statement that it was "appalled" by her remarks and launched a fierce and successful social media campaign to vindicate her with a complete video of her whole speech.[6]
- On the right, a social media campaign was waged to reinstate two prolife Claremont McKenna College students, banned by the neighboring and affiliated Pomona College, for videotaping tough questions put to a Planned Parenthood representative. Conservative students, outraged at what they saw as an

> abuse of the discipline process to shut down speech, mounted a Facebook campaign that recruited CMC students, faculty, and alumni to reverse the ban.[7]

In both cases, the perception of injustice against an individual drove the crowd. Whenever an affinity group believes that it has its very own Dreyfus affair, the resulting campaign will go viral—with increasing rates of "infection."

If the digital attack is not quite so hot-button, requiring only deflection, an effective way to enlist friends is to adopt an emotional stance that is the opposite of outrage. A good example occurred during the 2008 U.S. presidential campaign, after John McCain ridiculed Barack Obama in an ad as a vapid, Paris Hilton–like celebrity. Paris Hilton sent out a response to "the white-haired dude," a funny YouTube video that ended with her rattling off the elements of a plausible energy strategy that sounded more succinct and grounded than anything the two candidates were saying.

Who won? Paris Hilton won.

Google really won.

But it was the "friends" of Paris Hilton who helped her make her riposte go viral.

If you have a strong, supportive community of followers and trusted fans, they will automatically come to your defense when you are attacked. "Remember, George," the angel Clarence inscribed in the classic Frank Capra film *It's a Wonderful Life,* "no man is a failure who has friends."

The Seventh Shield of Digital Assassination: Virtual Silver Bullets or Olive Branches?

In this final shield, we work out a game plan for responding to a digital attack. A chart of action steps is on pages 235–36 to help master the elements of defense.

The first question that must be answered in the aftermath of an assassin's attack is whether or not to respond at all. Like encapsulated cancers or asbestos lining old buildings, sometimes it is best to leave an ugly post alone.

The reason, of course, is the Streisand Effect—the way in which an effort to repress something online winds up propagating it. Don't make matters worse by chatting online about or causing others to link to the offending site(s), which will only raise its prominence.

This is what happened to one property management company. It sued a woman for $50,000 in damages over a tweet about "moldy apartments." This lawsuit took a story that fewer than twenty-two people had seen and made the company's name a global search result for mold.

Or consider Liskula Cohen. She may have won a similar pyrrhic victory when she used legal means to force Google to unmask the blogger who called her the biggest "skank" in New York City. The upside? Cohen was allowed to proceed with her lawsuit to out the blogger, one Rosemary Port. The downside? Glenn Reynolds, a law professor, wrote on Instapundit, "I never would have heard the words, 'Liskula Cohen' and 'skank' together if it hadn't been for her blogger-outing litigation efforts."[8]

The first and biggest question is whether to ignore, appease, or counterattack a digital assassin.

- In deciding whether or not to act, ask yourself if the offending material is likely to have real-world negative consequences. Will it cost you that next job, a client, or a promotion?
- Second, who has seen it? Use Alexa.com or Quantcast to check the traffic of the offending site. Profile the site and its readership. Are these your constituents or crowd? Is something negative here likely to be seen by your cohorts? If the answer to these questions is no, then decide the safer play: To keep a close eye on the attack or to try to nip it in the bud?

When a digital attack occurs, first understand who is attacking you. Can you identify the attacker, or can you correlate his user name with a website or blog?

Does the attack appear organic, going viral over community anger over your perceived misdeeds, or cruel humor at your expense? Or do you see the repetition of keywords and text that indicates that you may be the victim of deliberate keyword stuffing?

Is there an organization behind this attack? If so, can donors be identified? Leaders of the organization give a clue to a possible hidden enemy who is subsidizing the attack.

Once these questions are answered, take the following steps:

- If the offending material is on a third-party website, go to the contact page of that website containing the offensive material and e-mail the web host. Send them a polite request to please remove the material. Explain why this information is inaccurate or harmful.
- Don't let anger seep into the conversation. Don't make accusations or threaten the webmaster.
- This same approach of sweet reason and appeal to fairness even extends to the actual attacker, if they can be identified. A threat might egg them on. Some vicious people delight in your entreaties, as a predator might enjoy the squeals of his prey. If it seems, however, as if the attack is based on a misunderstanding, politely set the attacker straight.
- If the webmaster or actual attacker agrees to remove the post—and they have not posted it on a major review site—ask them to use Google's public URL Removal Tool to eventually wash it out as a cache copy or snippet in Google's search results.
- Why are they attacking you? If this is a case of someone using mixed truth against you—and not a troll or a dedicated assassin—try to entice the person who made the post into an offline conversation. Let him know how hurtful his remark has been, without expressing legitimate anger. But while you are being reasonable, collect as much information as possible. For example, be sure and capture their IP address from any e-mails. In many cases, however, a reasoned, civil approach can do the job.
- Celebrities pay top dollar to separate fact from fiction and respond to rumors and lies on ICorrect. Find your equivalent. Don't post a response on a site where the message board can make you the equivalent of the clown in the dunking booth. In clarifying mixed truth, you may be forced to own up to facts you would rather not mention. Fully understand that a digital confession is forever. Will you make it worse by responding? If you have to explain some personal shortcoming to put it in context, at least make your statement on a site where you have some control.
- In running down a rumor, follow the example of McDonald's, which rebutted the ground-worm rumor by talking about the

quality of its beef. In an online world, it is best not to repeat the graphic terms of the charge; otherwise the offending keywords are boosted as search terms.

If these appeals fail, face the Streisand Effect head-on. Will responding make it worse? Is there enough truth to what is being said or shown that you will damage yourself by reacting at all?

If response is the plan, there are concrete steps you can take to blunt the attack.

- If the offensive material continues to rise in search engine rankings, hire a search engine optimization firm to try to bury it in the rankings.
- If the attacker must be unmasked, consider filing a Doe subpoena. If the IP address can be found, take the next step and subpoena the internet service provider to divulge the identity of the attacker. If the IP address represents a network, or if the Internet service provider has undertaken a routine change of addresses, or if the attacker has taken steps to cloak his identity, then you've hit a dead end. Understand that a lawsuit can cost thousands of dollars. It will enrage an attacker and his friends, possibly activating mirror sites. And it may require follow-through on the lawsuit, which will likely result in no real compensation. Still, some assassins are so egregious that you might feel their attacks merit nothing less than a lawsuit.
- Consider a ToS—or terms of service—response. At the bottom of most websites, next to a link to its privacy policy, is a link to its terms of service. For example, Popeater, the celebrity gossip site owned by AOL, states AOL's policy requiring you not to post anything "that contains explicit or graphic descriptions or accounts of sexual acts or is threatening, abusive, harassing, defamatory, libelous, deceptive, fraudulent, invasive of another's privacy . . ." This, by the way, includes a site dedicated to tracking the words and deeds of the likes of Charlie Sheen and Lindsay Lohan. Taken seriously, most ToS statements would exclude perhaps the lion's share of the Internet. Unless the post is pornographic or threatens violence, the likely response from most webmasters will be to yawn. Still, it

may be worth citing ToS language to appeal to a webmaster's sense of fairness. If the site would appear deeply offensive to an objective observer, a litigious response would be to threaten legal action against the hosting site for a violation of its own ToS for failure to remove the offending post if it clearly violates its own stated terms. Use litigation—and threats of litigation—sparingly, if at all.

- Another approach, if the site itself is defamatory to an extreme, send a snail mail letter to the legal department of the web hosting company that serves the website. Go to a WHOIS search site and enter the domain name of the offending site to reveal the web hosting company. Go to their main page and look up their ToS or acceptable use policy. Hosting companies have boilerplate ToS language. The web hosting service Go Daddy, for example, forbids users from posting anything that "promotes, encourages or engages in defamatory, harassing, abusive or otherwise objectionable behavior."
- If you are the target not of defamation that feels violent to you, but of actual threats of physical violence, the digital assassin has crossed into an area in which the law is fully on your side. Companies will respond to such ToS violations with alacrity, especially if you come armed with a court order.
- If your child or grandchild is the victim of a cyberbully, keep records of the attack, make a screen shot of it, print it out, and record identifying details about the attacker. Teach your children to try not to respond to such attacks. Any knee-jerk response could muddy the waters and make it less clear who is the victim and who is the attacker.
- If a cyberbully attack is irritating, take the matter up with the attackers' parents. If it is disturbing, consider taking it up with the school principal, depending on the policy of your school district. If violence is threatened, take it to the police immediately. For a tutorial, check out wikihow.com/Deal-With-Cyber-Bullying-As-a-Child-or-Teen, or check out the latest advice from Norton's Internet Safety Advocate, Marian Merritt, on cyberbullying.

Game Plan for Digital Defense

Here are the elements of a digital defense, boiled down to their essentials into a ready game plan.

Getting Prepared

Go back to school on social media.

- Understand how search engines work, how to create a blog and maintain it, use social networking sites and optimize search terms.

Understand yourself, the facts about your life and career that are discoverable through investigation, coincidence, or hacking.

- Know your digital profile from aggregators like Pipl, background sources, public databases, credit checks, Google searches, and free searches.
  - Identity checks: KnowEm
  - Message boards: BoardTracker, Boardreader, Omgili
  - Social media: Google Blog Search, Social Mention, IceRocket
  - Business: Yelp, Kosmix, sector specific trackers
  - News: Yahoo!, Google, "news" searches
  - Images: Google/Bing/Yahoo!, Google Maps and Street View, TinEye
- Boost your profile.
  - Create a "storefront" website.
  - Fill out Google Profile.
  - Open accounts on Facebook, LinkedIn, Twitter, Yelp, etc.
  - Link to plain vanilla data—professional associations, alumni groups, etc.
  - Sprinkle keywords in your network of sites that will help index positive and neutral material about you.
  - Link websites and social networking sites.
- Manage your profile.
  - Regulate your news and announcements.
  - Keep online conversations clean.

- If you are in a large business, develop a "war room" and a plan.
- Develop a list of real and virtual friends to call on if attacked.

In the Face of an Attack

- Approach the webmaster or digital assassin with a calm plea for relief.

  Upside

  Might clear up a misunderstanding

  Downside

  Might encourage more attacks.

- If the answer to your plea is yes, ask them to use Google's URL removal tool.

- File a Doe subpoena.

  Upside

  Might unmask your attacker for legal accountability

  Downsides

  Costs money

  Court will make you attest that harm merits subpoena

  Recovery unlikely

  Might enrage friends of assassin, create mirror sites

- A terms of service appeal to the webmaster or web hosting company.

  Upsides

  Possible near-term gratification

  If one site bans material for a ToS violation, you can use that precedent to argue to others that they should as well

  Downsides

  A bank shot

  Might enrage assassin, escalate attacks on other sites

- Obtain a court order, if the post contains a threat of violence.

  Upsides

  Stops attack

  Creates legal record of a threat

  Downside

  Might enrage an unbalanced person

One or none of these options may work. Even if they do, do not expect your digital profile to change overnight. The only strategy that always works in your favor 100 percent of the time is the positive approach of creating a reputational cushion.

The only way to obtain at least some protection is to create as much positive and descriptive information about yourself, link all your sites together, and then make as many organic links as you can to others.

- If driving the offensive material off your first search page is successful, that's a major victory.
- If only positive or neutral content is on your first three pages of search, that's a complete victory—for now. But keep in mind that anything negative in deep search can always move up in ranking.

Throughout, keep Postel's law of tolerance in mind if you should manage to get the upper hand. It reflects what John Seigenthaler did when he used legal proceedings to track down his digital assassin. "I called him on the phone, and told him I was pissed off and [asked] why did he do it," Seigenthaler says. "He teared up. It was just before Christmas and my wife was listening as I came into the house, and I was talking to him. She heard me react with surprise when she heard that they asked him to resign and she told me, 'It's just before Christmas, you can't let him lose his job.' I said, 'Pardon me, but can you tell me whose side you're on here?' "

The next day Seigenthaler called his assassin's boss and asked if the firm would take him back. The man was rehired.

As a result of Seigenthaler's classy way of handling the issue, his reputation online and offline has only been enhanced.

Managing Digital Platforms

Now we come to the actual keystrokes you need to undertake a tactical defense. The rest of the chapter deals with the means to grow and manage reputations on the most popular platforms: Facebook, Twitter, Yelp, Wikipedia. And it imparts the basics of good image management through the elements of search engine optimization.

Facebook

The section concerning the Fourth Shield, "The New and Improved You," explains the importance of developing an online presence. Have as many online sources of positive and truthful information about yourself established as possible. Doing so will provide greater leverage in the event that you are the victim of cyber character assassination.

One tool in that toolbox is a Facebook profile (for individuals) or page (categories: Local Business or Place; Company, Organization, or Institution; Brand or Product; Artist, Band, or Public Figure; Entertainment; Cause or Community). A critical question to answer when building out a Facebook profile is whether to use it primarily for business or personal use or perhaps for a combination of both.

Whatever purpose you choose, be sure to carefully manage what kind of information is disseminated on Facebook. Determine how much is shared (i.e., interests, photos, status updates, and so forth) down to individual friends. However, it is helpful to post only things that you ultimately could live with being available to the entire public.

Facebook has long faced criticism for its highly fluid approach to privacy controls. Google's Matt McKeon has a helpful chart that details these changes over time: http://mattmckeon.com/facebook-privacy.

Facebook substantially changed their privacy controls three times just between November 2009 and April 2010. The lesson here is to be vigilant. Monitor the Facebook Blog (http://blog.facebook.com) for changes and be sure to make adjustments accordingly.

To manage privacy controls, log into Facebook. In the upper right-hand corner is a tab "Account" with a drop-down menu. Select "privacy settings." As of this writing (summer 2011) there are five options to control who can see what information you share. We recommend using the "custom" level in order to fully understand what bits of data may be shared and to choose whatever makes you comfortable.

One final note on Facebook is the Facebook Connect platform. You may have seen other websites that offer the option to log into them via Facebook Connect (examples: www.WashingtonPost.com and www.Pandora.com). You may inadvertently log into one of these websites using Facebook, and then whatever you do on that website might be broadcast quite publicly. Actions like "liking" a piece of content (for example, an article or video) or making a comment would then be visible on that website and then reported back into Facebook, broadcast to your friends, and depending on your privacy settings, to the entire Internet.

Despite such risks, establishing a Facebook profile is an important way that you can claim a brand identity online as well as create communications that you control. If you haven't done so already, be sure to establish your vanity (or unique) Facebook URL by going to http://www.facebook.com/username. This will allow you to claim the URL www.facebook.com/yournamehere.

Facebook can easily enable evil clones, because anybody can create a profile with any name and any picture. Those attacking from a Facebook page may not be who they say they are.

Likewise, someone can spoof a profile that pretends to be you. The latter is even more reason to claim your own piece of digital real estate in order to bolster credibility should you need to deny the validity of an imposter.

Twitter

Twitter is another potential source of consternation for online victims. Many popular personalities and companies have been spoofed on Twitter. One way that Twitter has responded to this is to establish a "Verified" account. For example, if you look at President Barack Obama's Twitter page, http://twitter.com/BarackObama, the blue symbol indicates that his page legitimately represents the person it says it does.

Signing up for Twitter takes less than five minutes, but building influence to reach people in the case of a crisis takes patient and consistent effort (do it here: https://twitter.com/signup). Keep in mind that Twitter, like tennis, requires constant attention. Verbal volleys you send out will come back at you. Unless you are a mega-star, then, Twitter is not a broadcasting tool. It is a conversational media. For this reason, Twitter requires a commitment of time and resources that is not appropriate for everyone. If your Twitter account is not interacting and creating dialogue, it will not have long-term growth or any real traction.

Twitter messages can be up to 140 characters and may include links.

Build up a follower base—slowly and organically. Faster methods do exist but they tend to rely on less-than-aboveboard tactics.

First, publicize your Twitter account on other platforms, such as

Facebook, your blog, an e-mail to your contacts. Let people know what they can expect to get from following your Twitter updates.

Are you announcing company news? Giving your quick reaction to the day's news? Sharing the best must-read article?

Next, you can follow people that you are interested in and hope that they reciprocate. When seeking to build such a network, you must do more than just click "follow." You need to interact and engage. Respond to questions that others may pose or share your feedback to the content they are broadcasting. Twitter is more than a repeating station—it is social media, after all.

You have three primary means of communication on Twitter:

- The basic tweet
- An "@" reply
- The direct message

A basic tweet is typed into the box titled "What's happening?" (or into the tweet update section of your third-party application—more on that later). This is broadcast to all who have chosen to follow you and is placed in their "Timeline." The Timeline is displayed in reverse chronological order. Keep in mind that anyone following more than a few people will see a constant churn of new tweets.

The basic tweet is also publicly available, unless you choose to make your tweets private, and will be discoverable by anyone on the Internet. Technically, tweets may be deleted after being sent, *but like all content that is originally public on the Internet it can be cached and it is likely that someone can find it even after it is removed.*

The second way to publish a tweet is via an @reply, which is just a normal tweet that mentions another Twitter user. For example, the Washington Nationals, the Major League Baseball team, using their official Twitter account @nationals, tweeted: "Special #FF: RHP Stephen Strasburg @stras37 has joined the Nats Twitter Family. Give him a follow!"

Stephen Strasburg is a rising star pitcher who has just launched his own Twitter account, which is @stras37. So the Nationals' status mentioned Strasburg's account.

This means that the Nationals' tweet would show up under Strasburg's "@mentions," which is a search option on the home page of every

Twitter account. Any Twitter user can easily check to see if they have been mentioned in a tweet by clicking the @mention link.

The third method of communicating on Twitter is via direct message. Unlike the first two methods that are entirely public, this is private. It is the Twitter equivalent of an e-mail. It is as secure and private as your e-mail password.

In order to send a direct message your intended recipient must be following you. To send a direct message begin your tweet with the letter "d" and the name of the Twitter user you are messaging. For example: "d nationals hey there!"

In addition to directing tweets to specific individuals, you can also append your messages with hashtags. In the National's message mentioned above, they included "#FF" in their tweet. Anyone can create a hashtag by simply including the "#" sign before a word or phase (with no spaces). #FF refers to "Follow Friday," which is a Twitter cultural phenomenon where Twitter users recommend other interesting people to their own follows. Using those hashtags allows people to quickly search all of Twitter for any tweet that relates. It is just a shorthand indexing or labeling system.

The true power of Twitter comes alive in its integration with a myriad of third-party applications. These applications can help you search for keywords mentioning yourself or your company, organize your followers into manageable groups, schedule tweets so that you can maintain a digital activity during times in which you aren't literally in front of your Twitter-enabled device.

We recommend checking out two services: TweetDeck (http://www.tweetdeck.com) and Hoot Suite (http://hootsuite.com). There are many alternatives to these, but going to their sites and understanding how they work provide a good primer.

Yelp

The primary problems that people run into on sites like Yelp fall into two categories: spurious complaints and legitimate complaints.

Every business owner knows that there are those occasions where the company policy wasn't executed as it was intended. If you are receiving honest complaints about your business on a review site like

Yelp, then you have an opportunity to turn that negative review into a compelling positive story.

If you do not respond to these complaints—or worse, if you respond poorly—then you can further mire yourself in negativity. For a cautionary tale, a small bakery in Arizona was criticized by a first-time customer who posted a detailed negative review conveying why he felt the bakery wasn't up to snuff—poor service, reheated food, high prices, and so forth. The owner responded, and in the first sentence of her lengthy angst-filled response begins using ALL CAPS and name-calling.

Does Yelp Make Things Worse?

Some business owners might feel like the existence of websites like Yelp is at best an exhausting annoyance and at worse a serious liability. As we discussed in truth remix, some have even accused Yelp of extorting ad dollars in order to "help" business owners overcome negative reviews. The truth is that overall, Yelp's existence really is a net plus for business owners.

After all, consider what the world would look like if Yelp didn't exist. We live in a world where social networks allow everyone to be an instantly published critic and where colorful commentary can easily go viral. In a world without Yelp, local business owners would still face the problem of negative online reviews—only without an effective platform on which to respond.

Without Yelp, potential customers would still search for information on the Internet and would instead have to learn to muddle a hodgepodge of individual postings on various websites.

If anything, Yelp empowers business owners by organizing the way that customers share and discover reviews. Putting these reviews into an organized fashion makes it easier to keep track of what people are saying, while also allowing business owners the chance to respond directly—either privately or publicly—to anyone's comments.

Yelp has in fact developed algorithms that punish reviewers who appear only to have written into Yelp to grind their axes. These reviews are given a low quality score and are pushed to the bottom of a business's page and are hidden by default.

Responding to Yelp Negative Reviews

The primary thing to keep in mind when responding to negative reviews is to remain unemotional and businesslike to avoid escalating the situation. In the case of the small bakery, her over-the-top response only brought her further negative publicity. Threatening people or arguing with reviewers is very ill advised.

To begin, read Yelp's own guidelines on how to respond to reviews. These are thorough and include tips like keeping the following in mind as you consider responding:

1. Your reviewers are your paying customers.
2. Your reviewers are human beings with (sometimes unpredictable) feelings and sensitivities.
3. Your reviewers are vocal and opinionated (otherwise they would not be writing reviews!).[9]

They also give a host of examples of bad and good reviews for you to consider. The focus is—as when you are responding to anyone's negative emotions—listen first, then empathize, then focus on how things can be different next time.

Yelp stresses that you should avoid coming across as highly impersonal or corporate. Limit the public promise of coupons or freebies. Offering something complimentary by private message can in some cases be appropriate if it is accompanied by a sincere acknowledgment of the reviewer's concerns.

With the rise of social media, however, customers increasingly expect to have a conversation with the businesses with which they interact. The gold standard example that Yelp offers is when you can assure a customer that his feedback has contributed to shaping actual changes within your business. You will need a Yelp Business account (it's free) in order to interact with your reviewers. You can set that up here: https://biz.yelp.com.

As with Facebook and Twitter, claim your piece of the Yelp community before you run into problems. Establishing an active presence on Yelp in advance of any negativity will help generate goodwill that you can draw on when a crisis arises.

Wikipedia

Wikipedia entries are usually near the top of most search results. It is a radical experiment in human knowledge and crowd-sourcing that has largely been successful. We have shown, however, that it is subject to abuse. Though Wikipedia's standards for Biographies of Living Persons (BLPs) have been tightened up since the attack on John Seigenthaler, it pays to know how to correct abuses when they occur.

Creating BLP Entries

You must have a BLP before you can worry about inaccuracies in your BLP. There are various criteria, the most important of which is that a person must be "notable." Wikipedia says, "A person is presumed to be notable if he or she has been the subject of multiple published secondary sources which are reliable, intellectually independent of each other, and independent of the subject."[10]

You should never try to write your own BLP, an act of vanity looked down upon by the Wikipedia community. However, there is nothing to stop a friendly person from creating one if there are in fact legitimate published secondary sources about you that meet Wikipedia's criteria. Just keep in mind that once a BLP is created, *anyone* can edit it. There are many people with Wikipedia BLPs who wish they didn't have one.

If you are thinking about writing a BLP for someone else, then be sure to:

1. Read the BLP main article (http://bit.ly/BLPinfo).
2. Read the Wikipedia Manual of Style on BLPs (http://bit.ly/BLPstyle).
3. Follow formatting guidelines.

Formatting guidelines can vary depending on the level of public detail about the subject of a BLP.

Take Stephen J. Dubner, the coauthor of *Freakonomics* as an example. If you look at his Wikipedia entry, http://en.wikipedia.org/wiki/Stephen_Dubner, you will find it to be relatively brief with a short background and a few categorized lists of other information (books, affiliations, etc.). Now look at the "Edit" version of the Dubner's page: http://bit.ly/BLPexample. If you scroll down through the code, then you will see those same categories demarcated by double equal signs (e.g., "==Books==").

Unless you are writing a very short BLP, then you will want to organize the information into the most natural categories. Review other

BLP entries for help in choosing the most appropriate categories for the page you are creating.

Editing Existing Entries and Responding to Inaccuracies

Editing Wikipedia entries is a tricky business, a task to be approached with caution. Do not assume that it will be a quick or painless process.

The first step is to create a Wikipedia account. This can be done by clicking the link in the upper right-hand corner of any page on Wikipedia entitled "Log in / create account." Choose a user name and know that your IP address will be associated with any edits you make. While you don't have to give your real name, don't make any edits that would be embarrassing should your real identity be connected with them.

To make a change to a Wikipedia entry, either adding something that is missing or correcting an error, you need to have the details of whatever you are looking to have included be verifiable—details publicly available from a reliable published source. For more on verifiability, see this: http://en.wikipedia.org/wiki/Wikipedia:Verifiability. Self-published sources or nonpublic mediums are not acceptable.

If your information exists in a verifiable source, then the next step is to post it in Talk (the page title), Discussion (tab). Technically speaking, you can just hit the edit button and make the change you want immediately. But doing so decreases the odds of your edit will actually remain in place.

The Discussion or Talk page lets you raise a good faith concern with the community of editors of any particular page. The ideal scenario is that when the community of editors is presented with a verifiable source of information they will permit an edit to go forward. Especially for contentious edits, try to win over the support of the community in advance of making any changes.

See the Talk page on the "Coal" entry for examples of how users raise issues of concern to them before moving forward with their own edits (http://en.wikipedia.org/wiki/Talk:Coal).

On this page, one Wikipedia user, Bridgettttttte, says, "In certain parts of the world, pro-coal or anti-coal statements can get a person elected to a government office. I have a POV on this issue: Many of these people could not pass freshman chemistry! So, as an encyclopedia, how do we describe the political aspects of coal without bias?" Raising an issue this way will help generate some goodwill, deference, and trust from the user community as you make your case.

Whether you are making edits directly or engaging in dialogue on the Talk Page, you should never create multiple Wikipedia accounts to inflate the apparent support for your efforts. Attempts at this sock puppetry can be easily uncovered, causing a vicious boomerang (or at least an accusation of it, as a post alleged against Bridgettttttte).

The similar tactic of enlisting a friendly person to create accounts and weigh in on your behalf on Talk Pages, called meat puppetry, has its reputational risks (don't ask your sister to do it). But it is technically permissible and can lend critical momentum.

Again this strategy, like every action within Wikipedia, is not a foolproof solution; you might find yourself unable to ultimately get exactly what you want. Nevertheless, patience and calm persistence is critical to building support and credibility—the ultimate currency in the Wiki economy.

Search Engine Optimization (SEO)

When you search for a name or a company's name, Google or Bing uses a complicated algorithm to determine what links to display and in what order. You and potential character assassins can manipulate this algorithm for good or ill.

Keywords

One of the ways the search engine algorithms can be used in a forthright way for higher search results is by frequent but appropriate use of keywords in the copy on a website. One example is the blog Fuel Lines written by Michael Gass, which is dedicated to helping small to medium-sized ad agencies develop new business. Gass publishes a new post every few days and typically finds a way to incorporate the phrases "ad agency" and "new business" in every post title.

For example, Gass wrote three blog posts in a five-day period with the following titles:

- "Survey: Economy Improving, New Business Is Up for Small to Midsize Ad Agencies"

- "Study: 50% of Ad Agencies Generate New Business Through Networks and Referrals"
- "The History and Evolution of Social Media for Ad Agency New Business"

Note that the two key phrases aren't always immediately next to each other, but he finds a way to work them in. Doing this consistently enables Gass to completely dominate the rankings for the search term "ad agency new business."

There is an entire industry devoted to playing the keyword ranking game. To learn more about that check out tools like Raven (http://raventools.com) or SEOmoz (http://www.seomoz.org/tools).

For the purposes of this book, be aware that keywords can be specifically leveraged by repeatedly using them in copy on websites. Have influence over what content appears at the top of a search results page for any given keyword that is important to your name, product, company, or brand.

One way you can build up insurance against attacks is to consistently publish positive information with your name. This is where establishing social media profiles on Facebook, Twitter, and Linkedln can help tremendously, as they often can easily rise to the top of a search for someone's name. It is also why establishing a website or blog where you regularly post under your name builds up the number of search results that you have influence over.

The more laissez-faire your approach to establishing positive keyword references, the easier it is for potential assailants to hijack the search results page for your name or brand.

Link Juice and Authority

Keywords are just the beginning of the search engine rankings game. Another way that search engines determine what to place at the top of rankings is whether many people on the Internet associate a particular link with a particular keyword. This intentional associating between URLs and keywords can be called anchoring or using anchor text.

Search engines pay attention to the text phrases in which website links are embedded. For example, if I run a blog about personal finance, then I will want other websites to link back to my website and embed that link with inside terms like "getting out of debt" or "investing basics."

However, not all websites are created equal in the eyes of the search engines. As we've seen before, the more links pointing to a given website, the more authoritative that website becomes. So an anchor text link from a website like CNN or *The New York Times* carries greater influence on the search engine results page than MyObscureBlog.com.

Google Bombing and Bowling

This sort of anchoring strategy can be used for satire or for malice. Like the "French military victories" link, detractors can embed anchor text that links your name with a scandalous website. This intentional deceptive manipulation is sometimes referred to as Google bombing.

Google is constantly refining its search algorithms. Over the years, search engines have taken steps to mitigate the influence of this kind of anchor text manipulation—whether intended for good or bad—by punishing especially greedy anchor text generators. This punishment usually takes the form of being pushed down toward the bottom of a search engine results page.

Google bowling occurs when attackers go about manipulating anchor text (or other SEO strategies like link building) in a way that appears to be benefiting you or your company. As a result, Google will punish your website, burying your company or product at the bottom of the search results.

Monitoring Online Activity

Earlier we discussed ways to assess your existing online profile. That of course is just a first step. You must protect yourself online by actively monitoring the Internet for potential threats. Fortune 500 companies can spend tens of thousands of dollars per month for robust online monitoring reports. However there are easy-to-use and free solutions for individuals and small business to establish a basic ability to keep tabs on the constant churn of the Internet.

Google Alerts

Head over to http://www.google.com/alerts and you can enter your name—or any keyword of interest—and select a frequency by which you will be notified of new (or updated) websites that contain that keyword. This tool is a good way to easily stay up-to-date on what is being said about you or your company.

Social Mention

Like Google Alerts, Social Mention offers a similar service, but it tracks social networks and blogs. You can also sign up with them to receive alerts based on keywords of your choosing at http://socialmention.com/alerts.

Google Reader

In addition to Google and Social Mention Alerts, you can also create search tools from a variety of forums and other websites. For example, head to Twitter Search (http://search.twitter.com) and enter a keyword (e.g., "Chuck Norris"). The results page will show you the most recent tweets mentioning that keyword.

In the upper right-hand corner is a link "Feed for this query." Clicking on that will enable you to import an automatically updated feed of the latest tweets mentioning whatever keyword you are interested in following. Google and Social Mention Alerts can also be delivered via RSS feed.

RSS stands for really simple syndication because it works like an automated newswire. Whenever a new piece of content—be it a blog post, a tweet, or whatever—is published on a website that offers an RSS feed, then a copy of that same content is also sent to its RSS subscribers. One of the benefits of using RSS is that you can easily organize the content of many websites (or search engines) into one place.

When it comes to online monitoring, RSS feeds are useful because they can keep the barrage of updates separate from your e-mail inbox. To do this you need an RSS reader. RSS readers are like special inboxes that have "unread" and "read" items. You can put RSS content into file folders or flag it for later follow-up.

One easy-to-use and free reader is Google Reader (http://www.google.com/reader).

Domain Defense

Your domain is your base identity inside your website's URL, or uniform resource locator. All domain names are registered with a name and contact information of the owner, the administrative contact, and the technical contact. This information is publicly available for every website on the Internet and can be easily searched for free. You can do so by going to http://www.whois.net.

The Whois Database

Take the New Deals coupon website as an example. Go to www.whois.net and enter www.dealnews.com. While the owner is listed as dealnews.com, Inc., two human contacts are also listed. In addition to an e-mail address, there is a physical address and a phone number listed.

If a website is publishing negative and false information, then checking the Whois database is a good place to start. In some cases the website may not provide any means of communicating with them, so the Whois database can help you contact the owner. Also, it is possible that the owner of a website is unaware that there is negative information on their website about you. Smaller websites that may have been long since abandoned by their original owner are often easily hacked and malicious content can be uploaded onto their domain.

But beyond responding to attacks, it is important to check to see what shows up in the Whois database for your personal and company website. We have had clients who had a personal blog domain that listed their family's home address and phone number. Scammers can easily collect all publicly available information from Whois databases that can lead to identity theft. Moreover, if someone is trying to seek you out personally, then having that information available may be a security issue.

Private Domain Registration

Keep your domain registration private. But how? To own a domain, you are required to include contact information, which is then publicly available. By using a service like Domains by Proxy, you can keep your domain registration private. For an annual fee, they will publish their own information, but forward any e-mails or letters to you.

The obvious downside of a service like this is that if you are trying to identify the owner of a website, they may have private registration as well. You will still be able to send them information, but their identity won't be revealed unless they contact you.

Domain Poaching

Another piece of information that is publicly available in the Whois database is when any domain was registered, when it was last renewed, and when it will expire. This data makes it easy for scammers to monitor when domains are about to expire and they can swoop in and purchase your domain out from under you.

The critical steps that you need to prevent this from happening are twofold: make sure that you have your domain registrar account set to auto renew, and make sure that your credit card or other payment information is up-to-date. Even if you have your domain set to auto renew, if on the day the registrar attempts to charge your credit card only to have it bounce back that the card is expired, then domain poachers can capitalize on your mistake.

Domain Theft

While domain poaching can be frustrating and is a borderline legal gray area, outright domain theft is also common (despite being obviously illegal). The most common method of domain theft occurs when a thief initiates a domain transfer.

Honest domain owners may want to transfer their domain from one registrar to another for a myriad of reasons: cost savings, different features, better customer service. In order to conduct a domain transfer, the owner generates a transfer code from the current registrar. This code is then sent to the e-mail address associated with the domain name. Once you have that transfer code you can enter it into a new registrar and the controls are moved.

Therefore, all a crook needs to do is to gain access to the e-mail address associated with any domain that they want to transfer. E-mail addresses can often be hacked with ease because most passwords aren't complex enough.

The first line of defense against domain theft is to create a secure passcode of the sort we discussed earlier for your e-mail account. The second is purchasing a "domain lock" service from your registrar. This kind of service typically carries an annual fee for which the registrar will prevent any transfer codes from being generated unless you go through a laborious unlocking process.

Laws of the Land—A Refresher

Again, on the Internet, the buck stops nowhere. Any legal recourse available to those who have endured wrongful behavior is through a patchwork of state, federal, and international law. The most famous and most often used online legal statute is the Digital Millennium Copyright Act or DMCA.

This law protects copyright owners from having their material unlawfully used online. The most common way that copyright owners attempt to deal with infringement is by sending a "cease and desist" or "take down" letter to the website hosting the illegal content. You can read a summary of the DMCA here: www.copyright.gov/legislation/dmca.pdf.

It should be noted that there are major exceptions to the law. The Safe Harbor provision, also known as DMCA 512, limits the liability of websites who may find themselves accidentally hosting copyrighted materials. The advocacy group Chilling Effects helpfully documents the requirements for a website to be granted the Safe Harbor exception:

A service provider who hosts content must:

- have no knowledge of, or financial benefit from, infringing activity on its network
- have a copyright policy and provide proper notification of that policy to its subscribers
- list an agent to deal with copyright complaints[11]

The Communications Decency Act of 1996

The most relevant section of the Communications Decency Act for those facing online attacks to their reputation is Section 230. This law rarely provides any satisfactory means of recourse, as there are broad protections for website owners. Website owners are not obligated to remove any content created by visitors to their sites. This user-generated content exception means that an anonymous person can post libelous or other harmful content on a website and the liability for that act remains with that person alone.

As with any human activity, it is easy to get discouraged by the catalog of horrors that is the Internet. And yet for all its misuses, digital media is a liberating technology that brings people together as never before and allows them to transform vast mountains of data into useful knowledge.

The web contains all wisdom, all faith, and all science, not just the darker precincts of the human psyche. It is no better or worse than the people who create it every day.

To comment, share your stories or solutions, and to stay current, join us at DigitalAssassinationBook.com.

Notes

1. The Digital Mosh Pit

1. John Seigenthaler, "A False Wikipedia Entry," Editorial/Opinion, *USA Today*, November 29, 2005, http://www.usatoday.com/news/opinion/editorials/2005-11-29-wikipedia-edit-x.htm.
2. Linsey Davis and Emily Friedman, "New Jersey Governor Wonders How Rutgers 'Spies' Can Sleep at Night After Tyler Clementi's Suicide," ABC News, September 30, 2010.
3. Tamara Linse, "A Senator's Suicide," *Casper* (WY) *Star-Tribune*, November 1, 2004.
4. CNET news.com, October 23, 2008; Jim Goldman, "Steve Jobs Talks New iPods, Health: My One on One," TechCheck, CNBC.com, September 9, 2008, http://www.cnbc.com/id/26628547/Steve_Jobs_Talks_New_ iPods_Health_My_One_on_One.
5. Tom Krazit, "Engadget Sends Apple Stock Plunging on iPhone Rumor," CNET Asia, May 16, 2007, http://asia.cnet.com/reviews/mobilephones/0,39050603,62013674,00.htm.
6. Howard Kurtz, "Clinton Hoax Retracted," *Washington Post*, January 22, 1999.
7. Patrick Byrne, "Roddy Boyd Sucks It Like He's Paying the Rent (Fortune Magazine)," DeepCapture.com, October 10, 2008, http://www.deepcapture.com/roddy-boyd-sucks-it-like-hes-paying-the-rent/; Patrick Byrne, "Today's Yawn: Scoffers of Law Rocker-Gradient Ignore Court Order & Roddy Boyd Shills, Exhibit Z," DeepCapture.com, January 14, 2010, http://www.deepcapture.com/rocker-gradient-scoff-at-law-and-roddy-boyd-shills/.
8. Roddy Boyd, "America's Nastiest CEO," The Big Money, January 19, 2010, http://www.thebigmoney.com/articles/judgments/2010/01/19/americas-nastiest-ceo.
9. Bethany McLean, "Phantom Menace," *Fortune*, November 14, 2005.
10. "About Deep Capture," http://www.deepcapture.com/about-deep-capture.
11. McLean, "Phantom Menace"; Joe Nocera, "Overstock's Campaign of Menace," *New York Times*, February 25, 2006; Susan Antilla, "Overstock Blames with Creepy Strategy," Bloomberg.com, February 21, 2007, http://www.bloomberg.com/apps/

news?pid=newsarchive&sid=aLDKLcXDf9PU; "Copper River Partners Settles Lawsuit with Overstock.com, Inc.," PR Newswire, December 8, 2009, http://www.prnewswire.com/news-releases/copper-river-partners-settles-lawsuit-with-overstockcom-inc-78832152.html.
12. Tom O'Neil, "How Far Have Oscars' Campaign Budgets Dropped?," Gold Derby (blog), *Los Angeles Times,* February 12, 2009, http://goldderby.latimes.com/awards_goldderby/2009/02/oscars-campaign.html#more.
13. Claire Atkinson, "Friending Oscar," *New York Post,* January 10, 2011.
14. Nikki Finke, "Much Ado About Oscar," *New York,* March 15, 1999.
15. "John Nash's Beautiful Mind," interview with Mike Wallace, *60 Minutes,* CBS News, March 17, 2002, http://www.cbsnews.com/stories/2002/03/14/60minutes/main503731.shtml; David Kohn, "Nash: Film No Whitewash," *60 Minutes,* CBS News, March 17, 2002; Matt Drudge, "Universal Rips Drudge After Nash Bash," March 8, 2002; Tom Tugend, "An Anti-Semitic Mind?" *The Jewish Journal,* March 14, 2002.
16. Rick Lyman, "A Beautiful Mind Meets Ugly Oscar Tactics," *New York Times,* March 16, 2002.
17. Ibid.

2. America's First Bloggers

1. Socialnomics09, "Social Media Revolution 2," accessed February 16, 2011, YouTube, http://www.youtube.com/watch?v=lFZ0z5Fm-Ng&feature=related.
2. "Memorable Quotes for *Thirteen Days* (2000)," Internet Movie Database, accessed February 17, 2011, http://www.imdb.com/title/tt0146309/quotes.

3. The First Sword: New Media Mayhem

1. Interview with Leo Yakutis by Mark Davis, October 8, 2010.
2. Interview with James Lee by Mark Davis, November 1, 2010.
3. Andy Greenberg, "The Streisand Effect," Forbes.com, May 11, 2007, http://www.forbes.com/2007/05/10/streisand-digg-web-tech-cx_ag_0511streisand.html.
4. Steve Lohr, "Library of Congress Will Save Tweets," *New York Times,* April 14, 2010.
5. Interview with Bill Livingstone by Mark Davis, October 10, 2010.
6. Perezhilton.com, January 27, 2010.
7. *Generation M2: Media in the Lives of 8- to 18-Year-Olds,* Kaiser Family Foundation, January 20, 2010, http://www.kff.org/entmedia/mh012010pkg.cfm.
8. Verizon Business RISK Team, 2009 Data Breach Investigations Report, http://www.verizonbusiness.com/resources/security/reports/2009_databreach_rp.pdf.
9. "Report: Most Companies Unprepared for Quick Response to Attack," DarkReading.com, October 5, 2009, http://www.darkreading.com/security/vulnerabilities/220301057/index.html.
10. Bill Gertz, *Washington Times,* February 17, 2000. Central Intelligence Agency Inspector General, Improper Handling of Classified Information by John M. Deutch, Report of Investigation (unclassified), February 18, 2000.
11. Frank Wolf, "Wolf Reveals House Computers Compromised by Outside Source," press release, June 11, 2008; "Rep. Wolf: China Hacked Congressional Computers," FoxNews.com, June 11, 2008, http://www.foxnews.com/story/0,2933,365635,00.html.

12. "Pentagon Source Says China Hacked Defense Department Computers," FoxNews .com, September 4, 2007, http://www.foxnews.com/story/0,2933,295640,00.html.
13. Andrew LaVallee, "AT&T Counters Verizon Ads with Luke Wilson's Help," Digits (blog), *Wall Street Journal,* November 20, 2009, http://blogs.wsj.com/digits/2009/11/20/att-counters-verizon-ads-with-luke-wilsons-help/.
14. Andy Soltis, "It's 'Starve Wars,'" *New York Post,* January 20, 2010.
15. Kathy Kristof, "Diet Smackdown," CBS MoneyWatch.com, January 20, 2010.
16. Jack Neff, "Burt's Puts Bees in Bonnet of Skin-Care Marketers," *Advertising Age,* January 31, 2008; mcmilker, "Attack the Ingredient Not the Brand—Is Burt's Bees' New Campaign on the Right Track?," Ecopreneurist.com, February 12, 2008, http://ecopreneurist.com/2008/02/12/attack-the-ingredient-not-the-brand-is-burts -bees-new-campaign-on-the-right-track.
17. *Advertising Age,* February 1, 2008.
18. L. Gordon Crovitz, "Facebook's Anti-Google Fiasco," *Wall Street Journal,* May 15, 2011; Sam Gustin, "Boom! Goes the Dynamite Under Facebook's Google Smear Campaign," *Wired,* May 12, 2011.
19. *Trial Lawyers, Inc.: A Report on the Lawsuit Industry in America, 2003,* Manhattan Institute for Policy Research.
20. "About Us," Huffington Post Investigative Fund, beta version accessed February 13, 2011, Huffpostfund.org./about-us.
21. "About," Franklin Center for Government and Public Integrity, http://www .franklincenterhq.org/about/.
22. Mike Hess, "Talking Poop, Nudity and Twitter with Robin Williams and Bobcat Goldthwait," PopEater.com, August 20, 2009, http://www.popeater.com/2009/08/20/talking-poop-nudity-and-twitter-with-robin-williams-and-bobcat/.
23. Mary Foster, "James O'Keefe, Accomplices Plead Guilty in Landrieu Break-in, Get Probation, Community Service, Light Fines," Huffington Post, May 26, 2010, http://www.huffingtonpost.com/2010/05/26/james-okeefe-pleads-guilty-sentenced _n_590559.html.
24. "Congressman Conyers Reads Playboy on Plane to DC," YouTube.com, November 25, 2010, http://www.youtube.com/watch?v=l9yhHiRc4-4.
25. "KFC Sink Trio Finger Lickin' Fired," Sky News, December 12, 2008, http://news .sky.com/skynews/Home/World-News/KFC-Bath-Prank-Three-Girls-Fired-From -California-KFC-After-Bathing-In-Restaurant-Sinks/Article/200812215178233.
26. Patrick Vogt, "Brands Under Attack: Marketers Can Learn from Domino's Video Disaster," *Forbes,* April 24, 2009.
27. Ibid.
28. A. J. Daulerio, "Duke 'Fuck List' Author Gets Potential Book, Movie Deals," Deadspin.com, October 1, 2010, http://deadspin.com/#!5653266/duke-fuck-list -author-gets-potential-book-movie-deals.
29. AOL Legal Department, Decisions & Litigation, *Zeran v. AOL* Opinion in the United States District Court for the Eastern District of Virginia, Alexandria Division, http://legal.web.aol.com/decisions/dldefam/zeranopi.html.
30. *Zeran v. America Online Inc.,* 129 F.3d 327 (4th Cir. 1997).
31. "Quotes for Alfred Pennyworth (Character)," Internet Movie Database, accessed February 15, 2011, http://www.imdb.com/character/ch0000204/quotes.

4. The Second Sword: Silent Slashers

1. Glaukôpis, "HBO's Rome ep 5," Glaukôpidos (blog), September 27, 2005, http://glaukopidos.blogspot.com/2005/09/hbos-rome-ep-5.html.
2. Suetonius, *The Twelve Caesars,* trans. Robert Graves (New York: Penguin, 1957), 231–32.
3. Ibid.
4. Portrait of Nero, from Paavo Castrén and Henrik Lilius, *Graffiti del Palatino,* ii, *Domus Tiberiana* (*Acta Instituti Romani Finlandiae,* IV) (Helsinki: Akateeminen Kirjakauppa, 1970), http://commons.wikimedia.org/wiki/File:Nero-graffito.jpg.
5. Mary Beard, *The Fires of Vesuvius: Pompeii Lost and Found* (Cambridge, Mass.: Belknap Press of Harvard University Press, 2010), 59.
6. Ibid., 202.
7. "The Writing on the Wall: Graffiti," quoting from the *Corpus Inscriptionum Latinarum,* vol. 4, *Destruction and Re-discovery,* accessed February 20, 2011, http://sites.google.com/site/ad79eruption/the-writing-on-the-wall.
8. Ibid.
9. Ibid.
10. Jamie Schram and Lukas I. Alpert, "Bar Goon's Slash and Smash Past," *New York Post,* July 31, 2008.
11. George Rush, "Outed Blogger Rosemary Port Blames Model Liskula Cohen for 'Skank' Stink," *New York Daily News,* August 23, 2009.
12. Owen Thomas, "Model Sues Google over 'Skank' Blog Post," Gawker, January 6, 2009, http://gawker.com/#!5124621/model-sues-google-over-skank-blog-post.
13. Jose Martinez, "Model Liskula Cohen Sues Google Over Blogger's 'Skank' Comment," *New York Daily News,* January 6, 2009.
14. David Margolick, "Slimed Online," Portfolio.com, February 11, 2009, http://www.portfolio.com/news-markets/national-news/portfolio/2009/02/11/Two-Lawyers-Fight-Cyber-Bullying.
15. Ibid.
16. Ellen Nakashima, "Harsh Words Die Hard on the Web," *Washington Post,* March 7, 2007.
17. Amir Efrati, "Students File Suit," Law Blog (blog), WSJ.com, June 12, 2007, http://blogs.wsj.com/law/2007/06/12/students-file-suit-against-autoadmit-director-others/.
18. Christopher Andrew and Vasili Mitrokhin, *The Sword and the Shield: The Mitrokhin Archive and the Secret History of the KGB* (New York: Basic Books, 1999), 245.
19. Interview with Sir Martin Gilbert, Pave the Way Foundation, http://www.barhama.com/PAVETHEWAY/gilbert.html.
20. Ibid.
21. Ion Mihai Pacepa, "Moscow's Assault on the Vatican," *National Review,* January 25, 2007, http://www.nationalreview.com/articles/219739/moscows-assault-vatican/ion-mihai-pacepa.
22. Andrew Ferguson, "You Don't Say?," *Forbes Life,* November 8, 2010.
23. Susan Stellin, "Hoteliers Look to Shield Themselves from Dishonest Online Reviews," Itineraries, *New York Times,* October 26, 2010.
24. Peter Martin, "Boyfriend Uses Netflix to Exact Revenge on Cheating Girlfriend," Cinematical: News (blog), moviefone.com, December 2, 2010, http://blog.moviefone.com/2010/12/02/boyfriend-netflix-girlfriend-cheating/.

25. Danny Sullivan, "Google Bombs Aren't So Scary," Search Engine Watch, March 18, 2002, http://searchenginewatch.com/2164611.
26. Farhad Manjoo, "Google Link Is Bush League," Wired, January 25, 2001, http://www.wired.com/science/discoveries/news/2001/01/41401.
27. Caroline McCarthy, "Stephen Colbert Finally Drops a Google Bomb," CNET News, April 19, 2007, http://news.cnet.com/8301-10784_3-9710844-7.html.
28. Chris Bowers, "A Different Way to Make a Big Difference in 2010," Daily Kos, October 8, 2010, http://www.dailykos.com/story/2010/10/08/908577/-A-different-way-to-make-a-big-difference-in-2010; Neil Stevens, "Tech at Night: Google, Daily Kos, Net Neutrality," RedState, October 11, 2010, http://www.redstate.com/neil_stevens/2010/10/11/tech-at-night-google-daily-kos-net-neutrality-2/.
29. http://blog.searchenginewatch.com/101013-085400.
30. Neil Stevens, "Google, Daily Kos, Net Neutrality," Redstate.com, Tech at Night, October 9, 2010, http://www.redstate.com/neil_stevens/2010/10/09/tech-at-night-google-daily-kos-net-neutrality/.
31. Saul D. Alinsky, *Rules for Radicals: A Practical Primer for Realistic Radicals* (New York: Vintage, 1989).
32. Gordon Willard Allport and Leo Joseph Postman, *The Psychology of Rumor* (New York: Henry Holt, 1947), 33.
33. Ibid., 3.
34. Fredrick Koenig, *Rumor in the Marketplace: The Social Psychology of Commercial Hearsay* (New York: Auburn House Publishing Company, 1985), 15.
35. Ibid., 132.
36. Ibid., 101.
37. Ibid., 40.
38. Ibid., 47.
39. Associated Press, "Procter & Gamble Awarded $19.25 Million in Satanism Lawsuit," FoxNews.com, March 20, 2007, http://www.foxnews.com/story/0,2933,259877,00.html.
40. Bernard Hart, "The Psychology of Rumour," *Proceedings of the Royal Society of Medicine* 9 (March 28, 1916): 20.
41. QuadsZilla, "GoogleBowling SEO Black Hats for Hire," SEO Black Hat (blog), http://seoblackhat.com/category/googlebowling/.
42. Ibid.
43. John Seigenthaler, "A False Wikipedia Entry," Editorial/Opinion, *USA Today*, November 29, 2005, http://www.usatoday.com/news/opinion/editorials/2005-11-29-wikipedia-edit_x.htm.
44. "Golfer Sues over Vandalized Wikipedia Page," Smoking Gun, February 22, 2007, http://www.thesmokinggun.com/documents/crime/golfer-sues-over-vandalized-wikipedia-page.
45. Philippe Naughton, "Wikipedia Founder's Fling with Columnist Ends in Nasty Public Breakup," *Times* (London), March 4, 2008, http://www.foxnews.com/story/0,2933,334652,00.html.
46. Ibid.
47. "Rachel Marsden and Jimmy Wales' Sex Chats and Break-up E-Mail," Huffington Post via Valleywag (blog), March 3, 2008, updated March 28, 2008, http://www.huffingtonpost.com/2008/03/03/rachel-marsden-and-jimmy-_n_89566.html.
48. Jordan Golson, "The Goodbye Email from Jimmy Wales's Girlfriend," Valleywag

(blog), Gawker, March 2, 2010, http://gawker.com/valleywag/?_escaped_fragment_=362814/the-goodbye-email-from-jimmy-waless-girlfriend.
49. Cade Metz, "Jimbo Wales Dumps Lover on Wikipedia," Register, March 3, 2008, http://www.theregister.co.uk/2008/03/03/jimbo_wales_rachel_marsden.
50. "Wikipedia: Biographies of Living Persons," Wikipedia, accessed February 22, 2011, http://en.wikipedia.org/wiki/Wikipedia:Biographies_of_living_persons.
51. Margolick, "Slimed Online."
52. Ibid.
53. Ibid.
54. Koenig, *Rumor in the Marketplace*, 16.
55. Ibid., 59–60.
56. Margolick, "Slimed Online."
57. John Markoff and David E. Sanger, "In a Computer Worm, a Possible Biblical Clue," *New York Times*, September 30, 2010.

5. The Third Sword: Evil Clones

1. Anna Vander Broek, "Managing Your Online Identity," Forbes.com, June 2, 2009, http://www.forbes.com/2009/06/01/manage-online-reputation-technology-identity.html.
2. http://www.chasemasterson.com/about.html.
3. *Carafano v. Metrosplash.com, Inc.*, 339 F.3d 1119 (9th Cir. 2003).
4. Ibid.
5. Ibid.
6. Interview with confidential source, by Mark Davis, October 8, 2010.
7. Peter Hannaford, "False Free Speech," Media Matters, *American Spectator*, September 8, 2008, http://spectator.org/archives/2008/09/08/false-free-speech.
8. Melody Y. Hu, Eric P. Newcomer, and Monika L. S. Robbins, "Allegations Cloud Harvard Republican Club Race," *Harvard Crimson*, November 19, 2010, http://www.thecrimson.com/article/2010/11/19/email-mclean-mckinsey-martinez/.
9. Hamilton Nolan, "Dirty Tricks at the Harvard Republican Club," Gawker, November 19, 2010, http://gawker.com/#!5694275/dirty-tricks-at-the-harvard-republican-club.
10. Hu, Newcomer, and Robbins, "Allegations Cloud Harvard Republican Club Race."
11. Sarah Lai Stirland, "Decoy Election Websites Pretend to Root for Your Candidate," Politics: Online Rights, Wired, November 6, 2007, http://www.wired.com/politics/onlinerights/news/2007/11/spoof_forums ; Kevin Poulsen, "Backlash Comparison: Who's Nuttier, Apple Fanatics or Ron Paul Enthusiasts?," Threat Level (blog), Wired, November 6, 2007, http://www.wired.com/threatlevel/2007/11/whos-nuttier-ap/.
12. "Bass Aide Resigns After Posing as Democrat on Blogs," WMUR.com, September 26, 2006, http://www.wmur.com/politics/9936715/detail.html; Anne Saunders, Associated Press, "Bass Aide Resigns for Fake Website Postings," *Concord Monitor*, September 27, 2006, http://www.concordmonitor.com/article/bass-aide-resigns-for-fake-website-postings.
13. http://www.hollywoodreporter.com/thr-esq/jake-gyllenhaal-claims-defamation-by-190274.
14. Isaiah Wilner, "The Number-One Girl," *New York*, May 7, 2007.
15. Tom Krazit, "Engadget Sends Apple Stock Plunging on iPhone Rumor," Crave (blog), CNET News, March 16, 2007, http://news.cnet.com/8301-17938_105-9719952-1.html?tag+mncol;3n.

16. Corey Grice, "23-year-old Arrested in Emulex Hoax," CNET News, August 31, 2000, http://news.cnet.com/2100-1033-245192.html; "Telecommunications: Prison Sentence in Hoax," Technology Briefing, *New York Times,* August 8, 2001.
17. Mike Hughlett, "Fake News Release Targets General Mills in Possible Stock Swindle," *Star Tribune* (Minneapolis–St. Paul), June 16, 2010.
18. Mike Hughlett, "General Mills Hoaxer Surfaces," *Star Tribune* (Minneapolis–St. Paul), June 18, 2010.
19. "Javelin Pharmaceuticals: US Supreme Court Split—Rules in Favor of Big Pharma," Business Wire, Benzinga, June 18, 2010, http://www.benzinga.com/press-releases/10/06/b340226/javelin-pharmaceuticals-us-supreme-court-split-rules-in-favor-of-big-ph.
20. "Phony New Releases on the Rise," Capitol Communicator, June 21, 2010, http://www.capitolcommunicator.com/News/tabid/116/EntryID/1078/Default.aspx.
21. Hughlett, "Fake News Release."
22. Gennaro D'Amato et al., "Facebook: A New Trigger for Asthma?" *Lancet,* 376, no. 9754 (November 20, 2010): .1740, doi:10.1016/S0140-6736(10)62135-6.
23. *United States of America v. Lori Drew,* Grand Jury, U.S. District Court for the Central District of California, February 2008, CR08-00582.
24. Christopher Maag, "A Hoax Turned Fatal Draws Anger but No Charges," *New York Times,* November 28, 2007.
25. Jennifer Steinhauer, "Woman Who Posed as Boy Testifies in Case that Ended in Suicide of 13-Year-Old," *New York Times,* November 20, 2008.
26. Jonann Brady, "Exclusive: Teen Talks About Her Role in Web Hoax that Led to Suicide," *Good Morning America,* ABC News, April 1, 2008, http:/abcnews.go.com/GMA/story?id=4560582&page=1.
27. Ibid.
28. Kim Zetter, "Judge Acquits Lori Drew in Cyberbullying Case, Overrules Jury," Threat Level (blog), Wired.com, July 2, 2009, http://www.wired.com/threatlevel/2009/07/drew_court/.
29. Ibid.
30. Ibid.
31. Offenses Against the Person, Missouri Revised Statutes, Chapter 565, Section 565.225, August 28, 2010, http://www.moga.mo.gov/statutes/C500-599/5650000225.HTM.
32. Mattathias Schwartz, "The Trolls Among Us," *New York Times Magazine,* August 3, 2008.
33. Rodney D. Sieh, "FPA EX: Emails Tie Lib. Officials to LISCR Deal Bribery; U.S. Help Sought in Probe," FrontPage Africa, August 20, 2008, http://webcache.googleusercontent.com/search?q=cache:V6UWFnZeDU8J:www.frontpageafrica.com/newsmanager/anmviewer.asp%3Fa%3D7118%26print%3Dyes+"FAP+EX:Emails+Tie+Lib.+Officials+to+LISCR+Deal+Bribery%3B+U.S.+Help+Sought+in+Probe,"&cd=1&hl=en&ct=clnk&gl=us&client=safari&source=www.google.com.
34. Ibid.
35. Aaron Leaf, "Liberian Saga: Angry Court, Jailed Editor, President's Speech," CPJ Blog (blog), Committee to Protect Journalists, January 27, 2011, http://www.cpj.org/blog/2011/01/Liberia-saga-court-jail-editor-sirleaf.php.
36. Ian Grant, "Cybersquatters Launch 10,000 Attacks a Week on Top Brands," Computer-Weekly.com, February 28, 2008, http://www.computerweekly.com/Articles/2008/02/28/229627/Cybersquatters-launch-10000-attacks-a-week-on-top-brands.htm.

37. Interview with James Lee, by Mark Davis, November 1, 2010.
38. Interview with Bill Livingstone, by Mark Davis, October 5, 2010.
39. Ibid.
40. *Kevin Spacey v. John Zuccarini,* National Arbitration Forum, claim no. FA010300 0096937, May 8, 2001, http://www.adrforum.com/domains/decisions/96937.htm.
41. Memorandum in Opposition to Preliminary Injunction, Alitalia–Linee Aeree Italiane S.P.A. v. William Porta, United States District Court for the Southern District of New York, 00 civ. 9731, http://www.citizen.org/litigation/article_redirect.cfm?ID=1898.
42. Barry Hurd, "United Airlines CEO Glenn Tilton Under Attack—By Pilot Union," Reputation Examples (blog), Social Media Reputation, August 18, 2008, http://socialmediareputation.com/2008/08/united-airlines-ceo-glenn-tilton-under-attack-by-pilot-union/.
43. http://untied.com.
44. Clifford Krauss, "Oil Spill's Blow to BP's Image May Eclipse Its Cost," *New York Times,* April 29, 2010.
45. Ann Gerhart, "BP Chairman Talks About the 'Small People,' Further Angering Gulf," *Washington Post,* June 17, 2010.
46. Alan Mascarenhas, "BP Global PR vs. BPGlobalPR," *Newsweek,* July 4, 2010.
47. Upright Citizens Brigade, "BP Spills Coffee," UCB Topical video, 2:48, accessed February 25, 2011, http://www.ucbcomedy.com/videos/play/6472/bp-spills-coffee; Upright Citizens Brigade, "BP: Rich Fish," The Brig video, 1:13, accessed February 25, 2011, http://www.ucbcomedy.com/videos/play/6409/bp-rich-fish.
48. Upright Citizens Brigade, "Zuckerberg's Facebook Apology," Diamonds, Wow! video, 1:54, accessed February 25, 2011, http://www.ucbcomedy.com/videos/play/6425/zuckerbergs-facebook-apology.
49. Ben Jackson, "Kit Kat Manufacturer Nestlé to Stop Using Oil After Graphic Greenpeace YouTube Video Airs," *Sun* (London), May 18, 2010.
50. "Bhopal Disaster—BBC—The Yes Men," YouTube video, 5:30, from BBC World TV, posted by "razorfoundation," January 2, 2007, http://www.youtube.com/watch?v=LiWlvBro9eI.
51. The Yes Men, http://theyesmen.org.
52. Ryan Gilbey, "Jokers to the Left, Jokers to the Right," *Guardian,* July 17, 2009.
53. The Yes Men, http://dowethics.com.
54. Ibid.
55. The Yes Men, "WTO Announces Formalized Slavery Market for Africa," accessed February 25, 2011, http://gatt.org.
56. Dave Gilson, "The Yes Men Hack the iPhone," *Mother Jones,* November 19, 2010, http://motherjones.com/mojo/2010/11/yes-men-iphone-congo.
57. David Zax, "Yes Men Attack Apple, Advertising Special 'Conflict-Free' iPhone," Fast Company, November 19, 2010, http://www.fastcompany.com/1703966/yes-men-attack-apple-advertising-special-conflict-free-iphone.
58. Kate Sheppard, "The Yes Men Punk the Chamber," *Mother Jones,* October 19, 2009, http://motherjones.com/mojo/2009/10/yes-men-punk-chamber; "The Yes Men Pull Off Prank Claiming US Chamber of Commerce Had Changed Its Stance on Climate Change," democracynow.org, October 20, 2009, http://www.democracynow.org/2009/10/20/yes_men_pull_off_prank_claiming; "Fox Business Network on Chamber Climate Hoax," YouTube video, 1:39, from a broadcast on Fox Business Network, posted by "eviltwinbooking," October 19, 2009, http://www.youtube.com/watch?v=rF3Kks8O_Mk.

59. (No byline), CNBC.com, "GE Rebuffs Tax Refund Report as 'Hoax,'" April 13, 2011, http://www.cnbc.com/id/42570045.
60. Evan Buxbaum, "New York Post Not Laughing at Climate Change Spoof," CNN.com, September 22, 2009, http://articles.cnn.com/2009-09-22/us/new.york.fake.newspaper_1_climate-change-climate-meeting-new-yorkers?_s=PM:US.
61. "The Yes Men—Exxon Hoax: Vivoleum," YouTube video, 9:59, from a broadcast on bnetTV, posted by bnetTV, June 19, 2007, http://www.youtube.com/watch?v=WkLzK13rI-Y.
62. Stuart Elliott, "Prankster Lampoon Chevron Ad Campaign," Media Decoder (blog), *New York Times*, October 18, 2010, http://mediadecoder.blogs.nytimes.com/2010/10/18/pranksters-lampoon-chevron-ad-campaign.
63. The Yes Men, "Help Us Keep Chevron's Campaign on the Skids!," TheYesMen.org, accessed February 25, 2011, http://theyesmen.org/blog/help-us-keep-chevrons-campaign-on-the-skids.
64. Interview with "Steve" by Mark Davis, November 27, 2010. All names and identifying details of the story of "Steve" and "Linda" have been changed.
65. http://www.senatorsimitian.com/images/uploads/SB_1411_Fact_Sheet.pdf.
66. Aaron Kelly, "Consequences of Filing a False DMCA Takedown Request," Aaron Kelly Intellectual Property Law Blog (blog), Lawyers.com, December 8, 2010, http://intellectual-property.lawyers.com/blogs/archives/10363-Consequences-of-filing-a-false-DMCA-Takedown-Request.html.

6. The Fourth Sword: Human Flesh Search Engines

1. Mary Kay Magistad, "China Web Attacks Get Personal," phonetic transcript of a radio broadcast, *PRI's The World*, 1/15/10, http://www.theworld.org/2010/01/china-web-attacks-get-personal/; Venkatesan Vembu, "The Meow Murderess Brought to Heel," DNAIndia, March 18, 2006, http://www.dnaindia.com/world/report_the-meow-murderess-brought-to-heel_1018584.
2. Jonathan Krim, "Subway Fracas Escalates into Test of the Internet's Power to Shame," *Washington Post*, July 7, 2005.
3. Isaiah Wilner, "The Number-One Girl," *New York*, May 7, 2007.
4. Magistad, "China Web Attacks Get Personal."
5. Mattathias Schwartz, "The Trolls Among Us," *New York Times Magazine*, August 3, 2008.
6. "Jail for Lab Boss Attacker," BBC News, August 6, 2001, http://news.bbc.co.uk/2/hi/uk_news/1494924.stm; Andrew Alderson, "The Men Who Stood Up to an Animal Rights' Militant," Telegraph.co.uk, January 17, 2009, http://www.telegraph.co.uk/news/uknews/law-and-order/4276376/The-men-who-stood-up-to-animal-rights-militants.html.
7. "A Controversial Laboratory," BBC News, January 18, 2001, http://news.bbc.co.uk/2/hi/uk_news/1123837.stm.
8. Marco Evers, "Britain's Other War on Terror: Resisting the Animal Avengers," Spiegel Online, November 19, 2007, http://www.spiegel.de/international/europe/0,1518,517875,00.html.
9. "A Controversial Laboratory," BBC News.
10. Zoe Broughton, "Seeing Is Believing—Cruelty to Dogs at Huntingdon Life Sciences," *Ecologist*, March 2001, http://findarticles.com/p/articles/mi_m2465/is_2_31/ai_71634854/?tag=content;col1.

11. Ibid.
12. David Harrison and Daniel Foggo, "Terrorists Target Lab's Shareholders," Telegraph .Co.Uk, December 3, 2000, http://www.telegraph.co.uk/news/uknews/1376731/Terrorists-target-labs-shareholders.html.
13. Evers, "Britain's Other War on Terror."
14. Harrison and Foggo, "Terrorists Target Lab's Shareholders."
15. "Animal Rights or Wrongs," The Money Programme, BBC News World Edition, October 23, 2001, http://news.bbc.co.uk/2/hi/programmes/the_money_programme/archive/1602541.stm; "Pressure Builds on Animal Tests Lab," BBC News, January 16, 2001, http://news.bbc.co.uk/2/hi/uk_news/1120259.stm.
16. Jo-Ann Goodwin, "The Animals of Hatred," *Daily Mail* (London), October 15, 2003, transcribed at DawnWatch.com, http://lists.envirolink.org/pipermail/ar-news/Week-of-Mon-20031013/008215.html.
17. Harrison and Foggo, "Terrorists Target Lab's Shareholders."
18. Goodwin, "The Animals of Hatred."
19. Ibid.
20. Megan Murphy, "Activists in Live Testing Trial Deny Blackmail," FT.com, October 6, 2008.
21. Evers, "Britain's Other War on Terror"; "A Controversial Laboratory," BBC News.
22. Confidential interview with security consultant by Mark Davis, November 2010.
23. Heather Tomlinson, "Huntingdon Delays Listing After Attacks," Guardian.co.uk, September 8, 2005, http://www.guardian.co.uk/business/2005/sep/08/research.animalrights.
24. Goodwin, "The Animals of Hatred."
25. Fran Yeoman, "Extremists Face Long Jail Sentences After Blackmail Conviction," *Sunday Times* (London), December 24, 2008, http://www.timesonline.co.uk/tol/news/uk/crime/article5391798.ece.
26. Confidential interview with security expert by Mark Davis, November 2010.
27. Anonymous, "I Had a One-Night Stand with Christine O'Donnell," Gawker, October 28, 2010, http://gawker.com/#!5674353/i-had-a-one+night-stand-with-christine-odonnell.
28. Andrew Sullivan, "Defending Christine O'Donnell," Daily Dish (blog), *Atlantic*, October 29, 2010, http://andrewsullivan.theatlantic.com/the_daily_dish/2010/10/smearing-christine-odonnell.html.
29. Interview with Carol Howard Merritt, by Mark Davis, December 16, 2010.
30. Carol Howard Merritt, "Why Evangelicalism Is Failing a New Generation," Huffington Post, May 1, 2010, http://www.huffingtonpost.com/carol-howard-merritt/why-evangelicalism-is-fai_b_503971.html.
31. Leslie Katz, "Calif. Court Drops Charges Against Dunn," CNET News, March 14, 2007, http://news.cnet.com/Calif.-court-drops-charges-against-Dunn/2100-1014_3-6167187.html.
32. Interview with Tom Kellermann, by Mark Davis, November 18, 2010.
33. Amanda Hess, "Web Site Attempts to Convince Gay Priests to Stop Being Hypocrites," *Washington City Paper*, November 19, 2009, http://www.washingtoncitypaper.com/blogs/sexist/2009/11/19/web-site-attempts-to-convince-gay-priests-to-stop-being-hypocrites/.
34. Stephanie Condon, "Wiki Site Wants Help Finding Dirt on Meg Whitman," Political Hotsheet, CBS News.com, March 9, 2010, http://www.cbsnews.com/8301-503544_162-20000195-503544.html.

35. Ginger Adams Otis, "Taliban's Chilling Hunt and Slaughter: Pak-Trained Killers 'Used Facebook' to Track Aid Group," *New York Post,* August 15, 2010.
36. Michael Bristow, "China's Internet 'Spin Doctors,'" BBC Mobile News, December 16, 2008, http://news.bbc.co.uk/2/hi/7783640.stm.
37. Ibid.
38. Matt Richtel, "In Web World of 24/7 Stress, Writers Blog Till They Drop," *New York Times,* April 6, 2008.
39. Damian Grammaticas, "Chinese Woman Jailed over Twitter Post," BBC News Asia-Pacific, November 18, 2010, http://www.bbc.co.uk/news/world-asia-pacific-11784603.
40. "PayPal Says It Stopped Wikileaks Payments on US Letter," BBC Mobile News Business, December 8, 2010, http://www.bbc.co.uk/news/business-11945875.
41. Schwartz, "The Trolls Among Us"; numerous troll sites.
42. Elinor Mills, "Hacker in AT&T-iPad Security Case Arrested on Drug Charges," CNET News, June 15, 2010, http://news.cnet.com/8301-27080_3-20007827-245.html.
43. "User Talk:Donations," Encyclopedia Dramatica, accessed February 26, 2011, http://encyclopediadramatica.com/User_talk:Donations.
44. David Margolick, "Slimed Online," Portfolio.com, February 11, 2009, http://www.portfolio.com/news-markets/national-news/portfolio/2009/02/11/Two-Lawyers-Fight-Cyber-Bullying.
45. "Pressure Builds on Animal Tests Lab," BBC News; "Jail for Lab Boss Attacker," BBC News.
46. The Torrenzano Group trademark.

7. The Fifth Sword: Jihad by Proxy

1. Brian Williams, "Questions Over Business Links: Greenie in Carton War," *Courier-Mail* (Brisbane, Australia), February 10, 1995; Bob Burton, "Sometimes Truth Leaks Out: Failed PR Stunts 'Down Under,'" PRwatch.org, 4th quarter 1996, http://www.prwatch.org/prwissues/1997Q4/badpr.html.
2. Williams, "Questions Over Business Links"; Jim Pollard, *Herald Sun,* February 9, 2007.
3. Interview with digital expert by Mark Davis, November 12, 2010.
4. Jo-Ann Goodwin, "The Animals of Hatred," *Daily Mail* (London), October 15, 2003, transcribed at DawnWatch.com, http://lists.envirolink.org/pipermail/ar-news/Week-of-Mon-20031013/008215.html.
5. Marco Evers, "Britain's Other War on Terror: Resisting the Animal Avengers," Spiegel Online, November 19, 2007, http://www.spiegel.de/international/europe/0,1518,517875,00.html.
6. Goodwin, "The Animals of Hatred."
7. Ryan Sager, "Keep Off the Astroturf," op-ed, *New York Times,* August 19, 2009.
8. Ben Smith, "The Summer of Astroturf," Politico.com, August 21, 2009, http://www.politico.com/news/stories/0809/26312.html.
9. Jim VandeHei and Paul Fahri, "POWs Shown in Film Join Swift Boat Group's Anti-Kerry Efforts," *Washington Post,* October 14, 2004.
10. Jim Kuhnhenn, "Chamber Emerges as Formidable Political Force," Associated Press, August 21, 2010, http://www.msnbc.msn.com/id/38797920/ns/politics-decision_2010/.
11. Michael Luo, "Left's Big Donors Gather to Plot Strategy," *New York Times,* November 15, 2010.

12. Interview with a political consultant by Mark Davis, December 15, 2010.
13. R. Jeffrey Smith, "The DeLay-Abramoff Money Trail," *Washington Post,* December 31, 2005.
14. Ibid.
15. Susan Schmidt, "Ex-Lobbyist Is Focus of Widening Investigations," *Washington Post,* July 16, 2004.
16. Dana Milbank, "One Committee's Three Hours of Inquiry, in Surreal Time," *Washington Post,* June 23, 2005; Alex Gibney, "The Deceptions of Ralph Reed," Atlantic.com, September 26, 2010, http://www.theatlantic.com/politics/archive/2010/09/ralph-reed-is-a-liar/63568/.
17. "About TVC," Traditional Values Coalition, accessed March 2, 2011, http://www.traditionalvalues.org/about.php.
18. Susan Schmidt and James V. Grimaldi, "How a Lobbyist Stacked the Deck," *Washington Post,* October 16, 2005.
19. Ibid.
20. James V. Grimaldi and Susan Schmidt, "Lawmaker's Abramoff Ties Investigated," *Washington Post,* October 18, 2005; R. Jeffrey Smith, "Foundation's Funds Diverted from Mission," September 28, 2004.
21. Susan Schmidt, "Casino Bid Prompted High-Stakes Lobbying," *Washington Post,* March 13, 2005.
22. Eric Reguly, "How Far to Go for Gold?," *Globe and Mail* (Toronto), last updated November 23, 2010, http://www.theglobeandmail.com/report-on-business/rob-magazine/how-far-to-go-for-gold/article1775540/.
23. "Environmental Benefits," QwikReport, Gabriel Resources, accessed March 2, 2011, http://www.gabrielresources.com/s/QwikReport.asp?IsPopup=Y&printVersion=now&XB0W=133378,128087.
24. Reguly, "How Far to Go for Gold?"
25. "Actual Situation in Rosia Montana," ProRosia Montana, accessed March 2, 2011, http://prorosiamontana.ro/voices-of-rosia-montana-actual-situation-in-rosia-montana/actual-situation-in-rosia-montana/.
26. Alan R. Hill, "The Facts of the Matter: Who Is Behind the Opposition to the Rosia Montana Project—And Why It Matters to All Romanians" (speech, Bucharest, Romania, September 5, 2007), http://www.gabrielresources.com/i/pdf/AlansspeechFINAL.pdf.
27. Reguly, "How Far to Go for Gold?"; "In Partnership: For the Economy," Gabriel Resources, accessed March 2, 2011, http://www.gabrielresources.com/benefits-econ.htm.
28. Cultural Benefits Report, Gabriel Resources, accessed March 2, 2011, http://www.gabrielresources.com/s/CulturalBenefits.asp?ReportID=128090.
29. "Cyanide Spill Reaches Danube," BBC News, February 13, 2000, http://news.bbc.co.uk/2/hi/europe/641566.stm; Reguly, "How Far to Go for Gold?"
30. Reguly, "How Far to Go for Gold?"
31. Ceremony Remarks, "Stephanie Danielle Roth: Romania Oil & Mining," Goldman Environmental Prize 2005 video 4:22, http://www.goldmanprize.org/node/158.
32. "Stephanie Danielle Roth: Romania Oil & Mining," Goldman Environmental Prize, http://www.goldmanprize.org/node/158.
33. Hill, The "Facts of the Matter."
34. Mary Katharine Ham, "The Forgotten Mammal," Townhall.com, January 26, 2007,

http://townhall.com/columnists/marykatharineham/2007/01/26/the_forgotten_mammal.

35. "Redgrave in Romanian Mine Rumpus," BBC News, last updated June 23, 2006, http://news.bbc.co.uk/2/hi/5110784.stm.
36. Reguly, "How Far to Go for Gold?"
37. Hill, "The Facts of the Matter."
38. Ibid.
39. Ibid.
40. Dorothy Kosich, "Soros Fund Holdings Favor Aluminum Corp of China, CVRD, Gold Stocks," Mineweb, August 15, 2007, http://www.mineweb.com/mineweb/view/mineweb/en/page60?oid=25124&sn=Detail.
41. Hill, "The Facts of the Matter."
42. Ibid.
43. Jesse Westbrook, "SEC Delays Proxy-Access Rules Amid Legal Challenge," *Bloomberg Businessweek,* October 4, 2010, http://www.businessweek.com/news/2010-10-04/sec-delays-proxy-access-rules-amid-legal-challenge.html.
44. "Help: How to Research Front Groups," SourceWatch, accessed March 2, 2011, http://www.sourcewatch.org/index.php?title=Help:How_to_research_front_groups.
45. Hill, "The Facts of the Matter."
46. Phelim McAleer and Ann McElhinney, "Green Lies and an Inconvenient Truth," *Irish Mail on Sunday,* February 18, 2007.

8. The Sixth Sword: Truth Remix

1. Murray Wardrop, "Young Will Have to Change Names to Escape 'Cyber Past' Warns Google's Eric Schmidt," Telegraph.Co.UK, August 18, 2010, http://www.telegraph.co.uk/technology/google/7951269/Young-will-have-to-change-names-to-escape-cyber-past-warns-Googles-Eric-Schmidt.html.
2. David Margolick, "Slimed Online," Portfolio.com, February 11, 2009, http://www.portfolio.com/news-markets/national-news/portfolio/2009/02/11/Two-Lawyers-Fight-Cyber-Bullying.
3. "About Us," Yelp, accessed March 4, 2011, http://www.yelp.com/about.
4. Ibid.
5. Interview with Washington, D.C., dentist by Mark Davis, November 21, 2010.
6. "About Us," Yelp.
7. Robin Wauters, "Yelp Hit with Class Action Lawsuit for Running an 'Extortion' Scheme," TechCrunch, February 24, 2010, http://techcrunch.com/2010/02/24/yelp-class-action-lawsuit/.
8. Leena Rao, "Complaints Against Yelp's 'Extortion' Practices Grow Louder," TechCrunch, March 17, 2010, http://techcrunch.com/2010/03/17/complaints-against-yelps-extortion-practices-grow-louder/.
9. "Yelp Elite Squad," Yelp, accessed March 4, 2011, http://www.yelp.com/elite.
10. Claire Cain Miller, "Yelp Will Let Businesses Respond to Web Reviews," *New York Times,* April 10, 2009.
11. Kirstin Downey Grimsley and Jay Mathews, "Executives' Privilege? In Boardroom, Sex Seldom Leads to Censure," *Washington Post,* September 16, 1998.
12. Adam Lashinsky, "Mark Hurd's Moment," *Fortune* online, CNNMoney.com, last updated March 3, 2009, http://money.cnn.com/2009/02/27/news/companies/lashinsky_hurd.fortune/index.htm.

13. Lashinsky, "Mark Hurd's Moment"; Connie Guglielmo, Ian King, and Aaron Ricadela, "HP's Mark Hurd Resigns After Sexual Harassment Probe," *Bloomberg Businessweek*, August 7, 2010, http://www.businessweek.com/news/2010-08-07/hp-chief-executive-hurd-resigns-after-sexual-harassment-probe.html.
14. Ben Worthen and Joann S. Lublin, "Woman in Hurd Case Regrets Dismissal," *Wall Street Journal*, August 9, 2010.
15. Ibid.
16. Ashlee Vance, "Boss's Stumble May Also Trip Hewlett-Packard," Technology, *New York Times*, August 8, 2010; Guglielmo, King, and Ricadela, "HP's Mark Hurd Resigns."
17. Ashlee Vance, "Oracle Chief Faults H.P. Board for Forcing Hurd's Resignation," Technology, *New York Times*, August 9, 2010.
18. Ashlee Vance and Matt Richtel, "H.P. Followed a P.R. Specialist's Advice in the Hurd Case," Technology, *New York Times*, August 9, 2010.
19. Ibid.
20. Jordan Robertson, "HP, Hurd Reach Settlement over Oracle Gig," *USA Today*, September 21, 2010.
21. Jesus Diaz, "How Apple Lost the Next iPhone," Gizmodo, April 19, 2010, http://gizmodo.com/#!5520438/how-apple-lost-the-next-iphone.
22. Peter Kafka, "Mobile Blogger 'Boy Genius' Unmasked, Acquired," MediaMemo, All Things Digital, *Wall Street Journal*, April 26, 2010, http://mediamemo.allthingsd.com/20100426/mobile-blogger-boy-genius-unmasked-acquired/; Jacob Schulman, "BlackBerry Storm 2 Dropping SurePress Screen?," Engadget, May 15, 2009, http://www.engadget.com/2009/05/15/blackberry-storm-2-dropping-surepress-screen/.
23. Engadget, July 27, 2009.
24. Wardrop, "Young Will Have to Change Names."
25. Seth Freeman, "Me and My Algorithm," op-ed, *New York Times*, January 17, 2011.
26. Jessica Bennett, "What the Internet Knows About You," *Newsweek*, October 22, 2010, http://www.newsweek.com/2010/10/22/forget-privacy-what-the-internet-knows-about-you.html.
27. Jeffrey Rosen, "The Web Means the End of Forgetting," *New York Times Magazine*, July 25, 2010.
28. Rosen, "The Web Means the End of Forgetting"; Brian Krebs, "Court Rules Against Teacher in MySpace 'Drunken Pirate' Case," Security Fix (blog), *Washington Post*, December 3, 2008, http://voices.washingtonpost.com/securityfix/2008/12/court_rules_against_teacher_in.html.
29. Wardrop, "Young Will Have to Change Names."
30. Ibid.
31. Noirin Shirley, "A Hell of a Time," NerdChic (blog), November 5, 2010, http://blog.nerdchic.net/archives/418/.
32. Comment by lucisferre, December 2010, on Noirin Shirley, "A Hell of a Time: Sexual Assault at Tech Conferences," on Reddit, accessed March 5, 2011, http://www.reddit.com/r/programming/comments/e20ct/a_hell_of_a_time_sexual_assault_at_tech/c14nozg.
33. "Killed in Stevenson Home, Girl Shot Accidentally by Former Vice President's Grandson," *New York Times*, December 31, 1912.
34. Joseph Cummins, *Anything for a Vote: Dirty Tricks, Cheap Shots, and October Surprises in U.S. Presidential Campaigns* (Philadelphia: Quirk Books, 2007), 210.

35. John McArdle, "Florida, 'Taliban Dan' TV Ad Backfires on Grayson," *Roll Call,* September 30, 2010, http://www.rollcall.com/issues/56_33/atr/50384-1.html.
36. Kyle Western, *Men's Health,* 12/2010; Tom Espiner, "Private Browsing Tools Still Leave Data Trail," ZDNet Asian Edition, August 10, 2010, http://www.zdnetasia.com/private-browsing-tools-still-leave-data-trail-62201970.htm.
37. Samuel D. Warren and Louis D. Brandeis, "The Right to Privacy," *Harvard Law Review* 4 (December 15, 1890).
38. "Celebs Beware! New Pandora's Box of 'Personal' Drones That Could Stalk Anyone from Brangelina to Your Own Child," dailymail.co.uk, November 8, 2010, http://www.dailymail.co.uk/sciencetech/article-1327343/Personal-recreation-drones-developed.html.
39. "Man Pleads in Apparent Sextortion Case," Myfoxla.com, July 19, 2010, http://www.myfoxla.com/dpp/news/local/man-pleads-in-apparent-sextortion-case-20100719.
40. Anjeanette Damon and David McGrath Schwartz, "Sharron Angle Offers Juice to Tea Party of Nevada Opponent," *Las Vegas Sun,* October 5, 2010.
41. HKLawposterous.com; Dan Hicks, "Online Attacks Are Very Real Crises," Communicating Through a Crisis (blog), Institute for Crisis Management, March 10, 2009, crisisexperts.blogspot.com/2009/03/online-attacks-are-very-real-crises.html.
42. Cummins, *Anything for a Vote,* 120.
43. Ibid., 126.
44. Ibid., 52.
45. Richard H. Davis, "The Anatomy of a Smear Campaign," *Boston Globe,* March 21, 2004.
46. Suetonius, *The Twelve Caesars,* trans. Robert Graves (New York: Penguin, 1957).
47. Marcus Tullius Cicero, *Secondary Orations Against Verres,* Book 1, www.Uah.edu/student_life/organizations/sal/texts/latin/classical/cicero/inverrems1e.html.
48. Ibid.
49. H. Paul Jeffers, *An Honest President: The Life and Presidencies of Grover Cleveland* (New York: William Morrow, 2000), 106–107.
50. Ibid., 108.
51. Allan Nevins, *Grover Cleveland: A Study in Courage* (New York: Dodd, Mead, 1933); Jeffers, *An Honest President.*
52. Interview with Leo Yakutis, by Mark Davis, October 8, 2010.
53. Nevins, *Grover Cleveland,* 169.

9. The Seventh Sword—Clandestine War

1. "Estonia Hit by 'Moscow Cyber War,'" BBC News, May 17, 2007, http://news.bbc.co.uk/2/hi/europe/6665145.stm.
2. Interview with Leo Yakutis by Mark Davis, October 10, 2010.
3. Ashley Fantz, "Assange's 'Poison Pill' File Impossible to Stop, Expert Says," CNN U.S., December 8, 2010, http://articles.cnn.com/2010-12-08/us/wikileaks.poison.pill_1_julian-assange-wikileaks-key-encryption?_s=PM:US.
4. Tim Weber, "Cybercrime Threat Rising Sharply," BBC Mobile News, January 31, 2009, http://news.bbc.co.uk/2/hi/business/davos/7862549.stm.
5. "Ponemon Study Shows the Cost of a Data Breach Continues to Increase," Ponemon Institute, January 25, 2011, http://www.ponemon.org/news-2/23.
6. Bill Brenner, "Heartland CEO on Data Breach: QSAs Let Us Down," Q&A, CSO,

August 12, 2009, http://www.csoonline.com/article/499527/heartland-ceo-on-data-breach-qsas-let-us-down; "Alleged International Hacker Indicted for Massive Attack on U.S. Retail and Banking Networks," news release, U.S. Department of Justice, August 17, 2009, http://www.justice.gov/opa/pr/2009/August/09-crm-810.html; *Privacy in the Cloud Computing Era,* Trustworthy Computing: Policymakers, Microsoft, November 2009, http://www.microsoft.com/about/twc/en/us/Policymakers.aspx.

7. Network World, "Spear Phishers Hunting PR Firms and Lawyers, Says FBI," PC-World, November 18, 2009, http://www.pcworld.com/article/182536/spear_phishers_hunting_pr_firms_and_lawyers_says_fbi.html.
8. Julia Angwin and Jennifer Valentino-DeVries, "Apple, Google Collect User Data," *Wall Street, Journal,* April 22, 2011.
9. Julia Angwin and Jennifer Valentino-DeVries, "Race Is On to 'Fingerprint' Phones, PCs," *Wall Street Journal,* December 1, 2010.
10. Emily Steel and Geoffrey A. Fowler, "Facebook in Privacy Breach," *Wall Street Journal,* October 18, 2010.
11. Emily Steel, "Web Pioneer Profiles Users by Name," *Wall Street Journal,* October 25, 2010.
12. Ibid.
13. Steel and Fowler, "Facebook in Privacy Breach."
14. Julia Angwin, "The Web's New Gold Mine: Your Secrets," *Wall Street Journal,* July 30, 2010.
15. Ibid.
16. Niall Firth, "Facebook 'Accidentally Outing Gay Users' to Outside Firms Through Targeted Ads," *Daily Mail* (UK), October 22, 2010, http://www.dailymail.co.uk/sciencetech/article-1322916/Facebook-accidentally-outing-gay-users-advertisers.html#ixzz13OvImASl.
17. Angwin, "The Web's New Gold Mine."
18. "Privacy Fears as Eight in 10 Kids Have Photos Online," Breitbart.com, October 8, 2010, http://www.breitbart.com/article.php?id=CNG.c81a656973793fe072f583c520733516.841.
19. Cecilia Kang, "FCC Probes Google over Street View Program's Collection of Personal Data," *Washington Post,* November 10, 2010; Vanessa Allen, "Google Finally Admits That Its Street View Cars DID Take Emails and Passwords from Computers," Mail Online (UK), last updated October 28, 2010, http://www.dailymail.co.uk/sciencetech/article-1323310/Google-admits-Street-View-cars-DID-emails-passwords-computers.html.
20. Kim Zetter, "Hacker Spoofs Cell Phone Tower to Intercept Calls," Threat Level (blog), Wired.com, July 31, 2010, http://www.wired.com/threatlevel/2010/07/intercepting-cell-phone-calls/.
21. Luke Salkeld, "Scariest Speed Camera of All . . . It Checks Your Insurance, Tax and Even Whether You Are Tailgating or Not Wearing a Seatbelt," Mail Online (UK), November 3, 2010, http://www.dailymail.co.uk/sciencetech/article-1326035/Speed-camera-checks-insurance-tax-wearing-seatbelt.html.
22. Clark Boyd, "Cyber-War a Growing Threat Warn Experts," BBC News, June 17, 2010, http://www.bbc.co.uk/news/10339543.
23. "Partial List of Celebs Targeted by Hackers," TMZ.com, March 17, 2011.
24. Marian Merritt, "Alicia Keys MySpace Hack," Norton.com, November 15, 2007.
25. Marian Merritt, "Bots and Botnets: A Growing Threat," Norton.com, February 19, 2008, http://us.norton.com/familyresources/resources.jsp?title=bots_and_botnets.

26. Rik Ferguson, "Japanese Porn Extortion," CounterMeasures (blog), Trend Micro, April 14, 2010, http://countermeasures.trendmicro.eu/Japanese-porn-extortion.
27. Donald L. Evans, speech, Forum on International Property Rights Protection, January 13, 2005, http://www.america.gov/st/washfile.
28. "GM Daewoo-Chery Copyright Suit Settled," Asia Times Online, November 22, 2005, http://www.atimes.com/atimes/China_Business/GK22Cb04.html.
29. John Leyden, "Couple Charged over Hybrid Car Industrial Espionage Plot," *Register* (UK), July 23, 2010, http://www.theregister.co.uk/2010/07/23/hybrid_car_espionage_scam/.
30. Christopher Drew, "New Spy Game: Firms' Secrets Sold Overseas," *New York Times,* October 17, 2010.
31. Interview with security expert by Mark Davis, December 12, 2010.
32. Ryan Tate, "Apple's Worst Security Breach: 114,000 iPad Owners Exposed," Gawker, June 9, 2010, http://gawker.com/#!5559346/apples-worst-security-breach-114000-ipad-owners-exposed.
33. Thomas Claburn, "Cold Boot Attack Defeats Encryption Software," *InformationWeek,* February 21, 2008, http://www.informationweek.com/news/personal-tech/showArticle.jhtml?articleID=206801184&queryText=thomas%20claburn.
34. Interview with security expert by Mark Davis, November 4, 2010.
35. Interview with Bill Livingstone, by Mark Davis, October 5, 2010.
36. Interview with Tom Kellermann by Mark Davis, November 11, 2010.
37. Interview with security expert by Mark Davis, December 1, 2010.
38. "Political Hacktivists Turn to Web Attacks," BBC News, February 10, 2010, http://news.bbc.co.uk/2/hi/8506698.stm.
39. *Privacy in the Cloud Computing Era,* Trustworthy Computing: Policymakers, Microsoft, November 2009, 2, http://www.microsoft.com/about/twc/en/us/Policymakers.aspx.
40. Chuck Bennett, "Terror Target Breach," *New York Post,* December 6, 2010.
41. "Cyber Wars: US Is Stepping Up Defense Against Digital Attacks," Reuters, October 5, 2010, http://m.cnbc.com/us_news/39518423/1. Jim Wolf, "The Pentagon's New Cyber Warriors," special report, Reuters, October 5, 2010, http://www.reuters.com/article/2010/10/05/us-usa-cyberwar-idUSTRE69433120101005.
42. Fahmid Y. Rashid, "Cyber-Attacks Targeting Power, Gas Utilities on the Rise: Survey," IT Security & Network Security News, April 04, 2011.
43. Marshall Abrams and Joe Weiss, *Malicious Control System Cyber Security Attack Case Study—Maroochy Water Services, Australia,* Computer Security Resource Center, National Institute of Standards and Technology, July 23, 2008, http://csrc.nist.gov/groups/SMA/fisma/ics/documents/Maroochy-Water-Services-Case-Study_report.pdf.
44. "Staged Cyber Attack Reveals Vulnerability in Power Grid," YouTube video, 1:05, from a Department of Homeland Security video televised by CNN, posted by "fpzzuuulzgaxd," September 27, 2007, http://www.youtube.com/watch?v=fJyWngDco3g; "Cyber War: Sabotaging the System," *60 Minutes,* CBS News, first broadcast November 8, 2009, updated June 10, 2010, posted June 13, 2010, http://www.cbsnews.com/stories/2010/06/10/60minutes/main6568387_page5.shtml.
45. "Cyber Wars: US Is Stepping Up Defense," Reuters, October 5, 2010; Jim Wolf, "Pentagon's New Cyber Warriors," Reuters, October 5, 2010.
46. Ibid.
47. Mike DeBonis, "Hacker Infiltration Ends D.C. Online Voting Trial," *Washington Post,* October 4, 2010.

48. Michael R. Crittenden and Shaÿndi Raice, "Chinese Firm 'Hijacked' Data," *Wall Street Journal,* November 17, 2010; "Report: Massive Hack Targeted Government, Military," CBS News, November 17, 2010, http://www.cbsnews.com/stories/2010/11/17/world/main7062928.shtml.
49. Ellen Nakashima, "Chinese Leaders Ordered Google Hack, U.S. Cable Quotes Source as Saying," *Washington Post,* December 4, 2010.
50. "China Leadership 'Orchestrated Google Hacking,'" BBC News Asia-Pacific, December 4, 2010, http://www.bbc.co.uk/news/world-asia-pacific-11920616.
51. David Leigh, "How 250,000 U.S. Embassy Cables Were Leaked," *Guardian* (UK), November 28, 2010, http://www.guardian.co.uk/world/2010/nov/28/how-us-embassy-cables-leaked.
52. Javier Salido and Patrick Voon, "The Case for Data Governance," part 1 of *A Guide to Data Governance for Privacy, Confidentiality, and Compliance,* 4, Trustworthy Computing, Microsoft, January 2010, http://www.microsoft.com/privacy/datagovernance.aspx.
53. Open Security Foundation, "Data Loss Database—2009 Yearly Report," updated March 7, 2011, http://datalossdb.org/yearly_reports/dataloss-2009.pdf.
54. Shaun Waterman, "Gaps in Authority Hamper Military Against Cyber-Attacks," *Washington Times,* September 23, 2010.
55. Geoffrey Forden, "Russia's Nuclear Warriors: False Alarms on the Nuclear Front," NOVA Online, PBS, updated October 2001, http://www.pbs.org/wgbh/nova/missileers/falsealarms.html; Jonathan Schell, "The Forgotten Threat: 'Countdown to Zero' on Nuclear Weapons," *Nation,* July 27, 2010.

10. Swimming in the Silicon Sea

1. Interview with Ned Desmond, by Mark Davis, November 22, 2010.
2. Jaron Lanier, *You Are Not a Gadget: A Manifesto* (New York: Knopf, 2010), 32.
3. Stewart Brand, quoted in "Information Wants to Be Free . . . ," Roger Clarke's Web-Site (blog), amended August 28, 2001, http://www.rogerclarke.com/II/IWtbF.html.
4. Brian McRee, "The Cove (2009)—Dolphin Safe," Film Consumer (blog), July 12, 2010, http://www.thefilmconsumer.com/2010/07/cove-2009-dolphin-safe.html.
5. Interview with James Lee, by Mark Davis, November 1, 2010.
6. Matt McGee, "Google Removes Offensive Obama Image; Was It Justified?," Search Engine Land, November 19, 2009, http://searchengineland.com/google-removes-offensive-obama-image-was-it-justified-30165.
7. Interview with Leo Yakutis, by Mark Davis, October 8, 2010.
8. Interview with Rich Daly by Richard Torrenzano, January 19, 2011.
9. "Miniseries, Night 1," Battlestar Galactica Wiki, last modified November 22, 2009, http://en.battlestarwiki.org/wiki/Miniseries.
10. Arthur C. Clarke and Stephen Baxter, *The Light of Other Days* (New York: Tor Books, 2000).
11. Anita L. Allen, "*NAACP v. Alabama,* Privacy and Data Protection," EPIC Alert 15.13, last modified June 27, 2008, http://naacpvalabamaat50.org/.
12. Steven J. Horowitz, "Defusing a Google Bomb," Yale Law Journal Online 117, Pocket Part 36 (September 7, 2007), http://www.yalelawjournal.org/the-yale-law-journal-pocket-part/intellectual-property/defusing-a-google-bomb/.
13. Cass R. Sunstein, *On Rumors: How Falsehoods Spread, Why We Believe Them, What Can Be Done* (New York: Farrar, Straus and Giroux, 2009), 79.
14. Patricia Cohen, "Digitally Mapping the Republic of Letters," ArtsBeat (blog), *New*

York Times, November 16, 2010, http://artsbeat.blogs.nytimes.com/2010/11/16/digitally-mapping-the-republic-of-letters/.

15. Interview with Carol Howard Merritt, by Mark Davis, December 16, 2010.
16. Alexia Tsotsis, "To Celebrate the #Jan25 Revolution, Egyptian Names His First-born 'Facebook,'" TechCrunch, February 19, 2011, http://techcrunch.com/2011/02/19/facebook-egypt-newborn/.
17. Lanier, *You Are Not a Gadget*, 83.
18. Ibid., 87.
19. Zadie Smith, "Generation Why?," review of *The Social Network*, a film directed by David Fincher, with a screenplay by Aaron Sorkin, and *You Are Not a Gadget: A Manifesto* by Jaron Lanier, *New York Review of Books,* November 25, 2010.
20. Alexis Madrigal, "Literary Writers and Social Media: A Response to Zadie Smith," TheAtlantic.com, November 8, 2010, http://www.theatlantic.com/technology/archive/2010/11/literary-writers-and-social-media-a-response-to-zadie-smith/66257/.
21. "Pornography Statistics," Family Safe Media, accessed March 21, 2011, http://www.familysafemedia.com/pornography_statistics.html.
22. Nick Bilton, "Part of the Daily American Diet, 34 Gigabytes of Data," *New York Times,* December 9, 2009.
23. Roger E. Bohn and James E. Short, "How Much Information? 2009 Report on American Consumers," Global Information Industry Center, University of California, San Diego, updated January 2010, http://hmi.ucsd.edu/pdf/HMI_2009_ConsumerReport_Dec9_2009.pdf.
24. Murray Wardrop, "Young Will Have to Change Names to Escape 'Cyber Past' Warns Google's Eric Schmidt," Telegraph.Co.UK, August 18, 2010, http://www.telegraph.co.uk/technology/google/7951269/Young-will-have-to-change-names-to-escape-cyber-past-warns-Googles-Eric-Schmidt.html.
25. "Memorable Quotes for *Watchmen* (2009)," Internet Movie Database, accessed March 21, 2011, http://www.imdb.com/title/tt0409459/quotes.

11. The Seven Shields of Digital Assassination

1. The Torrenzano Group, LLC, trademark philosophy of doing business, 1996.
2. Ibid.
3. Ibid.
4. John Blossom, "Regulating the Ether: The FCC Confronts the Limits of Net Neutrality," ContentBlogger (blog), Shore Communications Inc., April 7, 2010, http://www.shore.com/commentary/weblogs/2010/04/regulating-ether-fcc-confronts-limits.html.
5. "Dave Carroll's Songwriting Revenge," News, Taylor Guitars, July 10, 2009, http://www.taylorguitars.com/news/NewsDetail.aspx?id=102; Mark Tran, "Singer Gets His Revenge on United Airlines and Soars to Fame," News Blog (blog), Guardian.co.uk, July 23, 2009, http://www.guardian.co.uk/news/blog/2009/jul/23/youtube-united-breaks-guitars-video.
6. Karen Tumulty and Ed O'Keefe, "Fired USDA Official Receives Apologies from White House, Vilsack," *Washington Post,* July 22, 2010.
7. "Political Retribution," *California Catholic Daily,* March 13, 2009, http://www.calcatholic.com/news/newsArticle.aspx?id=df9e1f03-ef76-49d3-bba0-ada8239b419c; interview with recent Claremont McKenna College students by Mark Davis, March 11, 2011.

8. Glenn Reynolds, "I Never Would Have Heard the Words 'Liskula Cohen' and 'Skank' Together," August 24, 2009, http://pajamasmedia.com/instapundit/83934/.
9. "Responding to Reviews," Support Center, Yelp for Business Owners, Yelp, accessed May 1, 2011, https://biz.yelp.com/support/responding_to_reviews.
10. "Wikipedia: Notability (people)," Wikipedia, accessed January 31, 2011, http://en.wikipedia.org/wiki/Wikipedia:Notability_(people).
11. "DMCA Safe Harbor," Chilling Effects, accessed February 5, 2011, http://www.chillingeffects.org/dmca512.

Index